Commercial Law Series

THE FRENCH STOCK EXCHANGE

A Practical Guide for Investors and Advisers

By
Thierry Schoen
Member of the Paris
and New York Bars
Clifford Chance, Paris

JOHN WILEY & SONS
Chichester · New York · Brisbane · Toronto · Singapore

Published in the United Kingdom by
Chancery Law Publishing Ltd
Baffins Lane, Chichester,
West Sussex PO19 1UD, England
National: Chichester 01243 779777
International: (+44) 1243 779777

Published in North America by
John Wiley & Sons, Inc.
7222 Commerce Center Drive
Colorado Springs CO 80919
USA

Other Wiley Editorial Offices

John Wiley & Sons, Inc., 605 Third Avenue,
New York, NY 10158-0012, USA

Jacaranda Wiley Ltd, 33 Park Road, Milton,
Queensland 4064, Australia

John Wiley & Sons (Canada) Ltd, 22 Worcester Road,
Rexdale, Ontario M9W ILI, Canada

John Wiley & Sons (SEA) Plc Ltd, 37 Jalan Pemimpin #05-04
Block B, Union Industrial Building, Singapore 2057

British Library Cataloguing-in-Publication Data

A catalogue record for this book is available from the British Library

ISBN 0-471-95550-7

Typeset in 10½/12pt Baskerville by Footnote Graphics, Warminster, Wiltshire
Printed and bound in Great Britain by Bookcraft (Bath) Ltd

This book is printed on acid-free paper responsibly manufactured from
sustainable forestation. At least two trees were planted for each one
used for paper production.

Contents

CONTENTS

CONTENTS

This publication is designed to provide accurate and authoritative information in regard to the subject-matter covered. It is sold with the understanding that neither the publisher nor the author is engaged, through the publication of this book, in rendering legal or other professional services. If legal advice or other expert assistance is required, the services of a competent professional person should be sought.

Foreword

In the move towards internationalisation which characterises the financial markets, it is appropriate to broaden one's knowledge of French securities regulations. Such laws are sometimes overlooked or inaccurately interpreted, possibly intentionally.

From a general viewpoint, the initial merit of Thierry Schoen's book is its demonstration that the Paris stock exchange environment is that of a legal regime.

Indeed, the history of the French stock exchange is a long one, an early milestone being the Edict issued by Philippe le Bel in February 1304 which regulated the activities of intermediaries in trade and currency exchange operations. Far better though to jump to the present day, and focus on the laws that have already withstood the test of time and now serve as the basis for today's securities market in France.

The Company Law of 24 July 1966 established a link between securities law and corporate law. The author rightly identifies this as the source of the rights of shareholders and, more generally, of holders of securities. He also identifies the requirement that a company which acquires a stake in another company should disclose its acquisition to the issuer and, if the latter is listed, that it should disclose its transaction to the Conseil des Bourses de Valeurs, which informs the market of the transaction.

It is interesting to note that the disclosures to be made when reaching certain levels of ownership in terms of capital or voting rights of an issuer were subject, in certain cases, to a disclosure requirement on the basis of a regulation of the Commission des Opérations de Bourse of 1981. There was already a concern that the public should be made aware of the increasing stake of certain shareholders in the capital of listed companies. This obligation to disclose the reaching of certain levels was dealt with again in a later law, and was supplemented in 1989 with a view to integrating the provisions of the European Directive regarding transfers of major holdings in listed securities. Furthermore, the rules governing the disclosure of shareholders' agreements concerning listed companies and those applicable to actions in concert appear in the Company Law.

As early as 1967, an ordinance created the Commission des Opérations de Bourse, whose task was to supervise the protection of savings invested in securities and to ensure the proper functioning of the markets placed under its control. This text has been supplemented several times, with the most significant modification being made by the Law of 2 August 1989 concerning the security and transparency of the capital markets. In fact, although the Commission already had wide-ranging powers (including that of overseeing the quality of disclosure and of carrying out inquiries into possible violations of securities laws), it appeared desirable that these powers be significantly broadened to keep pace with the expansion and increasing diversity of capital markets. The Commission des Opérations de Bourse was thus given the power to prohibit entities from infringing its regulations.

It also has the power to directly sanction those who violate its regulations. Since 1989, the Commission has imposed fines in such cases as insider trading, manipulation of share prices, misinformation and abuse of powers and mandates, to name only the most common violations. These sanctions are subject to appeal to the Paris Court of Appeals.

Reference should also be made to the Law of 22 January 1988 on the organisation of stock exchanges, which structured France's "Big Bang". This law created the Conseil des Bourses de Valeurs, the other authority responsible for the supervision of stockbrokers, market transactions and rules applicable to tender offers.

The French stock exchanges have therefore been regulated by a single institution for twenty-seven years. This fact reflects an organisational framework which has been tried and tested, most notably in the field of tender offers, to which the author has devoted the greater part of his study. The Conseil des Bourses de Valeurs organises procedures, and the Commission des Opérations de Bourse sees to it that disclosures made are adequate and transactions are correctly carried out. Since the promulgation of the Law of 2 August 1989, the actions of the Conseil des Bourses de Valeurs and the Commission des Opérations de Bourse have given substance to new concepts such as the mandatory offer and the action in concert. Thanks to its 1989 regulation, the Commission, supported by the Court of Appeals, has created respect for discipline and fairness in the course of tender offers.

The stock exchange environment has featured a new protagonist since 1988 – the Paris Court of Appeals, which hears appeals against decisions rendered both by the Commission des Opérations de Bourse and the Conseil des Bourses de Valeurs. Although the vast majority of tender offers take place without incident, certain of them, either because they are hostile or because they are not well received by minority shareholders, become controversial, and emotions run high. The Court of Appeals serves in these cases as a stage upon which, as in classical tragedy, the disputed transaction is played out according to unity of place, action and time; the Court is the forum in which passions may be expressed and thus soothed, such is the force with which the Court's decision puts a swift end to the battle. The body of precedents established by the Court of Appeals has supplemented and confirmed the decisions made by the stock exchange authorities, explicitly relating them to a body of legislation and providing a reference for the various parties taking part in a transaction.

The French market is, therefore, fully regulated, organised and controlled, and shares a common legal language with Anglo-Saxon markets. The Commission des Opérations de Bourse and the Conseil des Bourses de Valeurs have demonstrated the maturity of securities regulations in the financial markets and, under the supervision of the courts, have provided a regulatory framework for the smooth operation of the Paris stock exchange, thus contributing to its rise to a truly international status.

JEAN SAINT-GEOURS
Chairman of the
Commission des Opérations de Bourse

Preface

One reason for drafting a book in English on French securities law is that there is almost no literature or comprehensive documentation in English on the subject, even though almost one-third of the French securities market is said to be owned by foreigners. Foreigners also own one-third of the French stockbroking firms and almost 300 banking entities or branches operating in France are under foreign control. Furthermore, in the past ten years, a fair number of tender offers made in France have been launched by foreign acquirers.

Another reason for the book is that French regulations in the stock market area are (together with UK regulations) among the most sophisticated in Europe. For example, France and the United Kingdom are the only countries where mandatory offers exist (each shareholder who reaches the one-third level in a listed company being required to file a public bid). Most of the rules provided for in the "European Takeover Code", still to be adopted, are already implemented in France. Also, French rules concerning disclosures of holdings, shareholders' agreements and material facts are among the most advanced in Europe. Further, France has an elaborate body of jurisprudence concerning "action in concert" among market players which enables stockmarket authorities to prevent securities law fraud, such as "parking" of securities in undisclosed friendly hands.

The book will help practitioners (investment bankers, foreign shareholders of French listed companies, potential acquirers, investment funds, advisers, etc.) to assess key issues in the securities law area. It may also be useful if one wants to get an overview of the organisation and structure of French securities markets and authorities.

The book includes a comprehensive description of the basic securities rules governing tender offers, and describes the French securities markets, the French authorities and the players in this area. The book also discusses the rules governing public offerings of securities (including privatisation techniques), the newly implemented squeeze-out procedure and the rules governing insider trading.

In order to be as useful as possible, the book gives many examples of key transactions that have taken place in France and gives a general overview of the French business community and key players. It also discusses the various French "circles" that are keys to understanding the French financial market.

Attached to the book is the newly issued English translation of the Règlement Général of the Conseil des Bourses de Valeurs (the "General Regulation") prepared by the Société des Bourses Françaises. This key regulation should enable English readers to precisely assess a legal situation and form an opinion as to the main rules applicable to practical situations.

This book should enable the reader to grasp the basic concepts concerning tender offers in France and, more generally, acquisition and disposition of listed securities.

THIERRY SCHOEN
February 1995

Acknowledgements

A number of people have read the manuscript at various stages of its development. They are too numerous to be listed, but the author wishes to thank them all for their assistance and support.

The author also wishes to thank Julia M. Lichtblau, former Staff Correspondent of A.P. Dow Jones News Services in Paris and Jean-Michel Tron, Partner of Cleary, Gottlieb, Steen & Hamilton, for their careful, detailed and patient review of his successive drafts. The author also wishes to thank the late Jean L. Blondeel, Counsel with Cleary, Gottlieb, Steen & Hamilton and Honorary Chairman and President of Kreditbank S.A. Luxembourgeoise for his continuous support. Also to be thanked are Dominique Leblanc, General Manager of the Société des Bourses Françaises as well as Marc Outin and Wayne H. Smith, respectively *Responsable de l'Information* and *Chargé des Valeurs Etrangères* with the SBF, for their help.

Finally, the author wishes to thank his colleagues from Clifford Chance in Paris and London for their invaluable help.

Tables

TABLES

Chapter 1
Background to the French Securities Market

1. "Au début il n'y avait rien"

French securities regulations, and in particular rules governing tender offers in France are the *post facto* result of tender offers and takeover battles that have taken place over the past thirty years.

In the beginning, nothing existed. The first tender offer was made in France in 1964, at a time when there were no regulations or guidelines in the area. Surprisingly enough, the offer was for an American company listed in France, the Franco Wyoming Oil Company, which was controlled by French shareholders. Also, there were very few disclosure rules. Key shareholders of listed companies were not known to the public and very few disclosures were made by the issuers regarding price-sensitive information.

In 1966, following this offer, the sole securities authority at that time, the Chambre Syndicale des Agents de Change, the representative body of the stockbrokers' guild and known as the "Chambre", set down some basic guidelines concerning offers. This was done through an exchange of letters with the Ministry of Finance. The 1966 procedure was thereafter incorporated into the General Regulation ("Règlement Général") of the Compaignie des Agents de Change enacted in 1970.

In 1967, Ordinance No. 67–833 of 28 September 1967 (the "1967 Ordinance") created the Commission des Opérations de Bourse (the "COB"). Regulators were inspired by the US Securities & Exchange Commission ("SEC"), which had been established under the Securities Act of 1933. The COB was entrusted with monitoring the disclosures to be made by listed companies to protect investors. The purpose was to stimulate households' investment in securities and stimulate economic growth since French individuals seldom invested in securities, but rather in real estate or other traditional household investments. The 1967 Ordinance also regulated insider trading for the first time.

However, no sanctions were available against companies which failed to disclose key facts, and while the COB could publicly blame violators, it was not empowered to impose fines on them.

The first giant tender offer battle took place in 1969. It involved Boussois-

3

Souchon-Neuvesel ("BSN"), at that time a mainly packaging business but now France's largest food group and renamed "Groupe Danone". The company made an unsuccessful hostile bid for Saint-Gobain, a glass group.

In 1970, the COB issued its first regulation concerning tender offers to improve the information disclosed to the public during such operations.

In 1973, a short paragraph, drafted by the Chairman of the Chambre and the French Bankers' Association (Association Française des Banques – "AFB"), laid down the basis for the French standing offer or "*maintien de cours*" procedure (the successor of which is the "*garantie de cours*"). The procedure renders the offering of "tag-along" rights to minority shareholders compulsory in cases of acquisition of a controlling block ("*bloc de contrôle*") from one identified seller. This was the first type of mandatory tender in France. The purpose of the procedure was to allow minority shareholders to withdraw from a listed company in cases involving a change in control resulting from the sale of a controlling block by the main shareholders. Minority shareholders were also to be offered the same price as that paid for the controlling block. They got no such protection, however, when an acquirer took over a listed company through open market purchase. It was thus easy to get around the standing offer procedure by not entering into a contract with the controlling shareholder, but instead buying shares on the open market or filing a voluntary bid, coupled with agreements made with the target's main shareholders to tender their shares in the course of the offer.

In 1985, Law No. 85–705 of 12 July 1985 amending Law No. 66–537 of 24 July 1966 relating to commercial companies (the "Company Law") required any investors holding more than 5%, 10%, 20%, 33.33% and 50% of the capital of a company to publicly disclose their holdings.

This was the status of regulation up to 1988 before the French "big bang".

2. **1988: The French "Big Bang"**

Nineteen eighty-eight was the year of the deregulation of the French securities industry, when *agents de change* were replaced by *sociétés de bourse* by virtue of Law No. 88–70 of 22 January 1988 relating to stock exchanges ("the Stock Exchange Law").

Up to 1988, stockbrokers were individuals named "*agents de change*" who had an absolute monopoly over securities trading. They were appointed and removed by the Minister of Finance. Their status was governed by the Law of 28 April 1816. *Agents de change* had the right to nominate their successor in business, subject to the approval of the Compagnie des Agents de Change, the stockbrokers' guild. The number of *agents de change* was deliberately limited and new *agents de change* were appointed only when others retired or ceased to carry out their activities.

In the 1960s, most *agents de change* had created incorporated companies by grouping together as business partners. The company structure enabled them to raise funds with their clients and senior executives. However, *agents de change* were strictly required to retain majority control over these companies. While this form of doing business was adequate in the 19th century, it proved to be totally inadequate in the 1980s, when trading volume increased and heavy investment was needed in market technologies such as computer links and risk management. In the late 1980s, it became clear that it had not adapted to the requirements of modern markets.

In 1988, *agents de change* were replaced by companies named *sociétés de bourse* and credit and other institutions were progressively allowed to invest in (and thereafter register) brokers. One of the purposes of this corporate structure was to enable brokers to raise funds. Also, the Conseil des Bourses de Valeurs ("CBV") and its executive arm, the Société des Bourses Françaises ("SBF") replaced the Compagnie and the Chambre Syndicale des Agents de Change. The Stock Exchange Law abrogated most of the former legislation and regulations concerning the organisation of the stock exchanges. Shortly thereafter, most brokerage firms were put up for sale, and French or foreign financial institutions took over most *sociétés de bourse*.

The French "big bang" in 1988 shortly preceded the French tender offer fury.

3. **1988/1989: The French tender offer fury**

Nineteen eighty-eight was also the year of the major tender offers around the world and France was quickly drawn in, both through competing French interests and also through French links with other European groups. In Belgium, a major Belgian group, Société Générale de Belgique, was the subject of a hostile bid by Compagnies Européennes Réunies ("CERUS"), a French holding company controlled by Carlo De Benedetti, the Italian financial Chairman of the Olivetti Group. CERUS eventually failed when the major French financial and industrial holding company Compagnie de Suez (acting as a white knight) filed a competing bid and acquired a majority of Générale's shares by only a small margin. In France, the main battles were those described below:

(i) A "creeping" tender offer for LVMH

The most notorious tender occurred when the French fashion tycoon, Bernard Arnault, took over the world's leading fashion and luxury goods group LVMH-Moët Hennessy Louis Vuitton ("LVMH"). LVMH had been created the year before through the merger of two family-controlled groups, Louis Vuitton SA, a luggage manufacturer controlled by the Vuitton family, and the beverage group, Moët-Hennessy, of which 22% was owned by the

Hennessy family. A year before the merger, in a first attempt to protect Moët-Hennessy against a hostile raider, the company had publicly issued bonds with warrants to subscribe to shares on the international market. In fact, most of the bonds (or at least the warrants) were supposed to end up in friendly hands in order to enable the acquirers to step in to assist the company in case of a hostile raid. This device turned out to be one of the key factors of Arnault's successful raid one year later. Very soon after the merger, tensions appeared among the Vuitton and Hennessy clans and the management of the group, fearing a hostile bid, sought a stable group of shareholders. They chose Bernard Arnault, who was rapidly joined by the British group Guinness Plc.

Arnault's merger and acquisition ("M&A") activities began with his acquisition in 1985 of Compagnie Boussac Saint-Frères, a textile group that had been sold to Agache-Willot, another textile group specialising in the purchase of companies in financial trouble. In 1984, with the support of Messieurs Lazard Frères & Compagnie, France's powerful closely-held premier investment bank and the state-owned Crédit Lyonnais, France's largest commercial bank, Arnault took over Boussac Saint-Frères following its noisy bankruptcy with the help of significant State aid. Boussac had interests in the fashion industry and notably controlled Christian Dior, the French fashion house of world-wide renown. Boussac, which was in severe financial difficulties, had already sold Dior's perfume business branch to . . . Louis Vuitton in the early seventies.

With the support of Lazard, Arnault and Guinness organised a sophisticated holding structure which they baptised "Jacques Rober", and used it to make significant share purchases on the market. After acquiring 20% of LVMH's capital in July 1988, Arnault and Guinness declared that "they could acquire up to 30% of the company's capital, which did not constitute 'control' over LVMH". Both acquirers had, however, insisted that this statement was subject to any unforeseen events. In January 1989, following heavy stock market purchases, Arnault and Guinness held 39% of the stock of LVMH and 43.5% of the voting rights. This gave them *de facto* control over the target since they also held some of the warrants to subscribe to shares that had been issued in 1987 in an attempt to protect the company from hostile raiders. The members of the Vuitton family now held only 30% of the company's voting rights, while the Moët-Hennessy family (which comprises a wide-ranging group) held approximately 15% of the stock.

Arnault took majority control through other open-market purchases at the end of 1989. The head of the Vuitton clan, Mr. Henry Racamier, resigned after a vain effort to block an extraordinary shareholders' meeting to amend the company's by-laws in order to modify the management structure. Since Arnault and Guinness had not acquired LVMH shares from "identified" sellers, they were not required to launch a bid and buy out minority shareholders – which included the losers, the Vuitton clan. This was a salient example of "creeping tenders" (acquisition of control resulting from open-market purchases ("*ramassage*")).

6

(ii) Italians hit Epeda-Bertrand-Faure ("EBF")

Another interesting case was Valeo, a highly profitable company manufacturing spare parts for the automotive industry and a subsidiary of CERUS (the unfortunate bidder for Société Générale de Belgique). Valeo initiated a "hostile" (or at least unsolicited) bid for Epeda-Bertrand-Faure ("EBF"), an auto parts manufacturer with a luggage subsidiary because it believed that certain branches of EBF had "synergies" with Valeo. Meanwhile a syndicate of banks, led by the state-held Banque Worms, proposed Chargeurs SA, a diversified holding company led by Jérôme Seydoux, as a "white knight". While Seydoux's interest in the case was initially unclear (since Chargeurs had activities in textiles, shipping and entertainment and controlled an airline company), he turned out to have close links with Noël Goutard, Valeo's Chairman. Shortly after disclosing its intention to file a competing bid, and to the great distress of EBF, Chargeurs changed its mind and filed a joint bid for EBF with Valeo.

EBF then tried to find an alternative solution in the form of a leveraged buy-out ("LBO") organised by Crédit Commercial de France ("CCF"), a key player in the M&A area. A competing bid was launched through a holding company called Gefina (owned partly by Etablissements Michelin & Cie and Peugeot SA), which subscribed to loans arranged by Crédit Commercial de France. Key shareholders and the management of EBF retained their shares (which had double voting rights) and Gefina's bid was a success.

(iii) A Canadian/British battle over French Cognac

On 16 December 1988, the Canadian group Seagram, advised by Lazard Frères, entered into a "notarised" agreement with the Martell family with a view to purchasing 41% of the stock of Martell, France's number two Cognac producer, at FF2,500 per share. Since Seagram already held 11.59% of Martell, it reached the majority threshold and announced that it would file a standing offer to buy out the minority shareholders of Martell at that price. Seagram claimed that it could acquire the 41% block without recourse to a stockbroker since, at that time, purchases and sales resulting from notarised agreements could be made outside the exchange. This was not the view of the Chambre, which announced that it strongly disagreed and that its prior approval was needed. Seagram also tried to maintain that its purchase of the block was not a "mere purchase and sale" since the acquisition was subject to Treasury approval. This did not work either. On 24 December, another player also eagerly interested by Martell, the British group Grand Metropolitan or "Grand Met" filed a competing bid at FF2,650 with the help of Crédit Commercial de France. Seagram was finally forced to renounce its contractual rights and had to enter the tender offer arena. Through its French champagne company, G.H. Mumm et Cie, it filed a competing bid at FF2,975 per Martell share. Grand Met rapidly increased its bid to FF3,300 but Seagram finally won after filing a bid at

FF3,475 per share. As a result, Seagram had to pay almost FF1,000 more for each share than it had originally planned.

(iv) A battle over Télémécanique

On 4 February 1988, Schneider SA, a major French electrical equipment and construction group and one of the largest French groups headed by the prominent French business leader, Didier Pinault-Valencienne (or "DPV" to his intimates and the press) launched a hostile bid for La Télémécanique Electrique, an electrical equipment maker, at FF3,900 per share. Télémécanique's management opposed the bid and found a white knight in the guise of the state nuclear power plant builder, "Framatome" which filed a competing bid at FF4,300. Framatome's rationale for its bid was unclear since one of the purposes of its bid was to maintain existing management structures and co-operate in the computer area. Télémécanique also organised frequent demonstrations by its personnel in front of the Paris stock exchange building and Schneider SA's headquarters. Prior to the offer, Télémécanique had issued warrants to buy its shares to COFITEL, a shell company controlled by parties friendly to the management. Following the filing of the offer, COFITEL's shares were transferred to Framatome. Schneider immediately started summary proceedings and it was decided that the warrants held by COFITEL had to be placed in escrow and could not be exercised. Schneider also commenced an action on the merits in order to have the issue of warrants cancelled on the basis that it had been presented as being made for the sole benefit of employees of Télémécanique (whereas it was in fact reserved to friendly parties). Schneider also argued that the sale of the COFITEL shares resulted in an indirect sale of Télémécanique shares, a type of transaction which cannot take place in the course of a tender offer. In the meantime, Schneider finally out-bid Framatome by offering a price of FF5,500. Since Schneider won its tender, it withdrew from legal action.

(v) Unsuccessful Paribas bid for Navigation Mixte

One example of failure was the tender offer launched by Compagnie Financière de Paribas for Compagnie de Navigation Mixte "CNM" in 1989. Banque Paribas, one of the leading French *banques d'affaires*, filed a hostile bid for Compagnie de Navigation Mixte for the account of its parent, Compagnie Financière de Paribas, one of France's largest holding companies. The offer was initially made for FF1,850 and increased to FF1,887. In fact, Paribas was not able to acquire a majority but only 40% of the capital, since Crédit Lyonnais, Société Générale (France's second largest commercial bank), Framatome, French businessman Jean-Marc Vernes and Bouygues (a construction group) helped Mixte Chairman Marc Fournier by acquiring shares on the market at a price above the tender price. The stock market authorities claimed that these companies were "acting in concert" and asked them to file a competing bid instead of buying stock. They declined the request so were asked to certify in writing to the stock market authorities that they were not acting in concert with the target. They did this un-reservedly. The authorities were embarrassed by these transactions but were unable to demonstrate the existence of an action in concert and the legal presumption did not apply.

4. The 1989 Law relating to "transparency and security within the financial market"

In 1988 there was heavy criticism of the fact that acquirers could take over listed companies without being required to file a bid or public offer through open-market purchases (as was the case in the LVMH saga) or that friendly parties could effectively block a bid through open-market purchases (as was the case in the Navigation Mixte bid made by Paribas). In order to regulate the public offer business, Law No. 89–531 of 2 August 1989 (the "1989 Law") gave authority to the Conseil des Bourses de Valeurs to regulate the situation. For the first time, the law required the filing of a tender offer when an acquirer reached one-third of the issuer's capital or votes. According to the new rules, once an acquirer held this level, it was required to make a tender offer for two-thirds of the voting rights of the target (pre-holdings included), unlike the *garantie de cours* which required acquirers to bid for all of the stock of the target.

The 1989 Law also made other important changes:

- The notion of persons or entities "acting in concert" was defined. Under the new rules, persons or entities "acting in concert" became jointly and severally liable for compliance with laws and regulations breached by any member of the group and they could be collectively required to file a bid upon reaching the one-third level.
- Shareholders of listed companies were required to report to the CBV, and the latter was required to make public any agreements between them that contained provisions granting such shareholders "preferential rights" to purchase or sell shares;
- Market players were under a strict duty to promptly disclose to the public any price-sensitive information, subject to COB fines (see *infra*).

The 1989 Law also reinforced the rules governing threshold notifications by shareholders of listed companies when reaching the 5%, 10%, 20%, 33.33%, 50% and 66.66% levels. Penalties increased substantially and shares held in excess of the threshold requiring disclosure *automatically* lost voting rights for two years following the appropriate disclosure date. Further, acquiring voting rights in violation of these requirements became subject to civil proceedings for which the remedy could be partial or total suspension of the shareholder's right to vote any of its shares in the company for up to five years. Finally, the COB was granted substantial additional powers and was authorised to issue injunctions and fines (up to FF10,000,000 or ten times the amount of any profit made) in the case of a breach of its regulations.

The 1989 Law provided the basis for the current "modern" French tender offer rules. However, it contained a number of flaws and, as market players foresaw, the "two-thirds rule" resulted in minority shareholders being left with non-liquid stock that quickly decreased in value after most takeover bids. It took several years before the problems came into the open because the CBV kept granting exemptions to the mandatory tender rule either by acknowledging that there was pre-existing control by the acquirer or by being unable to demonstrate that an action in concert existed.

5. 1990/1992: loopholes in the 1989 Regulation: the department stores cases

(i) Galeries Lafayette acquires Nouvelles Galeries

The first mandatory tender in France following the 1989 regulation involved Nouvelles Galeries, a major group of department stores ("*grands magasins*"), controlling in particular the Bazar de l'Hôtel de Ville, a large store across from the City Hall in central Paris. This case was considered important since it was the first time the CBV imposed a mandatory tender by refusing to grant an exemption.

Nouvelles Galeries had three key shareholders: Devanlay, a textile group holding 41% of the voting rights, Galeries Lafayette, another group of department stores, holding 28.08% of the voting rights, and Proventus AB, holding a 16.5% stake. Proventus AB was a sophisticated Swedish investment group that had little by little built up its 16.5% stake. Proventus had tried to influence management but was treated as a foreign outsider and failed to gain a board seat. In April 1991, it sold its stake to Galeries Lafayette and Crédit Commercial de France who consequently held respectively, 38.42% and 5.83% of Nouvelles Galeries' voting rights. Galeries Lafayette immediately filed an application with the CBV in order to be exempt from launching a mandatory offer. The acquirer claimed that Devanlay had *de facto* control over Nouvelles Galeries (since it held a larger stake) and that it was not acting in concert with CCF. The CBV disagreed and required Nouvelles Galeries to launch a bid immediately. The bid was, however, on only a small portion of Nouvelles Galeries' capital since Galeries Lafayette and Crédit Commercial de France already held 44% and, as already noted the General Regulation, at that time, only required that offers be made for a sufficient number of shares to give the acquirer control of at least two-thirds of the voting rights.

Further, notwithstanding the fact that Galeries Lafayette and CCF together held 44% of the votes and could ultimately gain majority control following the acquisition of double voting rights, the court held that as long as they did not have a majority of the voting rights following the acquisition, the standing offer rules requiring a 100% bid were not applicable.

(ii) Pinault acquires Printemps

The Nouvelles Galeries case paved the way for French businessman François Pinault's bid for Au Printemps SA in 1991. The case showed the weakness in the law because the two-thirds rule made it so easy for an acquirer to escape the *garantie de cours* requirement and, consequently, bid on *all* of the stock. Pinault is a French entrepreneur backed by Crédit Lyonnais. Au Printemps SA, a department store located next to Galeries Lafayette on the major shopping street Boulevard Haussmann, was controlled by the Swiss Maus family which held 42.27% of the capital and 56.44% of the votes. The by-laws of Printemps granted voting rights to all shareholders holding registered shares for more than two years.

SAMAG and Maus Frères, two holding companies controlled by the Maus family, were the two main shareholders of Printemps. Simultaneously with the signing of a purchase and sale agreement with Pinault, Maus Frères transferred all of its Printemps shares to SAMAG, which caused the shares to automatically lose their double voting rights. Simultaneously, SAMAG transformed its registered shares into bearer shares. As a result, the total number of voting rights held by the Maus family decreased from 56% to 37% and SAMAG was subsequently sold by them to Pinault. Through this scheme, Pinault did not reach the majority level (which would have forced him to launch a *garantie de cours*) and was only required to file a mandatory offer on two-thirds of the voting rights of Printemps. He saved the equivalent of FF3 billion.

The CBV had approved the offer filed by Pinault but several minority shareholders challenged the CBV's decision on the basis that Pinault abusively avoided the standing offer rules under which he would have been required to offer to buy all shares tendered.

Despite the COB's criticisms of Pinault's behaviour, the court held that he was only required to bid on two-thirds of Printemps' shares notwithstanding the transactions that preceded the sale of SAMAG.

Following these and other transactions, the minority shareholders were left with only a portion of their initial stake, the value of which quickly decreased with a narrow market and no hope of exit. The two-thirds rule was, in fact, inadequate.

The rule was modified by an amendment to the General Regulation dated 15 May 1992, which now requires that all offers (whether voluntary or mandatory) be made on *all* equity securities.

This was the starting point of a tougher attitude by the French authorities, since some investors argued that the French market was a closed shop self-regulated by the leading banks (who in fact occupy most of the seats of the CBV) and that the CBV only hit small players, while heavyweights remained untouched. Also, foreign investors (who often took minority positions in French listed companies) and minority shareholders' associations complained that minority shareholders were insufficiently protected, in particular in cases of change of control. This led regulators to adopt a tougher attitude against market players.

6. **Regulators get serious**

(i) The CBV forces Bolloré to bid for Delmas-Vieljeux

The takeover of Delmas-Vieljeux by Bolloré Technologies took place in 1991, a few months after the Printemps bid.

Vincent Bolloré is one of the key figures of the "golden eighties" in France. One of the three French tycoons of the 1980s (the others being Bernard Arnault and François Pinault), he built up a multinational group in only a few years. His family was in the paper and tobacco industry, but he invested heavily in shipping. From 1986, Bolloré controlled SCAC, a shipping company that he successfully reorganised. Bolloré has been backed by Lazard Frères and Crédit Lyonnais.

With a FF5.5 billion turnover in 1990, Delmas-Vieljeux was the largest French shipping owner with nearly 50 vessels. Once controlled by the Vieljeux/Delmas families, Compagnie Financière Delmas-Vieljeux ("CFDV"), the parent company, was a listed company with no real stable shareholding. Little by little, the Bolloré group charmed its way into CFDV, acquired 22% of its equity and became its main shareholder. The other shareholder was Compagnie Privée d'El Rabah ("El Rabah"), a holding company formed among institutional investors (Crédit Lyonnais, the state oil companies Elf Aquitaine and Total, Axa and Pinault). The Vieljeux/Delmas families owned only 18% of CFDV.

Bolloré had tried to encourage a merger between SCAC and Delmas-Vieljeux to "develop synergies" and to help SCAC, which was much less profitable than Delmas-Vieljeux. Tristan Vieljeux, the Chairman of the group, was not at all enthusiastic.

After several months of tension, Bolloré managed to command a majority of CFDV's Board members and, in May 1991, he convinced the Vieljeux family to sell out its 17% stake. The transaction was organised in a clever way in order not to have to buy out minority shareholders. Of the 17% interest, Bolloré only acquired a 9% stake, bringing his holding to 31% (just below the one-third level), and El Rabah acquired 8%, holding 26% of the votes. Meanwhile, Crédit Lyonnais increased its stake in El Rabah from 10% to 20% in order to finance the latter's acquisition of CFDV stock. Bolloré and El Rabah contended that since neither held one-third of the votes (or shares) of CFDV, no mandatory tender offer had to be filed.

This time, the CBV disagreed, ruling that the three supposedly coincidental buyers (Bolloré, Crédit Lyonnais and El Rabah) were acting in concert. Bolloré was required to file a standing offer for both CFDV and its listed subsidiary, Delmas Vieljeux.

(ii) The Agnelli group loses control over Perrier: Nestlé wins

"In France, one never wins a tender offer battle in court" said a financial adviser to Reto Doméniconi, Vice-President and Chief Financial Officer of Nestlé SA, the Swiss food giant. This statement proved not to be entirely true in the Perrier battle.

Nestlé, one of the largest European companies and with a strong presence in France, had made the strategic decision to file a bid for Source Perrier SA, the internationally known sparkling water brand. Nestlé had hired Suez, the powerful French *banque d'affaires*. Nestlé had contacted its long-term French business partner, BSN (now "Groupe Danone"), and a meeting was organised at Lazard Frères (BSN's bankers) on 23 December 1992. A tender offer for Perrier appeared feasible since EXOR, the parent company of the target, owned only 35% of the capital and 40% of the voting rights. EXOR, once owned by the Menzopolos family, had been taken over by the Italian Agnelli group in the eighties. Also, Perrier indirectly controlled 6.68% of its own capital through SGP, one of its indirect subsidiaries. On the business side, BSN and Nestlé had agreed that, should Nestlé's offer be successful, Nestlé would sell Volvic (a subsidiary of Perrier and another mineral water brand) to BSN.

In order to maintain good relations, Nestlé and BSN decided to telephone Giovanni Agnelli at 6 pm on 3 January 1992 to let him know what they were planning. Lazard's Chief, Michel David-Veil, told Giovanni Agnelli that Nestlé might be interested in Perrier and an urgent meeting was requested. No tender offer was in the air, but Agnelli knew exactly what was going on. He turned out to be not at all co-operative, saying that his partners were difficult. Two hours later, "L'Avvocato" (the nickname for Agnelli) called Michel David-Veil back and said that he had to inform Jacques Vincent, the Chairman of both EXOR and Perrier, about the proposed meeting. This meant that from Nestlé's standpoint, things were getting out of control.

In the meantime, the 6.68% Perrier stake held by SGP had been sold to Saint Louis, a diversified holding company with interests in the sugar and food businesses. It later turned out that one hour after the phone call by Lazard's Chief, Jacques Vincent visited Gustave Leven (who was the retired Chairman of Perrier but still Chairman of SPG) at his home and had asked him to execute a proxy authorising the sale to Saint Louis of the 1,241,275 Perrier shares held by SPG. Gustave Leven did so and the sale was registered in haste the following Monday morning on the stock exchange before the opening of the market.

In retaliation, Nestlé and Suez filed a joint bid for Perrier and also filed lawsuits to have the SPG sale cancelled. Both hit home. The Commercial Court in Nîmes chose to apply the sanctions under the 1989 Law concerning voting rights for the first time. EXOR, Saint-Louis and other parties acting in concert were deprived of one-third of their voting rights for two years for failure to disclose the crossing of the one-third threshold. Following a succession of bids, the Suez/Nestlé team won the battle and took over Perrier.

(iii) A gigantic poison pill: the OCP case

Office Commercial Pharmaceutique, France's largest pharmaceutical distributor, looked like the perfect tender offer target. Eighty per cent of its stock was held by the public. But, behind that mild-mannered exterior lurked a grand poison pill. To deter raiders, OCP's management had contributed 80% of the company's activities to two *sociétés en commandite par actions* ("SCAs") which they controlled. The SCAs were held by OCP's management and headed by Mr. Duché, OCP's Chairman. The latter, who had been appointed for an indefinite term, could only be removed through an amendment of the SCAs' by-laws (which itself required management's approval) or for cause following a battle in court. By means of this structure, management was effectively able to retain control over most of OCP's business, even if there were a successful raid on the capital.

However, Gehe A.G., a German company active in the same area as OCP, had approached OCP's management, who agreed on the principle of a bid. In order to encourage Gehe in its decision to bid, OCP's management had granted options to Gehe to acquire the two SCAs, subject only to its acquiring a majority of the stock of OCP in the course of its offer. The tender offer had been ultimately filed and approved by the CBV.

It turned out that the bid angered France's insular pharmaceutical guild, who rallied French investors and drug companies to their side. A group of French and foreign investors, led by the CCF and supported by certain French pharmaceutical groups, prepared a competitive bid for OCP.

To gain time, the group also persuaded two OCP shareholders to sue the CBV and to have its approval of Gehe's offer cancelled. In the meantime, the group of French and foreign investors filed their competitive bid for OCP. In an unprecedented move, and to the astonishment of both plaintiffs and defendants, the Court of Appeals of Paris cancelled Gehe's offer on the basis that Gehe had been granted, through the options to acquire the SCAs, an unfair advantage *vis-à-vis* other potential bidders in violation of the spirit of free competition among bidders in a takeover battle – an all-important principle. The Court reasoned that the options would make competing bids more difficult for other acquirers since only Gehe had the right to acquire immediate control over the main portion of the target's business; competing bidders would have had to obtain management consent after the offer. Gehe filed a new bid at a higher price than CCF's offer and ultimately acquired OCP.

These are the main takeover battles of the last 15 years. Many more are to come, but France now has a mature regulatory system, the roots of which lie in four key principles.

7. **Four key principles**

The result of the foregoing transactions, cases and regulations is that the French securities rules and the tender offer game are now based on the following four principles that serve as guidelines for most decisions by the stock market authorities:

(i) Equality of treatment among shareholders

This is the most salient principle. It is the reason why all shareholders of the target have the right to be paid the same price as the seller of a controlling block in the context of a standing offer. Under this rule, no special benefit or premium may be granted to key shareholders in the context of an offer. Further, both minority and majority shareholders must be offered exactly the same kind of consideration.

(ii) Free competition among bidders

This is the key principle in each tender offer battle which results from the OCP case. It is now critical, in every tender offer, both as a practical and legal matter, to respect the principle of free competition among bidders in the context of tender offer battles. This is the cornerstone of the current French rules whereby all bidders are to be placed at the same level. Under this principle, options granted by the management to one bidder over key assets can result in a bid not being valid, as was held to be the case in the OCP case. Also the granting of irrevocable rights to acquire a substantial amount of the target shares may also have the same result.

(iii) Respect of target's interests

The interests of the target must always be a concern of companies involved in a tender offer. Under this rule, managers may not unreasonably organise defensive measures contrary to the shareholders' interests. Last-minute dilutions of the existing holdings of the target in key subsidiaries, or sales of substantial company assets, even if otherwise lawful, are subject to civil actions in the courts as well as the COB's scrutiny.

(iv) True and fair disclosure

Finally, all material facts, shareholders' agreements and financial figures must be truly, fairly and promptly disclosed by all interested parties whether in the context of an offer or otherwise. Under this principle, any agreement that "may" affect the evaluation or the outcome of the offer entered into among the shareholders of the target (or any persons acting in concert with them) must be disclosed to the companies involved, the CBV and the COB. Those agreements must also be immediately disclosed to the public through press releases. Secret agreements or understandings are no longer permissible and the public must be made aware, as promptly as possible, of any key information in relation to the offer.

Non-compliance with any of these four principles, most of which are set forth (or implied) in COB Regulation No. 89–03, can result in the imposition of injunctions and fines by the COB. Non-compliance can also constitute grounds for civil suits for damages or injunctive relief by all interested parties. It can even result in a bid being cancelled, as in the OCP case, or other legal remedies.

8. The Future – the European "Big Bang": the Investment Services Directive

The Investment Services Directive 93/22/EEC of 10 May 1993 will substantially facilitate access by foreign players to securities brokerage and, more generally, to investment banking in France.

The Directive will effectively allow European and non-European "investment firms", including foreign credit institutions, to offer investment services (including securities brokerage, M&A activities, underwriting and portfolio management) in France, subject to a mere notification to the French authorities. Foreign investment firms will be allowed to trade on the exchange, become members of the French clearing system and act as filing agents of takeover bids and other public transactions. Conversely, French investment firms will be authorised to offer investment services in other European States subject to a mere notification to the local authorities. The implementation of the Directive is likely to result in a greater interrelation among European and international key players in the area.

Chapter 2
Authorities, Players and Markets

France has a complex regulatory system which results from the key legislative changes that have taken place in the past ten years. One of the characteristics of the French system is that France has two parallel market authorities, the Conseil des Bourses de Valeurs ("CBV") and its executive arm, the Société des Bourses Françaises ("SBF"), on the one hand, and the Commission des Opérations de Bourses ("COB"), on the other. The functions of these authorities have evolved over time. It is essential to have an overview of the main characteristics of the authorities empowered to regulate the securities markets, as well as the key players in the area and the main aspects of French markets, in order to understand French securities law.

Most of the rules discussed below concern French companies, either *sociétés anonyme* ("SAs") or *sociétés en commandité par actions* ("SCAs") whose shares are traded on the official market, the second market or the over-the-counter market of French stock exchanges (these companies are hereinafter referred to as "publicly traded companies"). Foreign companies may also be listed on the French markets but are subject to specific rules.

1. The French stock exchange

The French stock exchange is a "paperless" and "floorless" market. It is divided into three markets: the official, the second and the over-the-counter market.

In the old days France had seven stock exchanges (*bourses des valeurs*). The Paris bourse was the only truly national exchange and by far the largest and most active stock market.

Six regional exchanges were located in Bordeaux, Lyons, Nantes, Nancy, Lille and Marseilles.

In the 1980s, French securities were de-certificated. Also, the various French exchanges had been earlier merged. These two events enabled the stock-market to become fully computerised. As a result, the French stock market is now essentially a "paperless" and "floorless" market. That is to say that

19

almost all transactions taking place on the French market are made through a computerised system (called the "CAC" system) through terminals located on the stockbrokers premises. The French exchange is divided into three securities markets or listings: the official market (*"cote officielle"*), the second market *"second marché"*) and the over-the-counter market, (or *"marché hors-cote"*). There is also an options market located within the premises of the Paris stock exchange, the MONEP.

(i) The official market

The official market is the main French market. It is divided into two main sub-markets, the spot or cash market, known as the *marché au comptant*, and the monthly settlement market, known as the *marché à règlement mensuel* or *marché* ("RM"). For transactions on the cash market, the seller must transfer the securities being sold the same day to the account of its broker, which then executes the trade on the market. Similarly, the buyer must immediately pay the purchase price to its broker. Both the second market and the over-the-counter market also operate as cash markets.

On the monthly settlement market, transactions are recorded on the trading date, but settlement is deferred until the end of the month in accordance with a calendar published annually by the SBF. Transactions on the monthly settlement market occurring before the so-called settlement date are usually settled between brokers at the end of the current calendar month during the settlement period. The settlement date is the first day of the settlement period. It is usually the sixth business day before the end of the month. The settlement period is a seven-trading-day period, the dates of which are determined annually by the SBF under Article 4-2-8 of the General Regulation. The last day of the settlement period is the last trading day of the month (Article 4-2-7 of the General Regulation).

Transactions taking place on the monthly settlement market must, as a general rule, be for a minimum amount of securities or a multiple thereof (Article 4-2-9 of the General Regulation). Therefore, special fees, which must be settled immediately, are applicable for transactions involving less than the minimum quota. It is likely that the "minimum quota" require-ment will progressively disappear in the future. Tests are being made by the French market authorities in this regard. Further, transactions on the monthly settlement market are subject to a margin requirement.

Listing on the official market requires approval by the CBV and the registration of a prospectus by the COB (see Chapter 10, p. 149 *et seq*). Delisting of securities listed on these markets also requires a decision by the CBV and, usually, the filing by the controlling shareholder(s) of a public offer to purchase the remaining shares held by the other shareholders (called an *offre publique de retrait* ("OPR")) (see Chapters 13 and 14 p. 195 *et seq*).

As far as French equity securities are concerned, the official market is reserved for companies that have published financial statements for at least three years and of which at least 25% of the total capital stock is held by the public as at the date of the listing or immediately thereafter (Articles 3-1-11 and 3-1-14 of the General Regulation). The cash market (*marché au comptant*) of the official market is for securities that are not eligible for trading on the monthly settlement market.

(ii) The second market

The second market is reserved for companies that have published financial statements for at least two years and of which at least 10% of the total capital stock is held by the public as at the date of the listing or immediately thereafter (Articles 3-1-28, 3-1-29 and 3-1-31 of the General Regulation). Listing on the second market also requires the CBV's approval, as well as the registration of a prospectus by the COB. Delisting of securities listed on this market also requires a decision by the CBV.

At the end of a three-year period following an initial listing on the second market, the CBV decides whether to transfer the securities to the official market, maintain the listing on the second market or delist the securities for trading on the over-the-counter market (Article 3-1-33 of the General Regulation).

(iii) The over-the-counter market (*"marché hors-cote"*)

No listing or delisting decision by the CBV exists for companies traded on the over-the-counter market, which is mostly an unregulated market. Securities may be traded upon the mere request of a prospective seller or buyer (Article 3-1-9 of the General Regulation). Such a request is made through a broker who simply issues a "buy" or "sell" order. The order then appears on the daily listing for non-listed securities and, if a transaction is carried out, a price is quoted. Likewise, there is no delisting decision for securities traded on the over-the-counter market since the listing would simply disappear if no trade was made during a period of at least one month.

Companies whose securities are listed (or traded on the over-the-counter market, when the company has more than 300 holders of securities) are subject to specific rules since they are classified as public companies (*"sociétés faisant appel public à l'épargne"*). Public companies are subject to extensive regulations governing disclosures and to the COB's supervisory powers (see p. 158 *et seq*).

(iv) French securities

Since 1984, French securities are no longer certificated. The actual delivery of securities is replaced by entries made on the books of the issuer or its agent (called approved intermediaries – *"intermédiaires habilités"*), generally credit institutions or brokers. All securities listed or traded on a French stock exchange are eligible for inclusion in the Société Interprofessionnelle pour la Compensation des Valeurs Mobilières ("SICOVAM") system, the French securities book keeping system. In this system, physical delivery of certificates is replaced by a transfer on the books of SICOVAM, with whom all approved intermediaries have accounts.

Most shares held by the public and traded on French exchanges are held in bearer form ("*au porteur*"). The name of a holder of bearer securities is not known to the issuer but only to the approved intermediary with which the holder has an account (with the exception of *titres au porteur identifiables* ("TPIs"); see p. 109 *infra*). On the other hand, holders of bearer shares may always elect to hold their shares in the registered form ("*sous la forme nominative*"). The registration of securities enables the holder to acquire double voting rights or a preferred dividend (in the case of common stock and if the issuer's by-laws so provide) and to receive corporate documentation (notices of shareholders' meetings and prospectuses) directly. In certain cases, including directors of listed companies pursuant to insider regulations, press companies and companies engaged in defence procurement, share registration is mandatory.

(v) The MONEP and MATIF

The Marché des Options Négociables de Paris ("MONEP") was created in 1987. The MONEP is an equity option market located within the building which used to house the floor of the Paris stock exchange. Puts and calls concerning a limited number of equity securities issued by the main French issuers, as well as the CAC 40 index (the French index for the most actively traded securities), are traded there. Another market located within the Paris stock exchange premises is the Marché à Terme d'Instruments Financiers ("MATIF") on which financial futures are traded.

2. Key market players

It is said that approximately one-third of the securities listed in France are owned by, or in the name of, non-residents. These non-residents include US and Japanese pension funds, parent companies of French companies under foreign control and financial institutions (also, one-third of stockbroking firms are owned by foreign institutions). Another third of the investors in the French markets are French institutional investors, the so-called *investisseurs institutionnels* ("*zins zins*"), including French insurance companies (mainly state-owned until the recent French privatisations). Insurance companies are required to own a minimum percentage of their assets in listed securities denominated in French francs. The last third is held by the French public.

The following section gives a brief description of French market players.

(i) Stockbrokers

Like agents de change before them, sociétés de bourse enjoy exclusive rights over purchases and sales of listed securities.

While shortly after the "Big Bang" in 1988 credit institutions had been allowed to have minority participation in stockbroker firms, credit institutions quickly took over most stockbrokerage firms. This takeover resulted from two main reasons. First, some brokers being forced into bankruptcy as a result of erratic stock market behaviour. Second, the SBF was discovered to have lost FF500 million because it had not properly covered its positions and investments on the MATIF, the French futures market. A recapitalisation of the SBF was needed and was subscribed mainly by French banks which, at this stage, effectively took over the stockbrokers' profession. As a result, most brokers are now controlled by credit or financial institutions and one-third of brokerage firms are owned by foreign entities (as of February 1995, out of 52 stockbrokers in activity, 17 were owned by foreign institutions).

(a) Licensing procedure

All brokers (with the exception of *agents de change* and their successors) have to be licensed by the CBV (Article 2-1-1 of the General Regulation). The licensing procedure involves the filing of a detailed application with the SBF, which verifies more particularly the financial means of the candidates (brokers are subject to various ratios), as well as the technical skills and reputation of the proposed managers.

This situation will be substantially modified as a result of the implementation in France of the European Investment Services Directive that will allow foreign players (including European investment firms and credit institutions) to act as stockbrokers in France without any licensing requirement and even without any physical presence in France (see paragraph (c) below).

(b) Activities

Like *agents de change* before them, *sociétés de bourse* enjoy exclusive rights over purchases and sales of listed securities. Transactions among brokers must be carried out on the exchange ("*en bourse*") at the listed price (with certain exceptions including for block trades). As noted above, this is mainly done by computer – through the CAC system.

Most *sociétés de bourse* are "broker-dealers clearers" ("*négociateurs compensateurs*"); they act both as brokers for clients and effectively trade securities on the exchange on the clients' behalf. Stockbrokers of that category have front, middle and back offices. Alternatively, since December 1991, stockbrokers may choose exclusively to act as brokers and leave actual trading, delivering of the securities traded and payment, to colleagues (see CBV General Decision No. 91-16 dated 11 December 1991). These are called "*négociateurs purs*". Another category are stockbrokers acting exclusively as traders for other colleagues; these are the "*compensateurs multiples*".

All transactions between brokers are centralised by the SBF and each broker is deemed to have purchased or sold the securities for any given transaction from or to the SBF, and thus ends up with a single debit or credit balance with this entity.

When a broker is involved in a transaction, it usually charges a special fee called *"courtage"*, the rate of which is set from time to time by the broker. Prior to 1988, the *courtage* was set by regulations issued by the French Ministry of Economy (since brokers enjoyed a legal monopoly) and all brokers were required to charge the same amount of fees to clients. One exception was that professional financial intermediaries (such as credit institutions) were entitled to a rebate (*"remise"*) on this fee, which could not be enjoyed by the institutions' clients.

Brokers are bound by professional secrecy rules and may not disclose the names of their clients, even to another broker who is a party to the transaction. Obviously, these professional secrecy rules may not be presented as objections to the COB.

Most stockbrokers also employ financial analysts and publish investment reports. They also frequently manage securities' portfolios on behalf of clients, as well as investment funds.

(c) The Investment Services Directive – The end of "French exclusivity"

The Investment Services Directive dated 10 May 1993 will greatly modify access to stock brokerage in France. In substance, the Directive liberalises the right of European investment firms to provide investment services (including securities brokerage) throughout the Community, including France, once they have been licensed in their home countries to conduct such activities. The Directive is to be implemented in the Member States by 1 July 1995 through legislation which must take effect no later than 31 December 1995.

The Directive will permit European firms to branch out freely or provide cross-border services within the Community on the basis of the licence obtained in their "home" Member States and continued supervision by the competent authorities of those States. This is the "single licence" and "home-country control" concept already in place for credit institutions on the basis of the Second Banking Directive. The Investment Services Directive requires prior notification of the host country, followed by a consultation between home and the host regulatory authorities. In substance, the host country may not oppose the application made by a duly licensed European investment firm.

Access to the European market for non-European firms will also be possible if reciprocity is ensured in the home country of the institution. If a Member State receives a request to authorise a non-Community investment firm, it will have to inform the competent authorities of the other Member States and the Commission. The authorisation will be withheld until the Commission has checked whether investment firms in every Member State enjoy reciprocal treatment in the home country of the applicant.

If the Commission finds that reciprocity is not ensured, it will be able to refuse the application.

The key provision is that Member States will be required to ensure that all European investment firms and credit institutions authorised to engage in brokerage, dealing or market-making activities in their home jurisdiction have access to membership of stock exchanges and organised securities markets of host Member States where similar services are provided, as well as membership of clearing and settlement systems that are available to members of such exchanges and markets. This access must be given by direct stock exchange membership through a local branch, or by indirect membership via a local subsidiary or the acquisition of an existing local member firm.

If a stock exchange does not require a physical presence for domestic members, *e.g.* where access may be had by electronic hook-up, foreign firms should have the same opportunity. Further, for Member States that do not allow domestic banks as securities exchange members, it will not be possible to deny access to their organised securities markets to qualifying credit institutions from other Member States.

(ii) Credit institutions

Credit institutions are the French banking institutions. They include banks, mutual banks (*banques co-opératives ou mutualistes*), saving institutions (*caisses d'épargne et de prévoyance*), municipal banks (*caisses de crédit municipal*), financial companies (*sociétés financières*) and specialised financial institutions (*institutions financières spécialisées*) such as the SBF. They are governed by Law No. 84-46 of 24 January 1984 relating to the activity and control of credit institutions.

Credit institutions enjoy exclusive rights to carry out banking activities on a habitual basis. These activities include the receipt of funds from the public; credit and lending activities; leasing activities; the granting of guarantees; and the issue and management of means of payment such as cheques and credit cards. All credit institutions are subject to the Second Banking Directive, which has been implemented in France, and which includes provisions similar to the ones applicable to investment firms as a result of the Investment Services Directive.

There is no distinction in France between commercial and investment banks and banks may (subject to certain ratios) freely invest in commercial and industrial companies. They may also engage in corporate finance activities and credit institutions and thus play an active role in the tender offer area as advisers and brokers. They control most of the stockbrokers and enjoy the exclusive right to file public offers with the CBV and draft prospectuses with the COB. Moreover, credit institutions frequently act as financial guarantors for the undertakings of bidders or lenders.

Credit institutions, whether directly or indirectly, also manage (or act as custodians for) investment funds which heavily invest in the securities markets. They further manage securities portfolios for clients' accounts and therefore play a major role in their investment strategy. Finally, most of the major French banking groups are affiliated with insurance or industrial groups.

(iii) French institutional investors

Institutional investors include insurance companies, investment funds, financial groups and others. They are said to own one-third of French securities.

Two categories of French investors are worthy of note. The first one includes French insurance companies that are required to maintain minimum investments in listed securities in order to enhance solvency. They must establish technical reserves that must be covered at all times by assets meeting various specified criteria, including securities listed on a stock exchange in an OECD Member State. They are thus heavy investors on the French securities markets.

The second category includes French investment funds that include *sociétés d'investissement à capital variable* ("SICAVs") and *fonds communs de placement* ("FCPs"). (These are generally collectively referred to as *Organismes de Placement Collectifs en Valeurs Mobilières* or OPCVMs.) The major difference between SICAVs and FCPs is that SICAVs are corporate entities subject to most of the rules governing SAs and FCPs are unincorporated funds that are not legal entities.

OPCVMS are required primarily to hold listed securities. An OPCVM may not invest more than 10% of its assets in warrants, deposit certificates (*bons de caisse*), mortgage certificates, promissory notes and non-listed securities. A security is considered "listed" for this purpose, and therefore not subject to a 10% ceiling, if it is listed either (i) on a stock exchange located in France or in a European Union Member State or (ii) on a stock exchange located in another country, provided that, in this latter case, the exchange has not been disapproved by the COB. Investment funds are always required to act in the best interests of their shareholders and are thus generally bound to sell securities held by them at the highest price possible (in the context of a tender offer or otherwise).

Holdings, industrial and financial companies also invest heavily in the stock market. As noted *supra*, there is no regulatory separation between banking, on the one hand, and industry and finance on the other. Thus major financial groups in France (such as Suez, Paribas, Lazard, BNP and Société Générale) frequently hold interests in industrial companies and there is a great degree of interrelation among the banking business and the industrial world (see "French circles" Section 4 *infra*).

(iv) Foreign investors

These are mostly investment and retirement funds, such as Japanese and US pension funds which are also said to represent one-third of the French market.

They are of great concern to the authorities since they manage immense funds and can truly influence overall market trends in France. In the context of the worldwide competition among stock exchanges, and more particularly the on-going battle for European leadership between Paris, Frankfurt and London, French authorities are trying to win back business from the rival London market through a step-by-step deregulation of the French market. Examples are the withdrawal of the stock exchange stamp tax duty in 1993 and the new block trade rules (see p. 188 *et seq*).

(v) Individual shareholders – the public

Individual shareholders (the public) are referred to as the "*petits porteurs*", literally "small holders" (including the *veuve de Carpentras* or Carpentras's widow; the French equivalent of the Belgian dentist). Individual investors represent approximately five million French individuals holding small quantities of securities. They are generally not well informed about market trends. They frequently complain that the disclosures made by issuers or other market players are overly complicated and presented in a language that only accounting experts, investment bankers and M&A lawyers can understand.

The number of individual French shareholders substantially increased as a result of French privatisations in 1986. For example, Compagnie de Saint-Gobain had over one million shareholders following its privatisation in 1986. French individual equity holders suffered a great deal as a result of the 1987 crash and the erratic behaviour of the stock markets in the following years. They are said to represent another one-third of the French market.

A small number of them have grouped themselves into non-profit associations ("*associations d'investisseurs*"). At this stage, there are only a few of them, such as the Association pour la Défense des Actionnaires Minoritaires – ("ADAM"). The ADAM is an association whose goal is to protect the interests of individual shareholders. It frequently takes part in legal actions initiated in the tender offer area when the interests of minority shareholders are at stake. Other examples are the Association Nationale des Actionnaires de France – ("ANAF") and the investment club federation (Fédération Nationale des Clubs d'Investissement).

Another 'gadfly' is Deminor, a Belgian consulting firm that specialises in advising minority shareholders. Unlike ANAF or ADAM, it is a commercial company.

These institutions have, so far, frequently challenged decisions made by key shareholders supposedly against the interests of minority shareholders. They are mostly successful in gaining press attention, but have never been successful in cancelling decisions made.

The shareholders' associations ("*associations d'actionnaires*") are a newly created structure that enables shareholders of one company to group themselves to collectively exercise minority rights such as the appointment of an expert to investigate a given transaction or the calling of a shareholders' meeting (see Chapter 12 *infra*).

3. Stock exchange authorities

The two main authorities in the stock market area are the Conseil des Bourses de Valeurs (and its executive arm, the Société des Bourses Françaises) and the Commission des Opérations de Bourse.

As already discussed above, there are several French authorities in the stock market area. The first one is the professional body in charge of organising and monitoring the market and its players, the Conseil des Bourses de Valeurs ("CBV"). Formerly controlled by independent brokers, it is now effectively controlled by French banks, which have taken over most Paris stockbroking firms. The CBV's executive arm is the Société des Bourses Françaises ("SBF"), which runs the market on a daily basis.

The second key body is the Commission des Opérations de Bourse ("COB"), created by the 1967 Ordinance governing the disclosures to be made by public companies. The COB has many of the same functions as the US Securities & Exchange Commission. It is an independent administrative agency, *i.e.*, it is, since the 1989 Law, independent from the French government, although its Chairman is appointed by governmental decree and he or she may not be removed, nor re-appointed.

The third player is the French State through its financial arm, the Treasury, the most powerful Department of the Ministry of Economy. A Representative of the State attends all meetings of the CBV but does not vote and the Treasury monitors all foreign investments in France.

Newly arrived is the Paris Court of Appeals, which has jurisdiction for most lawsuits initiated against both the COB and the CBV.

It is worth looking at these authorities in more detail.

(i) Conseil des Bourses de Valeurs

The CBV is a professional body which, through its General Regulation, covers licensing and conduct of brokers, listing and delisting of securities, trading procedures and tender offers.

The CBV is the main regulatory body of the French exchanges and is composed of ten members elected by brokers, plus one person representing listed issuers and one representative of the employees of stockbrokers and the SBF (Article 5 of the Stock Exchange Law). A representative of the government and the Managing Director of the SBF also attend the meetings of the CBV. In practice, since almost all brokers have been taken over by banks, most of the members of the CBV are representatives of French banking groups. The CBV has to meet at least eight times a year. In practice, however, it meets approximately every three weeks.

The Stock Exchange Law granted the CBV extensive regulatory authority that had previously been delegated to the Compagnie des Agents de

Change by the Ministry of Finance. It prepares and amends its own General Regulation (Règlement Général du Conseil des Bourses de Valeurs) which is the main body of regulation in the area (Article 6 of the Stock Exchange Law). The newly issued English translation of the General Regulation is attached to this book.

The CBV also issues so-called "General Decisions" ("*decisions generales*") which are sets of regulations implementing the General Regulation. It also issues "individual decisions" including the approval of a tender offer or the granting of an exemption from the mandatory tender rule. The CBV's decisions are published by the SBF by telecopy to interested parties and subscribers.

In general, the CBV has a real discretionary power to approve or disapprove a transaction and its debates are strictly confidential, except when it decides to issue a release. In practice, the staff of the SBF prepares a report concerning each decision that the CBV is to take concerning the question at hand.

In contrast to the COB, which has investigators and may carry out administrative enquiries, the CBV has no investigative powers. For example, when an offer is filed, the CBV does not (and in fact cannot) question representatives of the target or other interested parties.

(ii) Société des Bourses Françaises

The SBF is the operational body of French exchanges and the executive arm of the CBV.

The SBF is the successor to the Chambre Syndicale des Agents de Change, the executive arm of the Compagnie and was created in 1988 by virtue of the Stock Exchange Law.

The SBF is a so-called "specialised financial institution" (*institution financière spécialisée*), a term that covers credit institutions (such as banks) that have been assigned a public service mission. The SBF is responsible for the day-to-day operations of the French stock exchange. It is in charge of recording and acting as a clearing agency for transactions entered into by brokers (Article 10 of the Stock Exchange Law). The CBV has delegated substantial authority to the SBF in the daily supervision of tender and exchange offers. It is the key operational body of French stock exchanges. Its staff are frequently consulted and questioned by advisers and are in charge of preparing all matters dealt with by the CBV. The SBF is thus very influential.

(iii) Commission des Opérations de Bourse

The COB monitors the disclosures made by public companies and pursues securities law violators.

The COB has a different role than the CBV since it is in charge of promoting and enforcing French regulations governing disclosures. It was created in

1967 with a view to protecting individual investors in the French securities market.

(a) Organisation

The COB is headed by a Board (*"collège"*) composed of eight members and one Chairman (Article 2 of the 1967 Ordinance). The Board includes representatives of each of the following bodies: the Conseil d'Etat (the top French administrative court), the Cour de Cassation (the French Supreme Court), the Cour des Comptes (a French administrative body in charge of auditing administrations), the CBV, the Conseil du Marché à Terme (the supervisory authority for the future markets) and the Banque de France. Two members chosen on the basis of their professional qualifications also sit on the Board. Members of the COB may not be removed by the government.

The Chairman of the COB is appointed by governmental decree for a six-year period and his appointment may not be removed nor renewed. The Board usually meets twice a month and its deliberations are confidential unless it decides to publish a release concerning a particular transaction or when a matter raises broader issues. The COB has a staff of 230 persons and is organised into several departments in charge of investigations, disclosures, international affairs, legal affairs, accounting affairs, capital markets and public relations.

(b) Regulatory powers

The COB is empowered to issue regulations (règlements) applicable to publicly-traded companies and other players in the securities markets such as portfolio managers, and brokers (Article 4-1 of the 1967 Ordinance). It also issues instructions and recommendations. A key aspect of its activities is the enforcement of securities rules through its Investigation Department (Service de l'Inspection). The Investigation Department staff uses sophisticated computer systems to monitor market transactions on a real-time basis. There are two types of monitoring. The first one generally applies to all securities transactions and the other comes into play when abnormal prices or volumes are noticed or when a company is the subject of particular transactions. The COB is linked with the stockmarket computer network through several passive CAC terminals enabling it to follow all transactions made. The COB further uses a database enabling it to visualise on a computer screen events announced by an issuer before or after suspect transactions are made.

When unusual transactions are noted, the COB usually requests explanations from issuers or stockbrokers. If there is a suspected securities law violation, it can decide to initiate an investigation. COB's investigators are entitled to review (and obtain copies of) any relevant documents, and no professional secrecy rules may be invoked against them, except by lawyers. They have access to recordings made in trading rooms, confirmation tickets, client names and accounts, etc. The COB may also call witnesses and suspected violators to testify, with a minimum prior notice of six days. Witnesses and suspects may have legal assistance and minutes of the interviews are prepared and signed by the interested parties (Article 5B of the 1967 Ordinance).

Following an investigation, a report is made to the Board, which may either (i) decide not to pursue the matter, (ii) issue a fine or injunction, (iii) transmit the file to another professional authority (the CBV in the case of a stockbroker, or the Commission Bancaire in the case of a credit institution) or (iv) transmit the report to the criminal prosecutor (see *infra*).

Subject to judicial control, the COB may seize securities or bank accounts, request that a guarantee bond be issued or suspend professional licences. The COB may also carry out searches at violators' homes. In practice, these techniques are rarely used since parties tend to collaborate with investigators.

(c) Fines and injunctions

The COB may issue injunctions and fines in the case of a breach of its regulations if the breach results in either:

– an impairment of the market's operations;
– unjustified advantages for certain parties;
– inequality of treatment of investors;
– violation of disclosure requirements; or
– certain parties benefiting from improper acts of intermediaries.

Fines imposed may not exceed FF10 million or, where a profit has been made, ten times the amount of such profit, and a COB fine does not preclude criminal prosecution on the basis of the same facts (Articles 9-1 and 9-2 of the 1967 Ordinance). COB sanctions may be challenged before the Court of Appeals of Paris (Article 12 of the 1967 Ordinance). Sanctions issued by the COB are always publicly disclosed.

The COB is very keen on pursuing violators. In the years 1991, 1992 and 1993, the COB issued fines in 20 cases (ten of which concerned insider trading). Needless to say, these powers give substantial leverage to the COB in order to enforce its regulations and prompt fair behaviour by market players.

(d) Criminal prosecution

If a potential criminal violation is suspected by the COB (generally following an investigation), the Board transmits a report to the criminal prosecutor (the "Parquet"), who then initiates a criminal procedure against the violator. In fact, the COB is the main "supplier" of insider trading cases to the French legal system (so far, there have been 20 judgments rendered against insiders).

Criminal authorities may always request the advice of the COB (Article 12-1 of the 1967 Ordinance). In practice, the COB staff's advice is systematically sought in criminal cases concerning securities law and such advice is mandatory in the context of insider trading cases. Civil jurisdictions may also seek COB advice, which is not mandatory, but very frequently sought (Article 12-1 of the 1967 Ordinance).

(e) COB's releases, reports and opinions

The COB is entitled to disclose any opinion or comment concerning an issuer, a particular transaction or a securities law violation. In this regard, the COB may issue warnings ("*avertissements*") on the first page of prospectuses and is increasingly inclined to do so. For example, within the context of the OCP bid, the COB stated on the first page of Gehe AG's prospectus that Gehe had options to acquire key Gehe assets (Gehe's initial offer was subsequently cancelled by judicial decision for this reason).

Warnings usually concern:

(i)   the absence of a public market for securities offered to the public;
(ii) a material litigation concerning an issuer;
(iii) accounting and pricing issues; or
(iv) key information contained in the prospectus that the COB wishes to point out to the public.

The COB may also release opinions to the press, and these are reproduced in the COB's monthly reports. COB opinions have an important psychological impact on the parties involved since these are always scrutinised by the media.

The COB publishes an annual report which is delivered to the President of the French Republic. The report summarises the COB's activities, new regulations which have been adopted, and its recommendations for the future.

Upon request, pursuant to COB Regulation 90-07, the COB may issue no-action letters, called "*rescrits*", construing its regulations within the context of a specific transaction. If the COB states that a party in a given transaction is complying with its rules, it is precluded from taking any action against the party having requested the letter. The no-action letters are published (on a no-name basis) in the COB's monthly bulletins.

In practice, no-action letters are rarely used (the COB has, so far, issued only one no-action letter) since parties prefer to consult the COB on an informal basis where the advice remains confidential. The informal advice of the COB has *inter alia* the same result as a no-action letter for the concerned parties.

In case of a dispute, and with the consent of the parties concerned, the COB acts as arbitrator in the securities law area (usually among clients and financial intermediaries). Anyone can file a complaint with the COB (Article 4 of the 1967 Ordinance) and in fact it receives almost 3,000 complaints per year, most of which are without legal basis and simply result from poor understanding of market rules.

(iv) Court of Appeals of Paris

The Court of Appeals of Paris is a newcomer in the securities law area. Since 1988, it has had sole jurisdiction for all challenges to CBV decisions in the tender offer area (Article 5 of the Stock Exchange Law). A special Chamber of the Court specialises in stock market issues and its judges are thoroughly familiar with the tender offer game, since almost every takeover battle that has taken place after 1988 has ended up in court. There thus exists a substantial amount of case law in this field.

So far, except for the OCP-Gehe decision,[1] the Court has always upheld CBV decisions in the public offers area. This probably results from the fact that, in the Court's mind, the CBV is much closer to the market than the Court itself.

The Court of Appeals of Paris also has sole jurisdiction for all appeals made against COB decisions except for disciplinary decisions (Article 12 of the 1967 Ordinance). In the tender offer area, challenges to COB decisions are less frequent than challenges to CBV decisions, since the COB's role is mostly confined to registering prospectuses. Most challenges to COB decisions concern the issue of fines for insider trading and non-disclosures of material facts. The Court of Appeals generally tends to sustain decisions of the COB.

(v) The Treasury

The Treasury Department ("Trésor") of the Ministry of Economy is one of the most powerful administrative bodies in France, being the financial arm of the Ministry of Economy. It is staffed by powerful "Finance Inspectors" (see p. 37 *infra*) and is the guardian of France as regards foreign investors. The Treasury monitors foreign investments through the French foreign investment control scheme (see p. 175 *infra*). Thus all bids made by non-residents are subject to the Treasury's approval, which is largely discretionary as far as non-Europeans are concerned, although the attitude of the French authorities is becoming more and more liberal in this area. Further, representatives of the Treasury attend all meetings of the CBV and are very influential there.

On the other hand, the Treasury has lost part of its powers in the tender offer area as, until 11 March 1986, the Minister of Economy had the right to object to any tender offer within three days after approval thereof by the *Chambre* (former Article 183 of the General Regulation). This provision is now abrogated. Further, while prior to the 1989 Law, a representative of the Treasury attended meetings of the Board of the COB, this is no longer the case.

---

[1] *Mutuelles du Mans* v *OCP*, Court of Appeals of Paris, Section CBV, 27 April 1993, JCP éd. E. n° 25, 1993, II 457, note Viandier, Banque et Droit, p. 29, May–June 1993; Joly Bourse et Produits Financiers, n° 6, November–December 1993, note Marie-Anne Frison-Roche.

(vi) Several approaches to market regulations

There are some differences between the approaches of the three main authorities (CBV, COB and Court of Appeals of Paris) in regulating the French market.

The CBV and its executive arm, the SBF, have a practical close-to-the-market approach and are, in general, as close as possible to the concerns of issuers and acquirers. The CBV also tries to increase the degree of predictability in its decisions. It has considerable discretionary powers and is almost never bound to issue a decision one way or another. For example, it is never bound to grant an exemption to the mandatory offer obligation even if the applicant clearly falls within the technical scope of the exemption, nor to approve an offer. It has created certain techniques, such as the "action in concert" rulings, that have resulted in key innovations in securities law (see Chapter 4). It usually responds very quickly.

The COB has a different role since it is in charge of pursuing securities law violators. In view of its duties, the COB does not hesitate to require players to take steps to ensure equality of treatment among shareholders and free competition among bidders. It is recognised as an extremely powerful organisation and its Investigation Department is both respected and feared by market players. The COB has gained respect from players and it can be rather severe with violators. The fact that the COB can impose fines on violators of its own regulations appears shocking to certain practitioners since it is at the same time plaintiff and judge (*juge et partie*) on these issues. However, decisions are subject to appeal.

The Court of Appeals of Paris is a true newcomer. Most of the time, it tends to uphold decisions made by market authorities. As noted *supra*, a Chamber of the Court specialises in securities law issues and its members are thoroughly familiar with the tender offer game.

A number of checks and balances exist among the regulators themselves. For instance, when the CBV proposes any amendments or supplements to its General Regulation, these must be reviewed both by the COB and the Bank of France (the opinions of the COB or the Bank of France are, however, not binding on the CBV). They are thereafter officially enacted by the Minister of Economy, in practice after considerable consultation in the business community. These authorities are therefore able to co-ordinate their policies. Also, COB regulations are subject to approval by the Ministry of Economy.

4. The French business community – a "sociological approach"

It is essential for foreign investors to grasp two concepts:

(i) The French business community is composed of various circles of influence; and

(ii) "France is a small country and Paris is a village".

(i) Circles of influence

The first concept comprises certain concentric circles of influence which control the French capitalistic galaxy. They are:

– the State and industry;
– graduates of élite schools.

(a) The State and industry

In a simplified fashion it can be said that there are five categories in this circle, each of which operates according to its own logic.

A. The State-owned sector

The first category, with a decreasing influence, is the State-owned sector. Before the 1986 and 1994 waves of privatisation, the French State used to control key areas of the French economy, including the largest French companies such as Elf Aquitaine and Rhône-Poulenc and the largest French banks (Crédit Lyonnais, Société Générale, and Banque Nationale de Paris). It also controlled almost all insurance companies operating in France, including Union des Assurances de Paris, Assurances Générales de France and Groupement des Assurances Nationales as well as certain key "national" groups such as Electricité de France and Société Nationales des Chemins de Fer Français. The public sector is now shrinking rapidly but is still powerful. Both it and, to a certain extent, the privatised sector are largely staffed, at the executive level, with graduates from the élite French schools, ENA and Polytechnique (see *infra*). Some key institutions, such as the Caisse des Dépôts et Consignations, one of France's largest banks that renders public interest banking services, is also a heavy investor in the French securities market and sometimes acts as the French state financial arm on the stock market. It took part in the socialist raid on the recently privatised Société Générale in 1990, which turned out to be a total failure. The State-owned sector must please its shareholder, the French Government, and its decisions are not always predictable. In addition, it has limited financing from its parent since the French State usually runs a budget deficit.

B. Financial groups

The second category is comprised of entities controlled by certain financial groups out of which three are worthy of note. The first one, Compagnie de Suez, the largest French investment bank or *banque d'affaires* in French parlance, became heavily involved in major tender offer battles (*e.g.* such as the Société Générale de Belgique and Perrier bids). The second one is Maison Lazard Frères & Cie, the French arm of the Lazard galaxy. The third key player is Paribas, a powerful institution with heavy investment in French industry. Other players include Banque Nationale de Paris, Societé Générale, CCF, Credit Lyonnais, Demachy Worms & Cie and the increasingly powerful French branches of foreign institutions, most of which are of anglo-saxon origin.

As far as French institutions are concerned they also engage in M&A advice, capital market activities and (except Lazard) in commercial banking. They all control several banks and are often staffed with graduates of the French "élite" schools (see *infra*). Their key officers and partners sit on numerous boards of industrial companies sometimes affiliated with them and sometimes not. In fact, their sphere of influence goes way beyond their affiliated companies (subsidiaries and others) since, both on the advisory and on the commercial banking sides, they have ties with large groups of companies.

C. Privatised companies

The third category comprises the recently privatised multinationals. It includes very large groups or conglomerates, such as Elf Aquitaine, France's largest company, Rhône-Poulenc SA, Compagnie de Saint-Gobain and Renault, as well as, on the financial side, Banque Nationale de Paris, Union des Assurances de Paris and Société Générale. This category is being slowly integrated into the private sector and is changing its habits. Companies of this category keep on selling non-essential businesses and buying others.

D. Independent French industrial groups

The fourth category consists of the few independent French industrial groups. The category includes not only large companies, such as Peugeot SA, Lagardère Groupe and its subsidiary Matra Hachette, L'Orial, Total, Danone, Carrefour, Casino, Générale des Eaux and Lyonnaise des Eaux-Dumez, but also companies of a smaller size controlled by families, and local institutions such as Pernod Ricard, Taittinger, Dollfus Mieg et Compagnie, Paluel-Marmont or Rossignol SA. The small independent companies are, to a certain extent, part of a disappearing breed since a fair number of these are slowly being acquired by French or foreign multinational groups or financial institutions in the worldwide concentration movement. One expanding category in the independent sector is the newly created groups controlled by the French "tycoons". These are individuals who, with the help of financial groups have created empires in certain sectors in an astonishingly short time. The three most salient examples are Bernard Arnault, who now controls France's number one luxury goods group LVMH-Moët Hennessy Louis Vuitton; François Pinault, who controls a European-wide distribution network, including "Le Printemps" and FNAC; and Vincent Bolloré, who is active in the shipping and transportation businesses. All three are (or have been) backed by Lazard Frères on the investment banking side, and Crédit Lyonnais on the commercial banking side.

E. Foreign controlled companies

The fifth category is the foreign sector which includes companies controlled by European and American groups. It includes both very large companies and smaller companies. Most companies of this group are generally delisted through a squeeze-out procedure or otherwise shortly after their acquisition since foreign groups are not always at ease with minority shareholders in a listed subsidiary.

(b) Graduates of "elite" schools

This is the second circle, a true peculiarity of the French business community. It consists of the various powerful circles of alumni of certain French élite schools intended to educate candidates for the French civil service.

The first and probably most prestigious group consists of the French Polytechnique graduates. Polytechnique is the most eminent school. Although it is a military school, most of its graduates initially tend to enter top offices within the French administration (Ministerial Cabinets or the Treasury) and thereafter settle in the private sector. Many of these graduates are among the top executives of French banks and insurance companies.

The second group, which is at least as powerful as the first one, consists of the graduates of the Ecole Nationale d'Administration ("ENA"), the top French civil service school. The best ranking *énarques* (ENA's graduates) usually choose the prestigious Finance Inspection Department of the Ministry of Economy (and thus become the so-called "Finance Inspectors") or join one of the numerous departments of the French Treasury. More and more commonly, ENA graduates tend to leave the public sector after a short stay in the French civil service and are frequently hired by French banks and other market players who are attracted by their close links with policy-makers. They also traditionally occupy key functions in the public industrial or financial circle.

There are also sub-categories, such as graduates of Polytechnique who are also ENA graduates (among them former French President Valéry Giscard d'Estaing), or ENA graduates who have also graduated from the Ecole Normale Supérieure, a prime school for would-be professors, or polytechniciens who have entered the Ecole des Mines, who are very evident within certain companies such as Total, the oil company, or Péchiney, the State-owned aluminium company.

A true unity exists among these cliques; they constitute concentric networks of people with a strong tendency to co-opt classmates to key functions. They also display certain habits for instance, polytechniciens invariably call each other by their first name and say the familiar "*tu*" to their fellows. Other schools exist with similar alumni networks, but these are the circles with prime importance.

F. Other influential groups

In France, as in other countries, there are powerful family circles, and a limited number of French families control both key industrial groups and mid-size companies. For example, the French perfume company L'Oréal is largely controlled by the Bettencourt family (with the strong presence of Nestlé SA); Pernod Ricard is controlled by the Ricard family; a fair portion of Peugeot SA is still owned by the Peugeot family; and the Michelin family own part of Compagnie Générale des Etablissements Michelin, the world's largest tyre manufacturer. When investing in such a company, it is essential to understand the links between the families, their relatives and advisers.

Other categories include certain executive "clubs" in which key managers discuss and exchange ideas, the powerful and secret French freemasonry organisation, and links with political parties (certain groups tend to finance only certain parties and certain managers have close links with certain politicians).

(ii) A small community

The second concept to be understood by investors is that the French securities market is a place where all the players know each other, and meet and meet again. "One cannot lie twice among market players" runs a common saying. Indeed, they all meet frequently, whether within the circles discussed above, or for other reasons. This is reinforced by the great degree of cross-shareholding, co-operation and inter-relationships among French groups.

This scenario is important for anyone wanting to foresee players' re-actions. For example, a decision-maker would always want to satisfy persons within its "circle" and this would come before the willingness to please a foreign investor (or even a client) without strong ties in France. On the other hand, there also exist established enemies (banks who are always on opposing sides in public bids) or at least competitors who would be pleased to attack rivals.

Also, certain businessmen consider that there are reserved territories and would not allow third parties to enter certain business sectors.

Finally, within the village, there may be key arrangements among groups known as "the President's words" (*paroles de Président*) or "Gentlemen's agreements" and, although these are not easily enforceable in court, any defaulting party would run the risk of being condemned by its peers within the financial community (or its circle) if it broke its word. This can represent a far greater sanction than a legal sanction (which is uncertain, time consuming and gives adverse publicity).

The above account of habits and relationships within certain French circles is a very simplified version of reality. All the circles mentioned above are heavily inter-related and very influential and it is not always clear where a player stands or in which sphere they operate. However, this all needs to be taken into account by foreigners investing in France.

CONTENTS OF CHAPTER 3

Chapter 3
Acquisition of Shares in Listed Companies

Under current regulations, a buyer may acquire up to one-third of a listed company's capital or voting rights without having to bid for the remaining shares provided it is not acting in concert with other shareholders. A would-be acquirer can reach the one-third threshold by buying shares on the open market in a process called the "creeping" tender (*ramassage*). It is, in fact, sometimes the practice for a bidder to acquire an initial stake in a target company prior to commencing a formal tender offer. The low-key approach of the creeping tender has some appeal since any bid that is the slightest bit controversial (a foreign acquirer of the only company of its sort or a famous French brand) may instantly become a *cause célèbre* with front page coverage in *Les Echos* or *La Tribune*. However, creeping tenders have one significant disadvantage. If the market for the target's securities is too thin, open-market purchases are likely to push the price up, and this might increase the cost of a public offer (if it is eventually filed). Further, such purchases may indicate to the target that a hostile bid is on its way, enabling management to prepare its defences.

Another technique is to identify a block of shares for sale and purchase it directly from one or several shareholders. In this regard, the new regulation concerning block deals (enabling purchasers to acquire big stakes at a price other than the listed price) certainly constitutes a help for acquirers.

In both cases, the acquirer would generally be required to make its acquisition through a duly licensed French broker. In addition, when reaching certain levels of ownership (which may be as low as 0.5% of the target's voting rights), the acquirer may be required to disclose its ownership as soon as it reaches certain thresholds, if so provided in the by-laws.

1. The brokers' exclusivity

On pain of nullity and heavy tax fines, one cannot acquire securities listed on either the official or the second market without recourse to brokers. All transactions in listed securities must be made at the price listed on the exchange (subject to two exceptions; option contracts and block trades).

These provisions constitute the basis of the brokers' exclusive rights, usually referred to as the "French stockbrokers' monopoly" (*monopole des sociétés de bourses*).

(i) Scope of the brokers' monopoly

Purchases and sales of listed securities subject to the brokers' exclusivity and entered into without a broker are void. Further, parties to the transaction may be liable for a tax fine equal to twice the value of the securities transferred (Article 2 of the Stock Exchange Law) and any party acting as a broker that is not licensed as a *société de bourse* may be subject to imprisonment (two months to two years) and/or payment of a fine (FF3,600 to FF2,500,000 or one-fourth of either the value of the securities transferred or any damages paid).

(a) Affected securities

Brokers enjoy exclusive rights over purchases and sales of securities listed on an exchange by virtue of a decision of the CBV (Article 1 of the Stock Exchange Law). In other words, the monopoly only applies to securities listed on either the official or the second market ("listed securities").

Prior to the enactment of the Stock Exchange Law, the brokers' monopoly also applied to purchases and sales of securities traded on the over-the-counter market as long as a price for the securities had been listed by the Chambre within one month preceding the relevant transaction. However, the brokers' exclusivity thus no longer applies to securities traded on the over-the-counter market where listing does not require a decision by the CBV, nor does it apply to securities issued by private companies.[1]

(b) Concerned transactions

The brokers' exclusive rights apply to all "*negotiations*" (or brokerage transactions) and sales of listed securities, subject to limited exceptions.

The concept of negotiation corresponds generally to the English term "brokerage". It includes all purchases and sales that involve an intermediary. The intermediary may act as an agent, an auctioneer, a broker (or *courtier*), or an agent for an undisclosed principal (*commissionnaire*), as is usually the case in ordinary transactions involving brokers. It is useful here to look at the way in which stock is acquired in a listed company. Generally, a prospective investor would call up its bankers or financial intermediary to issue a trade order (*ordre de bourse*). Trade orders are either without indication of price, in which case the trade is made at the next listed price, or, more frequently, subject to price limits (a maximum price in case of a purchase and a minimum price in case of a sale). The intermediary would then transmit the trade order to a broker who would carry out

---

[1] *Le Républicain Lorrain* v *Etudes et Finances*, Commercial Court of Paris, 16 March 1990, JCP, 1990, éd. E, II, 15810.

44

the deal with another broker through the French stockbrokers' computer network.

The brokers' monopoly also applies to all direct or indirect sales of listed securities. Notwithstanding the direct or indirect provision, it seems possible to acquire the shares of a holding company, the sole assets of which are listed securities, without having to have recourse to a broker. This technique is sometimes used to allow a potential seller to sell listed securities indirectly at a freely agreed price. Another advantage of this structure is that the listed shares retain any double voting rights notwithstanding their indirect transfer. One example was the US company Emerson Electric's acquisition of Omet SA, a family holding company, whose main assets were 36.7% of the voting rights and 22.79% of the shares of Leroy-Somer just before it launched a bid for Leroy-Somer in 1989. This acquisition enabled Emerson to gain control over a substantial portion of the target's shares while retaining their double voting rights, since these were kept by Omet.

The brokers' monopoly does not apply to those transactions involving listed securities that are not viewed as "sales" for purposes of the Stock Exchange Law, namely:

- issue, underwriting or primary placement of newly issued securities, even when the placement of the securities is made by credit institutions;
- transfer of securities by gift or inheritance;
- swaps or exchanges;
- contributions in kind against shares ("*apports*");
- mergers; or
- spin-offs.

(c) Private sales registered with brokers; "upstairs trading"

If a prospective buyer is acquiring shares from identified sellers rather than through open-market purchases by *ramassage*, a brokers' registration of the transaction (called an "application") would typically be organised if it falls within the scope of the brokers' monopoly (Article 4-7-1 *et seq* of the General Regulation). Applications can also be made when a stockbroker acts as a principal in the context of a given transaction.

(d) Exceptions to the brokers' exclusivity

Purchases and sales of listed securities not subject to the brokers' exclusivity may be settled outside the stock exchanges through the mere delivery of transfer orders ("*ordres de mouvement*"), as in the case for sales of private stock.

The transactions involved are those which are:

- between two individuals;
- between an entity holding at least 20% of the capital of a another company;
- resulting from an agreement other than a mere purchase and sale agreement. This exception, which is referred to as the "complex transaction exception", is often used when the transaction concerning

45

listed securities is part of another transaction such as a joint venture or a transaction involving the acquisition of several companies. Seagram tried, without success, to follow this route in 1988 when attempting to acquire a majority of the shares of the French cognac producer Martell. Seagram finally gained control over Martell, but after a tender offer battle with Grand Met, and had to pay a higher price (see p. 7 *supra*).
– between affiliated insurance companies; or
– between companies or entities and the pension or retirement funds managed by them (Article 1 of the Stock Exchange Law).

The second set of exceptions concerns transactions taking place outside France since the brokers' monopoly only applies on a territorial basis. Clearly, the brokers' exclusivity does not apply to transactions involving securities listed in France carried out outside France among non-residents. The issue of whether a transaction is subject to the brokers' monopoly is more delicate when a transaction has both French and foreign connections. In this regard, a tax regulation issued in 1992 (that restates customary rules) states that the following presumptions are applicable to international transactions:

– Sales of listed securities occurring between two French residents are conclusively deemed to have been made in France regardless of where the parties make or purport to make the transaction. In other words, even in the case of use of a foreign intermediary or choice of foreign law, the transaction remains subject to the brokers' monopoly.
– Sales between a French resident and a foreign resident are presumed to take place in France when the securities being sold are issued by a French resident entity. Transactions on a foreign exchange of French listed securities which are also listed abroad between a French resident and a non-resident are, however, not subject to this presumption (Regulation 7 E, Division N, 15 May 1992).

It is important to note that most of the rules concerning the monopoly in the area of international transactions have not been tested before French courts and that the structuring of such transactions is to be approached with care. Notwithstanding this, there is an important market for French securities in London, where shares issued by the top French companies are quoted through the SEAQ International System.

(ii) Price determination

(a) General rule

Prices for listed securities cannot be set at will and the principle is that the transaction must be feasible on the exchange.

As a result of some particular rules of French law, one cannot provide in purchase and sale agreements for a sale of listed securities that is different from the listed price or a price formula (depending on a multiple of earnings) or for a fixed price (price plus interest, subject to floors or ceilings). These are provisions that render the transaction not always feasible on the exchange since (subject to the exception concerning option contracts and block trade) all transactions concerning listed securities must be effected at the listed price when the transaction is made.

For example, within the context of the registration of a private transaction (an "application"), the broker may only register the transaction if the transaction price is *inter alia* the same price as the listed price; the purchase and the sale must be effected within a price range in between the best offered prices on the market when the transaction is made (Article 4-7-3 of the General Regulation).

(b) First exception: option contracts

One exception to the same price rule is when option contracts (*"contrats optionnels"*) are registered with the SBF. Option contracts, which are a means to secure the price for a transaction, are put-and-call agreements between a prospective seller and a prospective buyer. Under these contracts, one of the parties may, at its own option, acquire or sell a specified amount of securities during the term of the contract. In order for an option contract to be eligible for registration with the SBF, its exercise price must be either:

- the listed price as of the date of registration of the contract with the SBF;
- the listed price as of the date of exercise of the option; or
- a price equal to the average of the prices listed between the date of registration with the SBF and the date of exercise.

The maximum term of an option contract is two years. Once the contract is registered with the SBF, the parties can close the transaction at the price provided for in the contract, during its applicable term, no matter what the market price is (Article 7-2-1 of the General Regulation).

(c) Second exception: block trades

In 1994, the CBV enacted regulations for transactions involving large blocks of French securities (General Decision, No. 94-06 of 10 August 1994). Previously for most block trades, acquirers and sellers were required to buy blocks at or very near the previous best quoted prices on the exchange's order-driven computer system. They had to take out all existing orders at the best spread, and publish promptly the price and size of the deal. These factors, along with a stamp tax on stock deals that was only modified in 1994, had encouraged the largest investors to do their big deals in French equities on London's SEAQ International System.

The new regulation distinguishes between two categories of block trades:

A. "Normal" block trades

This applies to block trades involving securities worth at least one million francs. It responds to market operators' demands for more leeway in pricing large deals, for delay in making the details public, and a more efficient way to buy large blocks of shares.

The new rules apply to the shares of 53 major French companies (companies included in the CAC 40 index and a few others) for deals of at least one million francs.

The CBV has set a "Normal Block Size", revised quarterly for each company based on trading volume. The market computer will use this to calculate average weighted buy and sell prices in relation to the market price. Block traders can price their deal at or within these ranges, which should be wider than the best spread quoted in the market for ordinary transactions, depending on the securities. Dealers notify market officials immediately, but publication is not for two hours or the next day, depending on block size.

B. "Significant" block deals

Another exemption allows the CBV to give permission for the largest transactions, such as those that precede a tender offer, to be executed at an off-market price.

Significant blocks (*"blocs structurant"*) are those equal to 10% at least of a company's capital, or worth more than FF500 million (Article 7-2-3 of the General Regulation and Article 3 of CBV General Decision, No. 94-06 of 10 August 1994).

For significant blocks, the buying and selling price spreads are to be within a 10% range of the best spread for individual shares. However, at the same time, there is an exemption allowing deals at prices not necessarily tied to the market, with prior permission from the CBV. This effectively allows the arrangement of purchases and sales at a price with no link with market price and allows much greater flexibility in closing arrangements for the purchase of majority blocks (within the context of mandatory tenders) or other significant blocks of shares.

Publication times are the same as for normal block deals, but can be extended to the third morning after the deal if the broker has not unwound its position.

This regulation removes a major constraint on pricing major deals, which often need to take factors into consideration other than the listed price. Previously, parties were forced to resort to questionable techniques to push the share price towards the desired level, for example, passing an impossibly large order at a certain price.

(iii) Stamp tax

When a transaction is subject to the brokers' monopoly, the broker is responsible for collecting the stamp tax (*"impôt de bourse"*). The stamp tax ranges from 0.15% to 0.3% of the price of the transaction and is payable both by the buyer and the seller. However, the stamp tax is no longer a real issue since the maximum tax liability is subject to a FF4,000 ceiling per transaction and a FF150 discount. In addition, no stamp tax is payable by non-residents, nor as regards transactions concerning securities traded on a "regional" stock exchange (outside Paris) nor on debt securities.

(iv) The future – The Investment Services Directive

The Investment Services Directive will deregulate the stock brokerage business throughout Europe. It includes an optional concentration rule that will permit a Member State to require financial transactions in financial instruments to be carried out on a regulated market. This is a key provision, as far as France is concerned, in view of the current French stockbrokers' exclusivity.

The concentration rule would, however, only apply if:

– the principal is a resident of the State in question;
– the investment firm proposing to complete a deal acts in that State through a subsidiary, a branch or on the basis of the freedom to provide services; and
– the financial instrument involved is traded on a regulated market of that Member State.

Member States will, however, be required to give their resident investors the right to opt out from this requirement, either by way of express authorisation to realise deals off-exchange or by means of a blanket waiver, but always in such a fashion that trades can be effected expeditiously. It is unclear whether these rules will be applicable in January 1996 (as is the case for the other provisions of the Directive), since the European Commission is due to evaluate the operation of the concentration rule by 31 December 1998.

2. **Disclosure requirements**

Operators on the French market are subject to increasing disclosure requirements and to COB and CBV scrutiny in this area. Certain rules apply when reaching certain levels of ownership (alone or in concert with others) that can be as low as 0.5%. On reaching 20%, the acquirer must disclose its intentions. In addition, notwithstanding the size of its holding, the acquirer is subject to a continuous disclosure requirement under rules issued by the COB. In addition, if the acquisition takes place in the context of a tender offer, other disclosure requirements apply (see Chapter 6).

(i) Notification of ownership ("*déclaration de franchissement de seuils*")

*Acquirers and vendors reaching (alone or in concert with others) 5%, 10%,
20%, 33.33%, 50% and 66.66% of the voting rights of a listed company
must disclose their holdings to both the CBV and the company.*

(a) Applicable sanctions

In the absence of proper disclosure, shares held in excess of the threshold
requiring disclosure automatically lose voting rights for two years following
the date on which the appropriate disclosure is finally made. If a company,
in its by-laws, has elected to establish thresholds below 5%, the by-laws
may provide that non-complying shareholders are deprived of their voting
rights only on demand by one or several shareholders whose holdings of
shares or voting rights are at least equal to the lowest threshold subject to
notification (Article 356-4 of the Company Law).

Acquiring voting rights in violation of these requirements may also be
subject to civil proceedings in which the remedy can be partial or total
suspension of the shareholder's right to vote for a period of up to five years
(Article 356-4 of the Company Law). This provision was first applied in the
Perrier takeover battle in 1992. In this case, EXOR was deprived of one-
third of its voting rights for two years by virtue of a decision of the Commercial Court of Nîmes for improper disclosure of the crossing of the one-third
threshold, jointly with six other companies acting in concert with it. This
decision helped Nestlé to acquire control over Perrier.[2]

Non-compliance with the notification requirements is also subject to
criminal penalties with fines up to FF120,000 being available.

(b) Triggering levels

The triggering levels specified by statute are 5%, 10%, 20%, 33.33%, 50%
and 66.66% of the voting rights and they automatically apply to each
publicly held company. Reporting obligations are linked to the percentage
of voting rights, rather than the percentage of shares, held by the shareholder (Article 356-1 of the Company Law).

An issuer may provide additional thresholds, which may be as low as
0.5%, in its by-laws. In such a case, any shareholder attaining such levels
is required to notify the issuer. However, no notification to the CBV is
required. Such purchases will thus not be disclosed to the public unless the
issuer does so (Article 356-1 of the Company Law).

The ownership level is to be compared to the total number of the issuer's
voting rights (*i.e.* the total number of voting rights held by all shareholders
entitled to vote, including double voting rights and excluding shares directly
or indirectly controlled by the issuer). In this respect, within 15 days after
each annual shareholders' meeting, any publicly traded company must
publish the total number of its voting rights in a special section of the

---

[2] *Nestlé/Indosuez* v *Others*, Commercial Court of Nîmes, 6 March 1992; Bulletin Joly, May
1992, p. 536, note Le Cannu.

French Official Journal, the Bulletin des Annonces Légales Obligatoires ("BALO") and report it to the CBV. The SBF then publishes a release in its bulletin. Further, if, during the period between two annual shareholders' meetings, the number of voting rights changes by 5% or more after any such publication, a new publication must be made by the company in the BALO (Article 356-1-1 of the Company Law).

Notification is required both when the shareholder exceeds one of the thresholds and when it falls below one of the specified levels. The rules apply regardless of the cause of the decrease or increase in the amount of voting rights held. The crossing of a threshold can result from a purchase or sale, a merger, a variation in the targets' total voting rights or a massive acquisition (or loss) of voting rights by another shareholder.

(c) What constitutes a disclosable holding?

In addition to the voting rights held directly, a shareholder must declare:

- those held by another person or entity for the shareholder's account;
- those held by a company under the shareholder's control;
- those held by persons or entities with whom the shareholder is acting in concert (see Chapter 4); and
- those that the shareholder can purchase at its own option (Article 356-1-2 of the Company Law).

Under these rules, undisclosed "parkings" of securities in friendly hands (*"portages"* in French parlance) are no longer possible since they would almost always result in a violation of the threshold notification rules.

(d) Timing for disclosure

Shareholders of companies whose shares are listed on either the official or the second market who attain the 5%, 10%, 20%, 33.33%, 50% or 66.66% levels must inform the CBV within five business days (*"jours de bourse"*) following the date when the triggering level was reached. In such a case, the SBF informs the public by publishing a notice in its releases.

Shareholders who attain these levels in a publicly traded company (including companies traded on the over-the-counter market) must also notify the issuer within 15 calendar days.

It is generally considered that, if a purchase of securities resulting in the reaching of a disclosable threshold is subject to prior administrative approval (*e.g.*, by the Treasury), the five-business-day period (as well as the 15-day period) only starts to run when the administration grants its approval.

(e) Directive regarding transfers of major holdings in listed securities

The French rules comply with the Directive regarding transfers of major holdings in listed securities adopted on 12 December 1988 and apply even stricter requirements than those provided for in the Directive.

The Directive also requires European companies which receive notice of a change of ownership to disclose that information to the public in each of the Member States in which its shares are officially listed as soon as possible, but no later than nine calendar days after receipt of the notice. European issuers listed in France are thus required to inform the CBV of any threshold notification received by investors within this time period. The CBV in turn informs the public of the threshold notification received.

It is worth noting here that the directive also amended Council Directive 79/279 of 5 March 1979, as last amended by Directive 82/148 on the conditions for the admission of securities to official stock exchange listing. Under that Directive, a company is required to inform the public of any changes in the structure of major holdings of its shares (both the shareholders and the breakdown of holdings) from information previously published on the subject as soon as such changes come to its attention. This disclosure is one of the conditions for the continued listing of securities.

(ii) Continuous disclosure requirements

Any party preparing a financial transaction that may have a substantial impact on the price of securities must promptly disclose it to the public. Disclosure may be delayed if legitimate grounds exist and if confidentiality can be ensured.

The continuous disclosure requirement is one of the essential elements of the COB's new rules based on the 1989 Law, and prompt, true and fair disclosure is now the rule of the game.

(a) Triple jeopardy

Persons not abiding by the above rule may be subject to fines of up to FF10 million (or, where a profit has been made, ten times the amount of such profit) imposed by the COB (Article 9-2 of the 1967 Ordinance).

The imposition of fines by the COB does not bar criminal prosecution on the basis of the same facts since persons knowingly disclosing untrue or fraudulent information which concerns the future or the situation of an issuer or the price of a security, and which is likely to have an influence on the price of such security, may be subject to the same sanctions as those applicable to insider trading. These sanctions include imprisonment ranging from two months to two years and fines ranging from FF6,000 to FF10 million, with a maximum of ten times the amount of any profits realised (Article 10-3 of the 1967 Ordinance).

Finally, if no disclosure has been properly made, the non-disclosing party (who would, by definition, be aware of inside information) would be subject to insider trading laws and thus strictly prohibited from acquiring or selling any of the securities concerned, in addition to being subject to the penalties applicable to insider trading (see Chapter 5).

(b) Prompt disclosure requirement

Any party preparing a financial transaction that may have a substantial impact on the price of listed securities is under a duty to disclose, as promptly as possible, the main terms of the proposed transaction (Article 5 of COB Regulation No. 90-02).

Such disclosure may only be delayed if legitimate grounds to do so exist and if the party is able to ensure the confidentiality of the information in question. In practice, an acquirer can keep material information confidential as long as it is able to ensure that:

– the transaction can effectively be kept confidential;
– only a limited number of persons are aware of it; and
– none of these persons carries out any transaction on the securities concerned (see insider trading rules, Chapter 5 *infra*).

As soon as there are leaks concerning the transaction (or trading in the securities concerned reaches abnormal levels in terms of price or volume), a disclosure needs to be made.

Disclosures are made through press releases that must be communicated to the COB at the time of their publication at the latest (Article 8 of COB Regulation No. 90-02). Such press releases are generally made public when the stock market is closed in order to minimise extreme price moves. Another possibility, in the case of a major information, is for the issuer to request that the SBF suspend trading temporarily prior to the issue of a press release. The information is then disclosed and can be publicised through the press and press agencies before the next opening of the stock market.

(c) Scope of disclosures

Current regulations state that all information disclosed to the public must be accurate, precise and sincere (Article 2 of COB Regulation No. 90-02).

The disclosure of inaccurate, imprecise or false information constitutes a breach of COB regulations and can result in the imposition of fines. One example is the Beaux Sites case. Beaux Sites was a real estate developer traded on the over-the-counter market that was in serious financial trouble. Its Chairman had spread rumours that led the market to believe that a sale of the company was imminent, and had issued several press releases stating that "discussions were taking place" or that "substantial modifications in the shareholding" could occur. He had even requested suspension of trading of Beaux Sites shares. In fact, it was later established that no serious negotiation had taken place with potential acquirers and that the only purpose of the disclosures was to keep stock prices high. The COB decided that this was a breach of the disclosure rules since the disclosures were not sincere, and the Chairman was heavily fined.[3] The COB also fined Beaux Sites, which quickly filed for bankruptcy.[4]

---

[3] COB decision of 29 September 1992, Bull. COB No. 262, October 1992, p. 21.
[4] COB decision of 29 September 1992, Bull. COB No. 262, October 1992, p. 28.

The COB usually requires that the disclosures made in France contain at least the same information as is contained in disclosures made on foreign markets. For example, if an American investor is required to make a public disclosure in the United States concerning a French acquisition, it has to make a similar disclosure at the same time in France.

In addition, any person who, having disclosed his intentions, changes his mind, must immediately disclose his new intentions (Article 6 of COB Regulation No. 90-02).

These rules may be enforced by the COB, which can request any party under a duty to carry out a public disclosure to properly do so, and even make such disclosure itself, if necessary. In this regard, the COB carefully reviews all disclosures made by market players through press releases, management interviews, press articles, and in the BALO.

(iii) Notification of intent ("*déclaration d'intention*")

On reaching 20% of the voting rights of a listed company, the acquirer must disclose its intentions.

Any acquirer of 20% or more of the voting rights of a company whose shares are listed on either the official or the second market must file a notice disclosing its future intentions. Such notice must be filed with the CBV, the COB, and the issuer. Regulations for filing deadlines are the same as those governing ownership notification described *supra* (Articles 1 and 2 of COB Regulation No. 88-02).

The notice of intent is then made public by the SBF and through a press release published by the acquirer in a financial newspaper having national circulation in France.

The notice must state whether or not the acquirer intends, within a period of twelve months, to:

– continue buying shares;
– acquire control over the issuer; and
– request a seat on the issuer's Board of Directors, Directorate or Supervisory Board (Article 3 of COB Regulation No. 88-02).

The notice must also disclose whether the acquirer is acting alone or in concert with other persons (Article 4 of COB Regulation No. 88-02).

Violations of the foregoing requirements are not subject to any criminal penalties. Non-compliance can, however, constitute grounds for civil suits for damages or injunctive relief. Further, since the requirements are laid down in a COB regulation, the COB may impose fines and injunctions on defaulting parties.

In practice, these press releases are sometimes imprecise as to the intended course of action of the acquirer. For instance the acquirer might state that "it does not intend to acquire control over the target, but reserves its right to modify its intent" or "it might acquire additional shares", etc.

(iv) Disclosure of shareholders' agreements

Shareholders must report to the CBV, for publication, any agreement granting "preferential rights" to purchase or sell shares.

Under Article 356-1-4 of the Company Law (which results from an amendment made by the 1989 Law), shareholders of a company whose shares are traded either on the official market or the second market (but not currently the over-the-counter market) are required to report to the CBV, and the CBV is required to make public, any agreement that contains provisions granting preferential rights to purchase or sell shares.

This provision covers any agreement that includes a right of first refusal, put-and-call options and other provisions relating to the sale of securities. By its terms, this provision applies only where two or more shareholders are parties to the agreement: an agreement between one shareholder and a third party would not *per se* be subject to this provision.

This rule is not subject to criminal penalties, but non-compliance can constitute grounds for civil suits for damages or injunctive relief.

When provided with such a shareholders' agreement, the CBV decides whether or not such shareholders are acting in concert (see Chapter 4). The decision is thereafter published together with the main terms of the agreement in the SBF bulletin.

In practice, prior to entering into shareholders' agreements, it is highly advisable for the parties to consult with the SBF as to whether the proposed agreement creates an action in concert. This is especially useful when it is unclear as to what the CBV's ruling will be.

Chapter 4
"Acting in Concert" With Others

Persons are acting in concert when they have concluded an agreement with a view to acquiring or transferring voting rights or with a view to exercising voting rights to implement a common policy with respect to management.

This is a key notion of French securities law, which results from the 1989 Law. This concept had been coined, but not defined, in previous regulations by the COB. Its purpose is to help market regulators to prevent frauds on disclosures, as well as the use of nominees *"faux nez"* in creeping tenders. It is a difficult but key concept under French law, and hence is frequently used in tender offer battles in order to challenge an opponent's behaviour.

1. Joint liability

Persons acting in concert are jointly and severally liable for compliance with all laws and regulations (and in particular stock market regulations) by any member of the group. They are also subject as a group to open-market purchase reporting and mandatory offer requirements.

The mere fact of entering into such an agreement may result in the parties being required to file a mandatory bid when they hold at least one-third of the company's shares or voting rights. Consequently, the question as to whether or not parties are acting in concert is essential and this is the first issue to address when entering into a shareholders' agreement.

2. The notion of "action in concert"

The notion of persons or entities "acting in concert" is purposely extremely broad. Under Article 356-1-3 of the Company Law, persons are deemed to be acting in concert when they have concluded an agreement "with a view to acquiring or transferring voting rights of a company or with a view to exercising voting rights to implement a common policy" with respect to management of such company.

The definition has two aspects: (i) acquiring or transferring voting rights, and (ii) exercising voting rights to implement a common policy.

(i) Acquiring or transferring voting rights

First, Article 356-1-3 covers "agreements with a view to acquiring or transferring voting rights", which is a bit troublesome since a literal reading of the first test would cover almost all situations in which parties enter into agreements providing for sales or purchases of shares.

As noted in Chapter 3 *supra*, however, the CBV, when provided with shareholders' agreements pursuant to Article 356-1-4 of the Company Law, issues a ruling on whether the signatories are acting in concert or not. The CBV does not generally rule that an action in concert exists in situations where a transaction is:

– a mere purchase and sale;
– an option; or
– a right of first refusal (except in particular contexts).

On the other hand, agreements providing for rules concerning the joint sale or acquisition of listed securities (through "tag-along" or "drag-along" rights) are generally viewed as creating an action in concert. Standstill agreements (*i.e.*, agreements providing for a cap on investments or prohibiting one party from acquiring stock in a listed company) are a special category and the determination is effectively made on a case-by-case basis. One generally considers that, if each party is able to decide on its own without having to get in touch (or negotiate) with other parties in order to implement the agreement, the clause does not create an action in concert. On the other hand, if the parties have to consult with each other prior to any acquisition or disposition of shares, the CBV generally rules that there is an action in concert.

(ii) Exercising voting rights to implement a common policy

The second test, covering agreements with a view to exercising voting rights to implement a common policy with respect to management, is less complex. Under this test, persons may be deemed to be acting in concert when they enter into shareholders' agreements whereby they need to discuss and agree in order to:

– allocate Board seats *and* top management functions;
– organise joint management of a company (through executive committees or otherwise).

On the other hand, the mere allocation of seats on the Board does not result in an action in concert.

(iii) Presumptions

Article 356-1-3 of the Company Law sets down a series of rebuttable presumptions of an action in concert. Thus an action in concert is presumed to exist in the following situations:

60

- between a company and its Chairman, its general manager, the members of its management committee, or its managers;
- between a company and another company under its control or under common control; and
- between the shareholders of a French *société par actions simplifiée* ("SAS") – a new form of limited liability company created by Law no 94-1 of 3 January 1994 whose by-laws afford almost total flexibility in the organisation of management and shareholders' rights.

The notion of control is defined in Article 355-1 of the Company Law whereby a company is deemed to control another company:

(i) when it holds, directly or indirectly, the majority of the voting rights in such company;

(ii) when the majority of the voting rights in such company can be voted pursuant to a shareholders' agreement "that is not contrary to the interests" of said company; or

(iii) when it has *de facto* control at shareholders' meetings through the voting rights that it holds.

In addition, a company is presumed to control another company if it holds, directly or indirectly, more than 40% of the voting rights of said other company and if no other shareholder holds, directly or indirectly, a greater number of voting rights. The COB can petition the courts in order to obtain a judgment acknowledging that a control relationship exists among two or more publicly–traded companies.

3. Certain cases

Below is a summary of certain key decisions in this area:

(i) Club Med

The first ruling made by the CBV concerned Club Méditerranée ("Club Med"), the famous French tour operator, which is listed on the official market of the Paris stock exchange. A shareholders' agreement, dated 17 May 1990, was made between the Edmond de Rothschild group, the Caisse des Dépôts et Consignations, Paribas, IFINT (part of the Agnelli group), Crédit Lyonnais, ROLACO (a Saudi group), Nippon Life Insurance Company, the employee fund of Club Med and Seibu Saison, which together held 45.52% of the voting rights. The agreement provided for mutual first-refusal rights, as well as an undertaking not to exceed 10% of Club Med's voting rights (shareholders exceeding this level were required to use best efforts to resell shares in order to decrease their holding to the required levels). The CBV held that neither the first-refusal clause nor the standstill provisions resulted in an action in concert among the signatories

(CBV's decision dated 17 May 1990, SBF release No. 90-1500). This ruling was generally approved by practitioners since it provided clear rules and retained the possibility of protecting listed companies from hostile bidders without creating a joint liability among the parties involved.

(ii) LVMH

The second ruling is one of the episodes of the LVMH saga (see Chapter 1). It concerned a first-refusal agreement entered into on 29 July 1988 among the Moët, Mercier and Hennessy families, on the one hand, and the Arnault group on the other. It was stated that the agreement was to create a "coherent" group of shareholders within LVMH. The CBV ruled that the agreement . . . created an action in concert among the signatories (CBV's decision dated 6 July 1990, SBF release No. 90-2204). Aside from the confusion created in the minds of market players, this ruling confirmed that the CBV could both agree to publish and issue a "concert ruling" concerning agreements entered into prior to the enactment of the 1989 Law.

(iii) S.A.E.

The third ruling increased confusion since the CBV confirmed that a first-refusal agreement could, in certain circumstances, result in an action in concert. It concerned S.A.E., a public contractor, which was the subject of a raid by a real-estate developer, the Pelège group, backed by Crédit Lyonnais (which held 14% of the stock). The other main shareholders (two banks, Paribas and Société Générale, a public contractor, Fougerolle and a financial company, Comptoir des Entrepreneurs) which together held 28% of the votes, entered into a first-refusal agreement in order to discourage the raiders. The agreement was then transmitted to the CBV, which ruled, to the great surprise of both the signatories and advisers, that the parties were acting in concert and had to file a joint threshold notification since they together held more than 20% of S.A.E. voting rights (CBV decision dated 26 December 1990, SBF release No. 90-4035). All signatories protested and sent separate letters to the CBV stating that they were not acting in concert, and suggested that the CBV should reconsider its position. The CBV confirmed its first ruling and decided that, since among the signatories of the agreement there were eight companies indirectly controlled by S.A.E. (holding more than 5% of the votes), the signatories were acting in concert (CBV decision dated 11 January 1991, SBF release No. 91-116). The rationale of the CBV's decision was probably that the signatories could not avoid discussion among themselves in order to monitor sales of S.A.E. stock to eventually be made by S.A.E.'s subsidiaries.

In this decision, the CBV also mentioned that if a threshold is reached as a result of the entering into an agreement, the five-business-day period that counts for the purposes of notification of ownership only begins to run when the determination (as to the existence of a concerted action) by the

CBV is officially published by the CBV (and not from the date of signing of the agreement).

(iv) Nouvelles Galeries

Another case concerned Nouvelles Galeries (see Chapter 1). In April 1991, Proventus had sold part of its 16.5% stake to Galeries Lafayette and part to Crédit Commercial de France ("CCF"). Following the purchase, the two acquirers held, respectively, 38.42% and 5.83% of Nouvelles Galeries' voting rights (44.25% overall). Simultaneously with the purchase, CCF had undertaken to resell its stake within the next six months and consult Galeries Lafayette in this regard. CCF had also granted a right of first refusal to Galeries Lafayette, on the understanding that the latter would indemnify CCF in case of a loss on the resale of the shares. Galeries Lafayette and CCF claimed that they were not acting in concert.

The Court of Appeals of Paris noted that CCF acted as financial adviser to Galeries Lafayette in this transaction (Galeries Lafayette was also a shareholder of CCF), had undertaken to sell its stake within the next six months (a rather short period) and was to consult with Galeries Lafayette in this regard. Further, CCF had granted a right of first refusal to Galeries Lafayette and Galeries Lafayette was to indemnify CCF in case of a loss on the resale of the Nouvelles Galeries shares. The court held that for these reasons CCF was acting in concert with Galeries Lafayette.[1]

(v) Delmas-Vieljeux

The Delmas-Vieljeux transaction took place a few months later (see Chapter 1).

Bolloré Technologies had become the main shareholder of Compagnie Financière Delmas-Vieljeux ("CFDV") by convincing the Vieljeux family to sell its 17% stake. The transaction had been planned so that Bolloré Technologies would stay below the magic one-third level that triggers the mandatory tender obligation. Of the 17% held by the Vieljeux family, Bolloré had acquired only a 9% stake (thus holding 31%) and El Rabah (a holding company) had acquired 8% (thus holding 26%), with the help of Crédit Lyonnais, which increased its stake in El Rabah from 10 to 20%. The acquirers claimed that they were not acting in concert and that, since neither Bolloré Technologies nor El Rabah had reached one-third of the votes (or shares) of CFDV, no mandatory tender was to be filed.

The CBV disagreed and ruled that Bolloré Technologies, Crédit Lyonnais and El Rabah were acting in concert. Consequently, the CBV required Bolloré to file a bid for CFDV (as well as for its subsidiary

---

[1] *Devanlay and others* v *Galeries Lafayette, CCF and others*, Court of Appeals of Paris, Section CBV, 24 June 1991; Flash JP, Gaz. Pal. 29 June 1991; JCPE 1991 II 215, Note Forschbach, Gaz. Pal. 17 Dec. 1991.

Delmas-Vieljeux). The CBV's ruling was based on the fact that the acquisition made by Bolloré resulted in a change in the strategy of the Delmas-Vieljeux group and a new distribution of Board seats. One key question was whether there was indeed an agreement between Bolloré, Crédit Lyonnais and El Rabah since no agreement had been disclosed. The CBV decided that the three companies could only have acquired the stock if they were in agreement as to the strategy to be followed by Delmas-Vieljeux. In addition, it was clear that Crédit Lyonnais had long been an ally of Bolloré's (Crédit Lyonnais is Bolloré's banker and holds interests in various companies of the Bolloré group).

(vi) Lagardère Groupe – the "contamination" rule

Under the contamination rule (*"concert en étoile"*), two parties can act in concert even if they have not met.

In 1993, Lagardère Groupe, a major French holding company controlling the French defence group Matra and the press group Hachette (now merged into Matra Hachette), was undergoing a major reorganisation as a result of the bankruptcy of La Cinq, the "fifth" French television station. In the context of the reorganisation, Arjil Groupe, the holding company controlled by Jean-Luc Lagardère, entered into a shareholders' agreement with The General Electric Company plc that included several provisions resulting in an action in concert (first-refusal rights, non-dilution provisions, co-ordination of key management decisions, etc.). At the same time, Arjil Groupe entered into a similar agreement with the German Daimler Benz group. When provided with both agreements, the CBV held that, since both agreements were aimed at keeping Arjil Groupe in control of Lagardère Groupe, the three parties were acting in concert (CBV decision dated 24 March 1994; SBF release No. 93-1068).

Chapter 5
Insider Trading

Market players must abstain from carrying out any transactions involving securities when aware of inside information.

Acquirers of securities listed in France (including securities traded on the over-the-counter market) are subject to extensive insider trading rules.

1. Types of Insider trading

(i) Double jeopardy

Persons engaging in insider trading in France are subject to two sets of rules, the *délit d'initié* and the *manquement d'initié*.

(a) Délit d'initié

Under Article 10-1 of the 1967 Ordinance, persons aware of inside information carrying out, or knowingly permitting others to carry out on their behalf, on the market, directly or indirectly, one or more transactions before the public become aware of such information, are subject to criminal sanctions (imprisonment ranging from two months to two years and fines ranging from FF6,000 to FF10 million, or ten times the amount of any profits realised by the insider) (this is the so-called "*délit d'initié*", a criminal violation).

(b) Manquement d'initié

Under Article 9-2 of the 1967 Ordinance, persons engaging in insider trading are in breach of COB Regulation No. 90-08 relating to the abusive use of inside information. They are subject to administrative fines issued by the COB (up to FF10 million or ten times the amount of any profit made).

It has been held by the French Constitutional Council that the double jeopardy rule is not unconstitutional, provided the total amount of the fines issued by the COB and the criminal authorities does not exceed in total FF10 million or ten times the amount of any profit made. It has also been held that the COB, when fixing the amount of its fine, is to take into account the gravity of the violation.

The COB is very keen on pursuing insider trading violators and, in the years 1991, 1992 and 1993, issued fines in ten instances. In the same period, there were 20 criminal court decisions made against violators.

(ii) "Insiders"

Article 10-1 of the 1967 Ordinance and COB regulations include parallel (but not exactly similar) definitions of the concept of an "insider".

(a) Article 10–1

According to Article 10–1, the first category of insiders (*de jure* insiders) includes persons holding certain positions as directors or officers within publicly traded companies. As far as SAs are concerned, these persons are the chairman, the directors and the general manager of SAs managed by a board of directors, and the members of the management committee and supervisory board of SAs managed by a management committee. As far as SCAs are concerned, *de jure* insiders are the managers and the members of the supervisory board. *De jure* insiders also include any individual appointed as a permanent representative of legal entities serving as directors or members of the supervisory board of an SA. In addition, *de jure* insiders include the spouses (when not legally separated) of any of the foregoing individuals.

The second category of insiders (*de facto* insiders) includes any person who would have access to inside information on the prospects of an issuer or its securities in a professional context.

Both of these are "primary insiders" punishable under Article 10–1 of the 1967 Ordinance.

(b) COB Regulation No. 90-08

COB Regulation No. 90-08 defines three categories of insiders (Article 1).

The first category is those persons aware of inside information as a result of their functions (as directors, officers or employees) with an issuer (compare *de jure* insiders above).

The second category covers persons possessing inside information in connection with the preparation or implementation of a financial transaction.

The third category includes persons who knowingly have access to inside information, directly or indirectly, through insiders of one of the two preceding categories. This latter category of insider ("tippees" in the US sense or "secondary insiders") are only subject to COB Regulation No. 90-08 (and not to Article 10-1 of the 1967 Ordinance), since they would not have access, "during the exercise of his or her profession" to the information.

(iii) "Inside information"

Again, there exist two parallel definitions of what constitutes inside information in the two applicable regulations. Article 10-1 defines inside information as information "on the prospects or the situation of an issuer of securities or on prospects of a security" not known by the public.

On the other hand, Article 1 of COB Regulation No. 90-08 defines the notion of inside information as a precise piece of information, which is unknown to the public, and which concerns an issuer, a security, a future or a listed financial product and which, if it was publicly known, could have an "influence" on the price of the security, future or financial product concerned.

(a) Certainty

One example of the COB's sanctions is the Delalande case. A Director of Delalande, a pharmaceutical product company, had been informed, during an informal meeting of the Board of Directors with the main shareholders of the company, that a tender offer was being prepared. During this meeting, the director had been provided with the proposed exchange ratio of the offer. The director in question subsequently acquired 4.9% of the stock of Delalande on the market through an entity that he controlled, prior to the announcement of the offer. The COB ruled that this constituted insider trading for the purposes of its regulations since the offer had "reasonable chances" of going through. As a defence, he claimed that he intended to prepare a competing bid and that the purchase was part of his strategy to file a competing bid for Delalande. The COB disagreed since there was no evidence that a competing bid was being prepared.[1]

(b) Preciseness

Article 10-1 of the 1967 Ordinance was held applicable in the Ruche Méridionale case. In November 1988, the subsidiary of a bank had acquired approximately 12% of La Ruche Méridionale for its own account. Two months later, the bank had filed a tender offer bid acting for the account of Rallye. A competing bid was then filed by Compagnie Financière d'Afrique Occidentale ("CFAO"), an affiliate of Pinault. CFAO ultimately over-bid Rallye and the bank tendered its Ruche shares to CFAO and made a FF90 million gain. Following an investigation by the COB, it appeared that, prior to the purchase of the Ruche shares, the bank had been informed by Rallye that, in an attempt to solve a commercial dispute among Rallye and La Ruche, Rallye was likely to acquire La Ruche stock on the market.

Before the criminal court, the bank argued that it had no precise piece of inside information when it bought the 12% stake since, at that time, the possibility of a tender offer battle was uncertain. The court agreed on the last point but held that, in view of their experience in the corporate finance area, they could easily guess that the take-over battle was likely and were thus guilty of insider trading.[2]

---

[1] COB Decision dated 22 December 1992, Supplement to Bull. COB No. 264 – December 1992.
[2] *Alibert, Cabessa, Deroy and Chauvin* v. *Ministère Public*, Court of Appeals of Paris, 9th Chamber, 15 March 1993, Gaz. Pal. 1993. 2. 356.

Both COB regulations and Article 10–1 concerning insider trading can thus apply even when the inside information in question is neither certain nor precise, but when there exists a reasonable possibility that a transaction might occur.

(c) Non-public information

When does a piece of information become public and cease to be inside information? One example is the case of the financial analysts' meeting during which Schneider's Chairman, Didier Pineau-Valencienne, announced forecast results that were substantially lower than those expected. This was due to heavy losses by one of Schneider's major subsidiaries, SPIE Batignolles, a real-estate developer. The announcement had been made in front of hundreds of financial analysts but prior to the issue of an official press release by Schneider. One analyst quickly ran out of the meeting and asked his stockbroker to immediately sell short SPIE Batignolles stock on the RM market. Since several analysts did the same, an investigation was made by the COB and one financial analyst was caught. The COB held that the analyst was in breach of COB insider trading rules, since the official press release by Schneider had not been made public when the analyst's trade had been made.[3]

This decision is in line with the COB's general policies whereby the only proper means of disclosing price-sensitive information is through an official press release. The mere fact that there are discussions in the press concerning a piece of information probably does not suffice to render a piece of information public for insider trading regulation purposes.

(d) Specificity

How specific must the inside information be to the issuer or its group? Case law applying Article 10-1 of the 1967 Ordinance seems to indicate that there can only be a violation of the Article when the inside information in question specifically concerns the issuer of the securities in play or its group. Although there is no case law on this point, the COB's position seems to be that Regulation No. 90-08 would be applicable even in cases where the information does not relate to one issuer but concerns a sector of activities or the economic environment generally.

(iv) "Disclose or abstain"

Insiders are under a strict duty to abstain from carrying out, or permitting others to carry out on their behalf, *any* transactions involving securities of any publicly traded company when they have knowledge of inside information concerning such company. The rule also applies to financial products related to such securities (including options, warrants and derivatives). Deals carried out under these circumstances are conclusively presumed to

---

[3] COB decision dated 24 June 1993, Bull. COB July/August 1993, No. 271, p. 88.

have been carried out on the basis of inside information. Insiders are thus under a strict duty to "disclose or abstain" (Article 2 of COB Regulation No. 90-08). This rule was established in the Métrologie International case, involving managers who had sold most of their shares in the company prior to the announcement of very poor results. The COB held that in these circumstances the managers had an "absolute" duty to abstain from any transaction on the stock.[4]

In practice, however, most of the insider trading cases (both under Article 10-1 and Regulation 90-08) concern situations where the violator had clearly traded on the basis of inside information and was almost certain to either make a gain or avoid losses.

Insider trading rules apply whether the transaction is made on the regulated market through a stockbroker (*en bourse*), or off the market (*hors bourse*) directly between two parties. Indeed, Article 10-1 was amended in 1988 and, while the prior wording mentioned that insiders were prohibited from carrying out transactions on the stock exchange market (*marché boursier*), the new wording now prohibits all transactions made on the market. In the Ruche Méridionale case, it was held that Article 10-1 was applicable even though the transactions were made off the market. This was also the reasoning of the COB in the Pierre Bergé case (see *infra*).

(v) "Long-arm" reach

French insider trading rules even apply to transactions taking place outside France when the transaction concerns securities listed in France. The rules also apply to transactions made in France that concern securities listed outside France.

(a) Transactions made outside France

One example is the Pierre Bergé case. Yves Saint Laurent is not only the genius designer of high fashion products, but also the corporate name of Yves Saint Laurent ("YSL"), a former SCA (now merged with Sanofi, a pharmaceutical company and a key subsidiary of Elf Aquitaine). The two managers of YSL were Yves Saint Laurent and Pierre Bergé, Saint Laurent's long-term business partner and an intimate of France's President, François Mitterrand. In 1993, while there were active rumours about the possible sale of YSL to L'Oréal that pushed stock prices up, Pierre Bergé sold 2% of the company's capital to YSL's finance director, Jean-François Bretelle, who in turn sold the shares to a private investor through a Swiss bank. All the transactions were done outside the French regulated market without recourse to a stockbroker at a price higher than the market price. Three days after the transaction, Pierre Bergé announced a significant

---

[4] *COB* v *Métrologie International*, Haddad, Fraiberger, Blaise, Moulin, Schwarzmann and Friedland; 20 April 1993, Bull. COB No. 269, May 1993, p. 21 et *seq*; and Court of Appeals of Paris, 12 January 1994, Bull. COB No. 277, February 1994.

decrease in the company's financial results. Following an investigation, the COB ruled that Pierre Bergé, who was presumably aware of the unannounced results when selling his 2% stake, was in breach of COB Regulation No. 90-08. It was decided that the COB regulation was applicable to the case even though the transactions were made without recourse to a stockbroker and outside France, and Pierre Bergé was given a FF3 million fine by the COB on 16 March 1994.[5] The Paris Court of Appeals confirmed the findings of the COB but decreased the amount of the fine to FF1 million, taking into consideration the fact that Pierre Bergé had been pressured by his bankers to reimburse certain debts.[6] He was also sued for noncompliance with the French stockbroker's exclusivity rules and a criminal case concerning the same facts is also pending before the Criminal Court of Paris.

(b) Transactions made in France on foreign securities

French insider trading rules also apply to transactions made on a foreign securities market, provided the transaction has some French connection. This was the case in the so-called "Péchiney" or "Triangle" nationwide scandal involving several intimates of François Mitterand.

While Péchiney was negotiating to acquire Triangle Industries, a US company listed on the New York Stock Exchange, and before the transaction was announced publicly, several government advisers (including Roger Patrice Pelat and Samir Traboulsi, a Lebanese intermediary and a key negotiator in the transaction) issued purchase orders to brokers for Triangle Industries stock. These orders were placed by telephone from France just prior to the announcement of the transactions and the buyers realised substantial gains within the context of the tender offer that followed the Triangle transaction. Following an enquiry by the COB, several criminal prosecutions were initiated in France but the suspected violators maintained that French courts had no jurisdiction over this matter since the transactions were made outside France. The French Supreme Court decided that Article 10-1 applied, since the trade instructions had been issued from France.[7] The Court applied former Article 693 of the Code of Criminal Procedure which provides that when one of the key aspects of a transaction is made within French territory, French criminal law may apply.

(vi) Defences

Under both the COB rules and Article 10-1, the criminal intent of the violators is irrelevant, as is question of whether they realised any profits. In the Métrologie International case (*supra*), the Directors did not realise

---

[5] *COB* v *Bergé*, 12 October 1993, Bull. COB, No. 277, February 1994, p. 31 *et seq.*
[6] *Bergé* v *Trésor*, Paris Court of Appeals, Section COB, 16 March 1994, JCP éd. E. 1994.II 605, Note Forschbach.
[7] *Traboulsi*, Cour de Cassation, Criminal Chamber, 3 November 1993, Gaz. Pal. 1993. 1. 221, note Marchi, Bull. Joly Bourse No. 2, 1993, p. 152.

any gain; they were found guilty, but not fined, on the basis of the "proportional pain rule".

The only excuse that appears available is when the transaction results from a clear and explainable industrial or financial strategy which obviously differs from the fulfilment of personal financial needs. For example, in the context of the LVMH saga, it was said that both clans could validly acquire LVMH shares on the market notwithstanding the fact that directors of the two groups were aware of the increasingly good financial results of LVMH which had not been made public.

This defence should, however, not be seen as allowing potential acquirers to purchase securities shortly before launching a takeover bid. One example is the Compagnie Foncière de la Banque d'Arbitrage et de Crédit ("BAC") case. Shortly before the purchase of a majority block of shares of Paris-Bail from a group of insurance companies at FF350, BAC had acquired shares of Paris-Bail on the exchange for prices ranging between FF278 and FF285. At that time, it appeared that both BAC and the insurance companies had reached an agreement in principle for the purchase of a Paris-Bail majority block at FF350. The COB held that the purchases made on the market were in breach of Regulation No. 90-08 and issued an FF800,000 fine against BAC.[8]

Still another example is the Zodiac case in which, while the acquirer had entered into a protocol providing for the acquisition of a majority block in the company, it had acquired shares on the market at a lower price than the price of the majority block shortly prior to the disclosure of the transaction.[9]

There are certain exceptions laid down in the Insider Trading Directive which were not adopted by the French securities regulators. The first concerns transactions carried out by or on behalf of a sovereign State or its central bank within the framework of their monetary policy, their exchange rate policy or the management of public sector debt. The second exception comes from the preamble to the Directive, which explicitly states that the Directive does not apply to the regular and *bona fide* activities of underwriters when stabilising a securities issue, to a stockbroker executing orders, or to research carried out by business analysts.

2. Improper communication of inside information

Insiders may not communicate inside information to third parties except within the context of their professional duties. Violations of this restriction are subject to imprisonment ranging from one to six months and/or a fine

---

[8] *COB* v S.A. *Compagnie Foncière de la Banque d'Arbitrage et de Crédit*, 17 September 1991, Bull. COB No. 250, September 1991, p. 7.
[9] *COB* v *Zodiac*, 1 March 1994, Bull. COB No. 279, April 1994, p. 25.

ranging from FF10,000 to FF100,000 and the COB's fines (Article 10-1 of the 1967 Ordinance and Article 4 of COB Regulation No. 90-08).

According to COB Regulation 90-08, publicly traded companies, banking institutions, brokers and other players must take all appropriate measures to avoid the improper use and diffusion of inside information. For example, the announcement of results to a large number of executives several weeks prior to the official disclosure of the results must be avoided. Similarly, the announcement of results to journalists within the context of a press conference while the market is open prior to publication of a press release must also be avoided.

3. **Price manipulation**

As in the case of insider trading, there are two parallel sets of rules applicable to price manipulation of listed securities.

(i) Article 10-3 of the 1967 Ordinance

Persons having directly or indirectly carried out an action with the purpose of affecting normal market operations by defrauding other persons may be subject to the same criminal sanctions as those applicable to insider trading (*i.e.*, imprisonment ranging from two months to two years and fines ranging from FF6,000 to FF10,000, or ten times the amount of any profit realised). It has been held that these provisions only apply when a violator acts with a view to defrauding the market.[10]

Such provision would prohibit any short sale carried out in order to decrease the price of a security not motivated by the situation of the issuer, followed by the purchase of a substantial amount of such securities, the profits being realised when the prices reach their market level. It would also cover artificial increases of a security price made shortly before a new issue of stock.

(ii) COB Regulation No. 90-04

COB Regulation No. 90-04 of 5 July 1990 provides that securities prices must be the result of deals made, and no one can issue a trade order with a view to artificially manipulating stock prices (Articles 2 and 3). The regulation also provides that trade orders must be consistent with the goals pursued by acquirers or sellers and the COB may request any party to publicly explain the purpose of a transaction (Article 4).

This regulation would be subject to the COB's enforcement powers and

---

[10] Tribunal de Grande Instance of Paris, 11th Chamber, 5 March 1993, RJDA 10/90, No. 813, p. 705.

the staff of the COB are of the opinion that the regulation would apply even if there is no intent to defraud on the part of the price manipulator.

4. **The requirement that *de jure* insiders hold their shares in registered form**

In order to enable stock market authorities to monitor transactions made by *de jure* insiders (board members, managing directors and so on), the regulations strictly require them to hold all securities issued by the companies in which they (or their spouses) hold office in registered form, as well as all securities issued by any publicly traded direct or indirect subsidiary of such company. This requirement also applies to shares held by the insider's children under 18 years of age (Article 162-1 of the Company Law).

The requirement must be complied with within one month following the appointment of the relevant insider (or spouse) or within 20 days of the insider's acquisition of the shares. Non-compliance is subject to a fine ranging from FF2,000 to FF60,000.

5. **Directive on insider trading**

The French rules on insider trading are in compliance with the Insider Trading Directive adopted by the European Council of Ministers on 13 November 1989 (to be implemented by 1 June 1992). In fact, French regulations impose even more stringent rules on securities law violators. The Directive defines "inside information" as information which has not been made public and which is of a precise nature, relating to one or more issuers of transferable securities or to one or more transferable securities, and which, if it were made public, would be likely to have a significant effect on the price of the transferable security or securities in question. For the purposes of the proposed Directive, "transferable securities" include futures, index contracts and options in respect of transferable securities which are admitted to trading on a "regulated" securities market open to the public.

The national rules must apply in particular to actions undertaken within a Member State's territory insofar as the transferable securities at issue are admitted to trading in a European Union securities market. This would include at a minimum transactions carried out on a regulated securities market situated or operating within such Member State. Also, the deals which are forbidden under the Directive are those effected through a professional intermediary. Member States, however, are free not to apply the prohibition to deals done off the stock market which take place without the involvement of a professional intermediary. As noted above, transactions made outside the regulated market remain subject to the insider trading prohibition in France.

6. International enforcement of insider trading rules

The regulatory authorities of the various Member States of the European Union and the European Economic Area are required to exchange all information relating to the investigation and monitoring of insider trading rules. This is true even if the information concerns alleged transactions or facts which would only be prohibited in the Member State requesting co-operation pursuant to the power of the Member States to adopt more stringent rules under the Directive on Insider Trading (Article 5 *bis* of the 1967 Ordinance).

In addition, the COB may also co-operate with other foreign stock market authorities, subject to reciprocity and on the understanding that such authorities are bound by professional secrecy rules similar to the French rules.

Requests for information can be refused for reasons of public order and security, *res judicata* and in the case of applications in respect of pending judicial procedures.

These are key provisions since almost one-third of the investigations made by the COB have an international aspect. For example, in the Péchiney case, where several foreign authorities carried out local investigations at the request of the COB, the latter entered into co-operation agreements with several foreign securities authorities, including the US SEC and various European authorities.

CONTENTS OF CHAPTER 6

Chapter 6
Regulation of Tender Offers

Takeover rules give minority shareholders an "out" in case of change of control.

Tender offers are the most spectacular events in the M&A area. They have their heroes, victims, "white knights" and peace-keeping bodies. Offers usually involve an immense amount of effort by the interested parties, their lawyers, bankers and other advisers within a very short time. When a public tender is not friendly, the transaction frequently turns into a legal and public relations battle. Sometimes, public administrations (or even politicians) come into play to try to pressure the parties involved.

Legally speaking, a tender offer is an offer made by a potential acquirer to purchase shares or securities held by the public. In a tender offer, the public is not bound to sell its securities but the acquirer is generally required to buy all securities tendered. One exception is the newly implemented squeeze-out procedure (*"retrait obligatoire"*) under which minority shareholders can be forced to sell their shares against the payment of an indemnity (see Chapter 14 *infra*).

A tender offer which is made on the sole decision of the bidder for the purpose of acquiring control (or a participation) over a listed company is called a voluntary bid (*"offre publique facultative"*). On the other hand, if an acquirer reaches certain levels of ownership in a listed company or executes an agreement resulting in an action in concert with key shareholders of a listed company the offer is called a mandatory tender offer (*"offre publique obligatoire"*). A mandatory bid of a special type is required when a majority block of shares is acquired from an identified seller. In such a case, the offer takes the form of a standing offer (*"garantie de cours"*) made under the simplified tender offer procedure (*"procédure simplifiée"*).

A tender offer can be made for cash, in which case it is referred to as an *offre publique d'achat* ("OPA"). It can also be a tender in exchange for other securities, in which case it is referred to as an *offre publique d'échange* ("OPE"). A tender offer may also be made for a combination of securities *and* cash (in which case it is referred to as a "combined offer") or for either cash *or* securities (in which case it is referred to as an "alternative offer").

Tender offers which are made for the purpose of acquiring a controlling interest in a listed company are either voluntary bids, mandatory bids or standing offers. Those made in order to acquire a minority stake (offers for no more than 10% of the voting shares or voting rights) or by a majority shareholder in order to reinforce its shareholding are governed by the rules applicable to the simplified offer ("*procédure simplifiée*").

A special category of offers are the public repurchase offers ("*offres publiques de retrait*") generally applicable when a shareholder holds more than 95% of a company's voting rights in order to ensure delisting of the company (or mandatory when the company undergoes substantial changes). The repurchase offer can generally be coupled with a squeeze-out procedure enabling the acquirer to buy out all minority shareholders.

Generally, tender offers are made on shares or securities listed on the official or second markets, as well as on shares or securities traded on the over-the-counter market. A tender offer can, however, also be made on the shares of private companies, in which case it is not subject to the General Regulation. An example of this is the tender offer initiated by Rhône Poulenc SA for Cooper in March 1994 and the position stated by the CBV in this regard in a release dated 30 March 1994.

Below is a discussion of the main regulatory aspects of tender offers.

1. **Standard tender offer procedure**

Offers governed by the "standard offer procedure" are to be made on all equity securities of the target, for at least twenty business days and at a justifiable price.

The standard tender offer procedure ("*procédure normale*") applies *inter alia* to voluntary tender offers and mandatory tender offers, unlike standing offers which are governed by simplified tender offer procedure. Each of these categories of public offer remains subject to distinctive rules which supersede the standard tender offer procedure on specific points.

(i) Irrevocability

Once filed with the CBV, an offer can no longer be withdrawn (Article 5-2-1 of the General Regulation).

A cash offer may not be subject to any corporate approval (board meeting or shareholders' meeting,[1] but for exchange offers see *infra*), nor can it be subject to due diligence. It may, however, be subject to applicable prior regulatory or administrative approvals (Trésor, German FCO or lapse of waiting period pursuant to the US Hart Scott Rodino Anti-Trust Improvements Act (see Chapter 11)).

As far as exchange offers are concerned, the filing of the offer only creates

---

[1] *Emess PLC* v *Thorn Emi PLC*, Court of Appeals of Paris, Section CBV, 13 July 1988, JCP, éd. E, 1988, II, 15337.

an obligation on the acquirer's management to make a proposal to the extraordinary shareholders' meeting to issue the securities proposed in exchange (Article 5-2-5 of the General Regulation). Banking institutions acting on behalf of the acquirer act as financial guarantors for the acquirer's undertakings in this regard (Article 5-2-1 of the General Regulation).

The Hubert Industries case is a good illustration of the irrevocability of a tender offer. On 2 April 1992, HFP had acquired 49.5% of the shares of Hubert Industries, a company traded on the over-the-counter market from the Hubert family. Hubert Industries, however, held, through one of its indirect subsidiaries, 0.6% of its own stock and the CBV considered that, as a result, since HFP controlled a majority block directly and indirectly (through Hubert Industries), it had to file immediately a standing offer for Hubert Industries (SBF release No. 92-1568 of 15 June 1992). HFP claimed that it was unaware of the indirect holding of the 0.6% of Hubert Industries and initiated legal proceedings in order to have the CBV decision cancelled. HFP also initiated legal action against the sellers of the 49.5% block in order to either obtain a substantial price reduction or have the sale cancelled. One month later, Hubert Industries was declared bankrupt. The Court of Appeals held that the mere fact that litigation existed between HFP and the sellers was totally irrelevant for securities law purposes, and approved the CBV decision to require HFP to file an offer.[2]

(ii) Main terms of the offer

(a) Offers to be made on all equity securities

The General Regulation requires that offers governed by the standard offer procedure be made on *all* equity securities (*i.e.*, all securities representing a portion of the capital of the issuer) and voting rights, as well as all securities which are convertible, exchangeable or which give the right to subscribe or purchase equity securities or voting rights. The offer has to be made for all shares (common and preferred), warrants to buy shares, investment certificates (*"certificats d'investissement"*), convertible or exchangeable bonds and voting rights of the target (Article 5-2-2 of the General Regulation). It is worth mentioning here that, since offers must now be made on all equity securities of the target, the latter would, if the offer were successful, run the risk of being delisted following the offer since it would no longer have a sufficient float. Therefore, in order to maintain the listing of publicly held companies, the CBV may grant a delay to the acquirer to reissue securities to the public at the end of the offer, during which no repurchase offer can be filed (see Chapter 13).

The history of this rule is worth a special mention. In the early days, as noted in Chapter 1, offers were not subject to many rules. Bids were

---

[2] *HFP* v *CBV*, Court of Appeals of Paris, Section CBV, 7 April 1993, Bull. COB No. 278, March 1994, pp. 45-47; see also COB release dated 26 August 1994, Bull. COB No. 282, July/August 1994, p. 36.

sometimes made on a small portion of the issuer's capital, leaving the target's shareholders with a fraction of their original holding.

Later on, it was provided that an offer should have as its goal the acquisition of shares representing at least 10% of the capital of the target. This percentage was reduced to 5% if the market value of the shares to be acquired equalled or exceeded FF10 million.

The 1989 Law then required that offers be made for a number of shares that gave the acquirer control (pre-offer holdings included) of no less than two-thirds of the target's voting rights. It was said, at that time, that one should not force acquirers to bid for all of the stock of targets since this would substantially increase the cost of takeovers, which would favour foreign industrial and financial groups which are wealthier than French companies. It was also said that a bid for all of the stock would result in the acquired company being automatically delisted following the offer and the French exchanges would lose business. This resulted in the enactment of the "two-thirds" rule.

This rule quickly proved to be inadequate since tender offers made two-thirds of the voting stock left minority shareholders with securities that decreased in value and liquidity as the result of a thinner market. Sometimes acquirers were even allowed to launch subsequent bids to reinforce their stake, at a lower price. The rule was also deficient since, in the case of a standing offer, the acquirer of a block of shares reaching a majority was required to make an offer for *all* the stock of the listed target (see Section 4 *infra*).

The first example of the issues raised by the two-thirds rule was the Nouvelles Galeries case, which was the first mandatory tender imposed by the CBV (see Chapter 1).

In April 1991, one of the key shareholders (Proventus AB) of Nouvelles Galeries had sold its 16.43% stake in part to Galeries Lafayette (which already held 22.8% of the shares and 28.08% of the votes) and to Galeries Lafayette's banker, Crédit Commercial de France, which held no Nouvelles Galeries shares prior to the acquisition. The two acquirers held respectively, following the purchase, 38.42% and 5.83% of Nouvelles Galeries' voting rights and it was ruled by the CBV (and confirmed by the Court of Appeals) that both Galeries Lafayette and CCF were acting in concert (see p. 99 *et seq*). Galeries Lafayette and its banker then applied for an exemption from the mandatory offer obligation, claiming that Devanlay (who held 33.43% of the shares and 40.79% of the votes) had *de facto* control over Nouvelles Galeries. The CBV disagreed and required Nouvelles Galeries to launch a bid. The bid, however, was only on that number of shares giving Galeries Lafayette (and CCF) control (pre-offer holdings included) of two-thirds of Nouvelles Galeries' voting rights (the bid had only to be made on 22.41% of the voting rights). Several shareholders of Nouvelles Galeries (including Devanlay, which had lost *de facto* control over Nouvelles Galeries since Devanlay and CCF were acting in concert, but was left with part of its stake) initiated actions before the Court of Appeals of Paris claiming that Galeries Lafayette and CCF had to file a standing offer for *all* the outstanding shares of Nouvelles Galeries since, by virtue of a provision of Nouvelles Galeries' by-laws, the acquirers would automatically acquire a majority of the votes, and then place their shares in registered form and wait for a two-year period. The court decided that the standing offer rule was not applicable in this case since the acquirers had not reached the majority level immediately following the acquisition of Proventus' shares.

Another example was the Pinault/Printemps transaction that took place shortly thereafter, which showed up the weakness in the law because the two-thirds rule made it so easy to escape the *garantie de cours* requirement and, consequently, bid for *all* the stock. Au Printemps SA was controlled by the Swiss family Maus (through SAMAG and Maus Frères) which together held 42.27% of the capital and 56.44% of the votes). The by-laws of Printemps granted double voting rights to shareholders holding registered shares for more than two years. Simultaneously with the signing of a purchase agreement with the Pinault group, Maus Frères transferred all of its Printemps shares to its sister company SAMAG, which caused the shares to lose their double voting rights. Simultaneously, SAMAG transformed its registered shares into bearer shares. As a result, the total number of voting rights held by the Maus family decreased from 56% to 37% and SAMAG was subsequently sold by the Maus family to Pinault. As a result of the transaction, Pinault did not reach the majority threshold of Printemps' voting rights (which would have forced him to launch a *garantie de cours* on all of Printemps' shares) and filed a mandatory offer on two-thirds of the voting rights of Printemps (less the 37% already acquired). He saved the equivalent of FF3 billion. The CBV approved Pinault's offer but several shareholders challenged the CBV's decision on the basis that Pinault abusively avoided the standing offer rules. Despite COB criticism of Pinault's behaviour, the court held that the transactions that preceded the sale of SAMAG were not abusive and approved the CBV decision.[3]

Following heavy criticism by minority shareholders' associations and the French and foreign financial press, the two-third rule was modified by an amendment to the General Regulation dated 15 May 1992 which now requires that all offers be made on *all* equity securities. The 100% rule is far more protective of minority shareholders than the two-thirds rule.

(b) Price

The key element of an offer is its price (or exchange ratio).

Although there is no specific rule or formula with respect to price, the General Regulation (Article 5-2-7) states that the CBV, in its review, is to use "objective criteria commonly used". Practice in this area requires the acquirer to justify its price through the multicriteria approach (*"approche multi-critère"*). The price of the offer is compared with:

---

[3] *Anastassiades and others* v *S.A. Pinault and others*, Court of Appeals of Paris, Section CBV, 10 March 1992, Bull. Joly, 1992, p. 425, Note Viandier; Droit des Sociétés No. 5, May 1992, Note Hovasse; Revue des Sociétés 1992, 229, Note Vasseur.

– the listed prices for the concerned securities (last listed price, average price over one month, six months and one year, weighted by trading volume, if needed);
– net asset value (reassessed to take into account undervalued assets) of the target (and subsidiaries); and
– price earning ratio (or PER) of other companies of the same business sector.

The review by the authorities is made on a case-by-case basis and other criteria are sometimes used such as the price of prior offers made on the securities concerned or valuations made by independent experts. The SBF's approach also depends on the target's activities; for example, as concerns holding companies, the PER may be irrelevant, and acquirers frequently have recourse to the reassessed net asset value of the underlying companies minus a discount.

The CBV generally requires a premium to be offered and it also generally insists that a premium should exist above the average price listed during the 60 business days preceding the offer. The last listed price is also frequently a minimum for the offer.

(c) Cash v securities

A tender offer can be made for cash or in exchange for other securities. It may also be made for a combination of securities *and* cash or for either cash *or* securities, in which case a decision must be made by the acquirer, with the approval of the CBV, as to whether the offer is primarily an exchange offer or a cash offer, since each of these is covered by separate sets of provisions of the General Regulation (Article 5-2-4 of the General Regulation).

In the case of an exchange offer, the authorities generally require that the securities offered in exchange be listed in France, although there have been a few cases where they were only listed abroad. In the latter case, the COB sometimes requires that foreign brokerage fees (which are significant for French residents placing a trade order on a foreign exchange) be borne by the acquirer. Alternatively, the authorities may be satisfied if the acquirer grants shareholders an option to sell the securities exchanged. It is also possible to provide that the securities proposed in exchange be listed shortly after the termination of the tender offer in order to grant "liquidity" to the tendering shareholders.

If it is the acquirer's securities that are offered in exchange, the acquirer must issue the securities promptly after the termination of the offer. Since the Law No. 94-679 of 8 August 1994, this can be done through a mere decision of the acquirer's board of directors or chairman. Further, there is no need for the decision to be made on the basis of a valuation report issued by a judicially appointed expert (the *commmissaire aux apports*) so long as the acquirer is listed in France or in a Member State of the European Economic Area or the OECD.

(d) Duration of offers

Offers must remain open for at least 20 business days (*"jours de bourse"*, *i.e.*, days during which the French exchanges are open) (Article 5-2-10 of the General Regulation).

When an offer is declared effective, the SBF publishes a release setting out the initial timetable for the offer (commencement, end, last day for filing of competing bids, delivery and payment schedule). The filing of a competing bid automatically prolongs the term of all prior offers pending if previous acquirers maintain their bids or increase the bid price.

The CBV has the flexibility to adjust termination dates for offering periods and may require accelerated bidding when a target has been in play for more than ten weeks. Also, the COB may always request that the CBV increase the duration of the offer to ensure proper disclosure (Article 5-2-10 of the General Regulation).

(iii) Filing with the CBV

A description of the proposed offer must be filed with the CBV by one or more credit institutions acting on behalf of the acquirer. These institutions act as guarantors of the acquirer's undertaking, which means that, if the acquirer is unable to buy the securities tendered, the bank has to do it. For this reason, banks always insist that all funds be readily available (or that a first-demand bank guarantee be provided) prior to the filing of the offer.

The documentation filed with the CBV must follow certain guidelines issued by the CBV (General Decision of the CBV No. 92-10 dated 1 October 1992). The offer file must describe *inter alia*:

- the identity of the acquirer (and persons acting in concert with it), together with a description of its activities and the identity of the credit institution(s) acting on its behalf;
- the purpose of the offer and the tender offer procedure that the acquirer intends to follow;
- the amount of securities and voting rights directly or indirectly held by the acquirer and persons acting in concert with it, as well as the securities (and voting rights) already held by the acquirer; and
- the terms of the proposed tender offer (including the price or exchange value and, in the case of a voluntary offer, the minimum amount of securities to be tendered in order for the offer to go through).

Upon filing, the acquirer must have applied for all the approvals from national and European regulatory bodies which are necessary for the transaction (see Chapter 11). Copies of all applications must be provided to the CBV when filing an offer. For example, as far as non-residents are concerned, this would include the mandatory exchange control filing with the Trésor (Article 5-2-5 of the General Regulation).

As soon as an offer is filed, the CBV informs the Trésor, the COB and the Antitrust Division of the Ministry of Economy of the main terms of the offer and suspends trading of the target and, if the acquirer is listed, of the acquirer (Article 5-2-1 of the General Regulation). Shortly thereafter, the SBF publishes a notice (the *"avis de dépôt"*) announcing the offer. The notice discloses the main terms of the offer, including the name of the acquirer, the banks acting on its behalf, the price (or exchange ratio) of the offer and the number of the target's securities already held by the acquirer.

(iv) CBV determination

The CBV is required to issue a determination regarding the acceptability of the proposed offer within five business days after filing (Article 5-2-6 of the General Regulation).

After review of the proposed price (or exchange ratio), the conditions of tender or exchange of a minimum number of shares and (in the case of an exchange offer) the state of the market for the securities proposed in exchange, the CBV may require the acquirer to revise its offer. The CBV enjoys broad discretion in this regard (Article 5-2-7 of the General Regulation).

The CBV is also entitled to require that the acquirer provide it with a deposit in cash or securities.

If the CBV approves the terms of the offer, it informs the public by means of a release published by the SBF (*"avis de recevabilité"*). Trading normally resumes two business days after publication of the approval notice in the SBF's bulletin (Article 5-2-8 of the General Regulation).

The offer only effectively commences two business days after the date when the necessary administrative and governmental approvals have been granted and the COB has approved the prospectus prepared by the acquirer. The commencement is announced to the market through an SBF release (*"avis d'ouverture"*). The release sets forth the calendar for the offer (Article 5-2-9 of the General Regulation).

(v) Prospectuses

(a) Acquirer's prospectus

A draft prospectus must be filed with the COB by the acquirer's bank no later than the day on which the SBF publishes its release stating that an offer has been filed with the CBV. The bank is required to sign the prospectus with the acquirer and guarantees that the information contained therein is complete and not misleading. The draft prospectus must also be delivered directly to the target.

The acquirer's prospectus must disclose:

- a basic description of the acquirer (corporate name, address, management (board of directors, etc), auditors and main activities);
- the acquirer's intentions concerning the target for the next twelve months in terms of industrial, financial and personnel management;

- whether the acquirer intends to maintain public trading in the target's securities or delist them through a repurchase offer or a squeeze-out;
- the duration of the offer;
- the price or exchange value proposed, together with the valuations made to compute such price or exchange value;
- the minimum number of securities the acquirer requires in order for its offer to be effective (in the case of a voluntary offer);
- the target's securities already held by the acquirer (or any person acting in concert with it);
- details concerning the financing of the offer (Article 7 of COB Regulation No. 89-03).

The prospectus must also include the acquirer's financial statements. Foreign acquirers' financial statements are to be translated into French. The acquirer's financial statements do not, however, have to be presented according to French accounting standards.

The acquirer must also disclose any agreement with third parties relating to the offer (which would include any undertakings by shareholders of the target to sell their shares to the acquirer) and the identity of the persons or entities acting in concert with it.

The COB is required to approve the draft prospectus within five business days after filing (Article 9 of COB Regulation No. 89-03) by issuing a *visa* (stamp) on the prospectus. If the acquirer does not comply with requests by the COB for additional information, the COB may extend this period to 10 business days or reject the prospectus. The COB then informs the public of its decision. Once approved, the definitive prospectus is immediately made available to the target by the acquirer (Article 10 of COB Regulation No. 89-03).

The acquirer must publish the prospectus in a financial newspaper having national circulation in France (*e.g.*, *Les Echos*, *La Tribune* or *l'AGEFI*) within four business days following the COB's approval. If all the shares of the target are held in registered form, the prospectus must be sent to all the shareholders. If less than all of the shares are registered, this requirement does not apply (Article 12 of COB Regulation No. 89-03).

(b) Target's prospectus

The target company is also required to file a draft prospectus with the COB no later than the fifth business day following delivery to the target of the acquirer's prospectus, as approved by the COB. It is possible, and in fact usual in the case of friendly bids, for the acquirer and the target to submit a joint prospectus to the COB.

The target's prospectus must include:

- a description of the target;
- a description of its shareholding both as of the date of the offer and as of one year beforehand, specifying the shares held by the target itself as well as by companies controlled by the target;

– any agreement known to the target's management that may affect the evaluation or the outcome of the offer; and

– the opinion of the Board of Directors of the target on the advantages or disadvantages for the shareholders of the offer, as well as information on the votes cast by the directors in reaching such opinion (dissenting directors are entitled to state their own position in the prospectus) (Article 11 of COB Regulation No. 89-03).

The prospectus must also include the target's financial statements. The COB must approve or reject the target's prospectus no later than the third business day after filing. The prospectus is then made available by the target to the public by publication or mail (as discussed *supra*) during the four business days following the COB's approval. The COB then informs the public of its decision.

(c) COB's review

In its review, the COB's primary function is to check whether the information contained in the prospectuses conforms to customary requirements and is adequate to inform the public. In this connection, the COB may request the publication of any additional information and make any comments on the prospectuses that it deems necessary through a warning (*"avertissement"*) on the first page of the prospectus. There are examples where the COB granted registration of a prospectus but suggested that the price was not justified or that the terms of the offer did not ensure equality of treatment among shareholders. The COB may also require (or at least exercise pressure) that the terms of an offer be amended, if the protection of the public so requires. The COB enjoys broad discretion in this regard and may refuse its visa (although there is no precedent for such a refusal).

(vi) Workers' committee

As soon as an offer is filed, the management of the target must inform the workers' committee (*"comité d'entreprise"*) of the terms of the offer. The committee may invite the acquirers to explain the purpose and the terms of its offer at one of its meetings (Article L 432-1 of the Labour Code).

(vii) Competing offers

A competing offer is a parallel tender offer for the target initiated by a third party. It must be filed with the CBV at least five business days before expiration of the initial tender offer. If the offer is for cash, it must be at least 2% higher than the initial tender offer. (Prior to the 1989 Law, competing offers had to be filed at least 20 calendar days before expiration of the initial offer and had to have a price or exchange value at least 5% higher than the initial tender offer, former Article 193 of the General Regulation.) However, if the initial offer is subject to a minimum number of shares being tendered, the new bidder may elect to offer the same price so long as it does not impose any minimum share requirement. By contrast, the increased bid requirement does not apply to an exchange offer.

All responses to a tender offer from the target's shareholders become null and void if a competing offer is announced (Article 5-2-15 of the General Regulation).

The person who made the preceding offer must declare its intentions (*e.g.* to improve the offer, maintain it, or withdraw it) not later than five business days after the date when the competing offer is launched (Article 5-2-15 of the General Regulation).

(viii) Increased bids

An increased bid is an amended cash offer launched by the acquirer. Such an offer may be made even if there has been no competing bid. An increased bid must be filed with the CBV before the expiration of the initial offer and must be at least 2% higher than the initial tender offer. However, if the initial tender offer is subject to a minimum number of shares being tendered, the increased bid may merely consist of an election to withdraw the minimum share requirement (Article 5-2-23 of the General Regulation).

The initiator of an increased bid must prepare an addendum to its original prospectus that must be filed with the COB on the same day the SBF publishes its notice that an increased bid has been filed. The addendum must be published two business days after the COB's approval (Article 13 of COB Regulation No. 89-03).

The target must publish the opinion of its Board of Directors or Directorate. The opinion must be filed with the COB and published two business days after the day on which the SBF publishes its notice that an increased bid has been filed.

These provisions do not apply if the price of its offer is increased as a result of open-market purchases by the acquirer (or parties acting in concert) during the pendency of the offer.

(ix) Supervision of transactions during an offer

Throughout the pendency of a tender offer, the companies involved (*i.e.*, the acquirer, the target and any person acting in concert with either of them) are subject to strict rules designed to ensure fair competition among all bidders as well as proper and prompt disclosure of material facts. The rules are as follows:

(a) Disclosure of purchase and sale of the target's securities

Companies involved in a tender offer and their directors and shareholders holding at least 5% of the voting rights of the target as well as any person acting in concert with either of them, must report to the SBF on a daily basis, all transactions carried out by them in the securities of companies involved in the tender offer. This requirement also applies to any person acquiring 0.5% or more of the capital or the voting rights of the target (Article 22 of COB Regulation No. 89-03). The SBF then publishes all such reports.

(b) All transactions to be made on the market

As soon as an offer is filed with the CBV, all transactions concerning the target's securities must be made on the market. Also, during the course of the offer no option contract may be registered and no broker's registration of private transactions (*applications*) may be made when the exchange is closed. The only exception is that option contracts filed prior to the commencement of the offer may still be exercised. Further, no one is allowed to acquire listed shares off the market (*hors bourse*) by acquiring holdings, the sole assets of which would be the target's securities or securities outside France (Article 5-2-18 of the General Regulation).[4]

(c) Transaction made outside ordinary course of business

The management of both acquirer and target are required to disclose to the COB any decision made or transaction initiated by them other than in the ordinary course of business. The COB then gives its opinion on how the public should be informed of such transactions. This would cover sale of substantial assets, mergers, joint ventures, distribution agreements and the like. The COB may express its views concerning such transaction publicly. In practice, the COB may even oppose the decision through its injunctive powers if it considers that the transaction is an unfair defensive measure taken by the management (Article 3 of COB Regulation No. 89-03).

(d) Press releases, interviews, etc

The management of the acquirer and the target must act with special care in their public statements (press releases, interviews, etc.).[5] They must receive the prior approval of the COB to publish any information other than that included in either the releases published by the SBF (announcing the offer, its time schedule, a competing bid or an increase in price) or the prospectuses (Article 6 of COB Regulation No. 89-03).

(e) Disclosures of key agreements

Any agreement that may affect the evaluation or the outcome of the offer entered into among the shareholders of the target (or any persons acting in concert with them) must immediately be disclosed to the companies involved, the CBV and the COB. This would cover arrangements between the target's shareholders and a white knight, new shareholders' agreements

---

[4] See also *Télémécanique* v *Schneider*, Court of Appeals of Paris, 18 March 1988, JCP, éd. E, 1988, II, 15248.

[5] *Framatome* v *Schneider*, Order of the President of the Commercial Court of Paris, 28 February 1988, Gaz. Pal., 1988, 2, 470.

and agreements concerning key assets of the target. For example, a joint-venture agreement that would include a termination clause in the case of a tender offer would fall within this category. Agreements of this type must also be disclosed to the public through press releases published in at least one financial daily having national circulation (Article 4 of COB Regulation No. 89-03).

(f) Enforcement

Brokers, banks and other intermediaries acting on behalf of clients tendering or exchanging securities must inform clients of all the provisions of COB Regulation No. 89-04 governing tender offers. The COB may make a request to any of these institutions to be provided with the identity of these clients, and professional secrecy may not be used as an excuse (Article 23 of COB Regulation No. 89-03).

(x) Termination of a tender offer

Shareholders may revoke sales orders previously placed by them through their brokers up to the last day of the offer. This is different from tenders taking place within the context of standing offers, which are final as soon as the tender is made and which may not be revoked.

The CBV has the flexibility to adjust termination dates for offer periods and may require accelerated bidding when a target has been in play for more than ten weeks (Article 5-2-21 of the General Regulation). Also, the COB may always request that the CBV increase the duration of the offer to ensure proper disclosure of material information (Article 12 of COB Regulation No. 89-03). This might take place when the COB approves a prospectus but wishes an independent expert to make a report on the target's valuation or other terms of the offer.

At the end of the offer period, the SBF centralises all tenders made through banks and brokers. Approximately ten business days after this, it publishes a release (*avis de résultat*) setting forth the results of the offer (Article 5-2-13 of General Regulation). If the acquirer previously declared that it reserved its right not to go through with its offer unless it acquired a minimum number of shares, it must then make its decision known, and this is immediately published by the SBF. If the offer is effective, the SBF transfers all securities tendered to the credit institutions acting for the account of the acquirer against payment of the purchase price. In the case of an exchange offer, the delivery of the securities is delayed until after the issue of the securities.

The acquirer effectively acquires the securities tendered on the day when they are registered in its name – usually shortly after the SBF has transferred them to the credit institution acting for the account of the acquirer.

Following a tender offer resulting in the acquisition of indirect control over listed subsidiaries of the target, the acquirer may be required to launch subsequent bids (in the form of *garanties de cours* or mandatory offers) for the subsidiaries, if these are "essential assets" for the target (see p. 94).

Also, following a tender offer or the acquisition of a controlling block, the majority shareholders may convene a shareholders' meeting to change the company's management or by-laws (Article 158-4° of the Company Law).

Prior to the 1989 Law, the originator of a tender offer could not initiate a new tender offer on the same target within 12 months following the end of the first offer, except to compete with a tender offer from a third party. This rule no longer exists.

2. Voluntary bids

In a voluntary bid, the acquirer may condition its offer on tender of a minimum number of shares; agreement to tender shares must be terminated in the event of a competing bid.

A voluntary bid is an offer made by an acquirer on its own behalf in order to acquire control over the target. Voluntary bids are usually friendly, but they can also be unfriendly. They are governed by the standard tender offer rules discussed above, except that the acquirer may make its offer conditional on the tender of obtaining a minimum number of shares or voting rights.

(i) Offer conditional on tender of a minimum number of shares

This is the so-called "*faculté de renonciation*" (right to renounce) whereby the acquirer discloses that it reserves its right not to go through with its offer if it does not hold or acquire, at the outcome of the offer, a certain number of the target's shares or voting rights (Article 5-2-5 of the General Regulation). This number can be the majority of the target's voting rights (in order to control decisions to be taken by ordinary meetings of the shareholders) or two-thirds of the voting rights (in order to control decisions to be taken by extraordinary meetings of the shareholders) but the acquirer is free to choose whatever number it wishes.[6] The threshold announced by the bidder must, however, be reasonable in view of the shareholding of the target and is subject to review by the CBV, which can refuse a proposed bid on that basis.

---

[6] Ordinary general meetings ("*assemblées générales ordinaires*") are competent to act on decisions of shareholders other than those requiring a modification of the by-laws. They consider such matters as the appointment or dismissal of members of the Board of Directors or the Supervisory Board, directors' fees, the appointment of the auditors, the issue of straight debt securities, the approval of financial statements and the allocation of profits and losses. Extraordinary general meetings of shareholders ("*assemblées générales extra-ordinaires*") are held to decide all amendments to the by-laws, such as any change in the corporate purpose, any increase or reduction in the corporate capital and therefore any issue of equity securities or securities convertible into equity securities, a merger or the dissolution of the company.

This type of offer is almost always used in the case of voluntary offers where the acquirer's purpose is to gain control over the target.

(ii) Agreements to tender shares

(a) General

In a voluntary offer, shareholders of a target may, by agreement, undertake to sell their shares to the party launching the offer. Agreements of this type would typically be executed shortly before a tender offer is launched and would have to be disclosed in the prospectuses. If executed after the commencement of an offer they would have to be disclosed immediately to the target and the public.

Usually, such agreements take the form of an undertaking to tender the shares to the acquirer if the latter files a bid within a short period and at a price at least equal to an agreed-upon minimum. If the bid is filed, the shareholder is bound to sell its securities.

(b) The debate

These agreements do not raise any particular issues when no competing bid is launched. However, if a competing bid is launched, by definition at some higher price than the initial bid, it will be worthless if the agreement to tender made between the shareholders and the initial bidder is irrevocable. This is one of the main debates of the past ten years within the French takeover arena. On the one hand, sellers wish to be able to choose buyers of their shares in a listed company and buyers want also to be sure to buy listed targets and the agreed-upon price. In a perfect world, no competing bidder shows up. If a competing bidder does show up, the situation is different. The sellers may change their minds in order to make higher gains (the price proposed by the competing bidder being by definition higher than the one proposed by the initial bidder) but the buyer may disagree. If the agreements to tender are irrevocable, the sellers would be bound to sell to the initial bidder. Also, this situation is arguably detrimental to minority shareholders who would not be in a position to benefit from a higher price. For this reason, the COB and the CSOP[7] have, in several instances, taken the position that agreements to tender must include a provision whereby they are terminated if a competing bid is launched.

On the other hand, one cannot force the controlling shareholder to put its shares up at auction if it wishes to sell its company. Indeed, shareholders

---

[7] Release of the CSOP dated 10 June 1988. The Comité de Surveillance des Offres Publiques (the "CSOP") was an advisory body in charge of interpreting or issuing recommendations concerning the existing regulations in the area of tender offers. It was authorised to issue releases to the public. The CSOP was created by an *Arrêté* dated 7 August 1978 to co-ordinate the attitude of administrative bodies in the case of tender offers which raised important economic issues. The CSOP consisted of: the Head of the Treasury; the President of the COB; and the Syndic of the Compagnie or their respective representatives. The CSOP last met in 1988 but did, in the past, issue key opinions in the tender offer area.

must be able to choose a buyer and there are other criteria involved in selecting a buyer than just the price (industrial strategy, personnel management, etc.).

In fact, the still to be adopted European Takeover Code (see 3(d) *infra*) provides that persons who have accepted a bid would be able to renegotiate in order to accept more attractive competing bids, unless domestic legislation permits the irrevocability of acceptance.

(c) Case law

Prior to the OCP case, case law[8] suggested that agreements to tender could be irrevocable even when they concerned a majority of the target's stock. However, in the OCP case, the acquirer (Gehe AG) had been granted irrevocable options to acquire control over the two main assets of the target (OCP), subject only to its acquiring a majority of the stock of OCP in the course of a tender offer. The tender offer had been approved by the CBV but the Court of Appeals of Paris cancelled this approval on the basis that Gehe had been granted an unfair advantage *vis-à-vis* other potential bidders. It is therefore unclear whether the voluntary offer procedure is still available if the acquirer is granted the right to buy a controlling interest in the target's shares during the course of the offer and if this right remains in force even if a competing bid is launched. An acquirer enjoying these rights would be deemed to have been granted an unfair advantage *vis-à-vis* other potential bidders since other acquirers would be deterred from making a competing bid. On the other hand, a voluntary tender offer may validly be filed by the acquirer if the undertakings to tender shares only concern a small portion of the issuer's capital.[9]

Therefore, on the basis of current case law, in the context of voluntary offers, acquirers can only be granted agreements to tender for a majority of the target's shares if the agreements include a provision whereby they are automatically terminated in the event of a competing bid.

3. Mandatory offers

Acquirers who alone or in concert hold one-third of the shares or voting rights of French companies listed on either the official or second market must file a bid unless an exemption is granted by the CBV.

Mandatory offers were created by the 1989 Law in order to force persons acquiring control of listed companies through open-market purchases or creeping tenders to launch a bid. Prior to the introduction of mandatory offers, the stock market authorities could only try to put pressure on persons

---

[8] See *France Valeurs and Biderman* v *Primistères*, Commercial Court of Paris, 28 July 1986, Rev. Sociétés, 1987, p. 580.
[9] *Balland and others* v *La Sucrerie Raffinerie de Chalon-sur-Saône and others*, Court of Appeals of Paris, 1st ch. Sect. CBV, 27 October 1993; RJDA 4/94, No. 422, p. 327.

carrying out creeping tenders to file a bid (or at least disclose their intent) but the acquirers almost never agreed (see LVMH's take-over by Financière Agache and Guinness plc, Chapter 1).

The French mandatory offer rules were inspired by two ideas:

(i) the draft proposal for a Thirteenth Directive made by the European Commission (the so-called "Europe Take-over Code"), which provides for a mandatory tender for all of the stock of a listed company when an acquirer reaches one-third of a target's voting rights (discussed in Section (iv) *infra*), and

(ii) the UK rule that provides for a mandatory tender on reaching 30% of the target's voting rights.

(i) The basic rule

Once an acquirer (or several acquirers acting in concert) holds one-third of the shares *or* voting rights of a French company whose shares are listed either on the official market or the second market (but not the over-the-counter market), it must immediately inform the CBV and commence a tender offer unless an exemption is granted by the CBV in this regard (see Section (iii) *infra*) (Article 5-4-1 of the General Regulation). Failure to do so results in the automatic loss of the voting rights held in excess of the one-third threshold.

The mandatory offer requirement may result from all types of transactions, such as the acquisition of securities on the market or through a block trade, the acquisition of double voting rights (resulting from the lapse of the two-year waiting period without any acquisition of shares), the subscription to newly issued securities, mergers, or contributions of assets in exchange for shares.

The mandatory offer may even result from the mere entering into of an agreement resulting in an action in concert among parties which together hold one-third of the shares or voting rights, even if the entering into of such an agreement is not coupled with any acquisition of securities (subject to an exemption, as discussed in Section (i) *infra*). It is interesting to note that, prior to May 1992, the mandatory tender offer obligation only resulted from "*acquisitions*" of shares or voting rights. The new regulation provides that the obligation may even result from the mere "*holding*" of shares or voting rights.

Mandatory offers are subject to the rules applicable to standard tender offers, discussed in Section 1 *supra*. In a mandatory offer, however, the acquirer cannot make its offer conditional on tender or exchange of a specified minimum number of shares and is hence bound to purchase all shares tendered, whatever the result of its offer.

(ii) Application in certain special cases

(a) When the acquirer already holds between one-third and one-half of the target

An acquirer (acting alone or in concert with other parties) whose holdings are already between one-third and one-half of the shares or voting rights is also required to make an offer if it increases its holdings by 2% or more during any one-year period, or if it becomes the majority holder of the company's shares or voting rights (Article 5-4-4 of the General Regulation). Acquirers subject to this provision must report to the SBF all changes in the number of shares or voting rights held. The purpose of this provision is to avoid the acquisition of control through creeping offers ("*ramassage*") by shareholders which already hold one-third of a target.

(b) Indirect acquisitions

The General Regulation includes a provision imposing a mandatory offer when an acquirer takes control of a company (whether publicly traded or not) and such acquirer, as a result of such control, holds, directly or indirectly, one-third or more of the shares or voting rights of a company listed on either the official or the second market. The rule results from Article 5-4-3 of the General Regulation, whereby acquirers:

> *are required to comply with the mandatory tender offer requirement when by acquiring control over a company, they acquire directly or indirectly more than one-third of the capital or voting rights of a French company whose securities are listed on the official market or the second market, if and when the securities of such French company held by the company acquired represent an essential part of its assets.*

In cases where the first company is a pure holding company whose sole assets are the shares of a listed company, this provision does not raise any issue. However, in the case of the acquisition of a company owning various assets, the applicability of Article 5-4-3 is more difficult to assess and the CBV has important discretionary powers to decide whether a holding is an essential asset or not. It is generally considered that a holding is deemed essential when it represents two-thirds or more of the total assets of the first company, provided the results generated by the second company contribute in the same proportion to the results of the first company. There are no clear-cut rules in this regard and other criteria might also come into play in order to compare the companies – such as the comparative results of the target and strategic values.

Another issue in the case of indirect acquisitions is that of the price to be offered to the shareholders of the indirect listed target. Here, the acquirer has to value the indirect target using the multicriteria approach (listed price, net asset value and PER) normally used for tender offers.

(iii) Exemptions to the mandatory offer rule

The CBV may grant exemptions from the mandatory offer requirement on a series of limited grounds set forth in Article 5-4-6 of the General Regulation. Most of these exemptions are aimed at exempting an acquirer from the mandatory tender obligation in situations where there is no real change of control of the target, whether the acquirer already held control prior to its acquisition or the company is still controlled by a third party.

Cases where an exemption may be available are where:

(i) the acquisition results from a gratuitous transfer of shares or voting rights (this would cover gifts and transmission through wills or inheritance).

(ii) the acquisition results from:
- the issue of new shares payable in cash reserved to specified parties (this exemption is aimed at allowing companies in financial trouble to find investors);
- a merger; or
- a partial contribution of assets;

provided these transactions are approved by the shareholders' meeting of the company concerned.

(iii) the acquisition does not exceed 3% of the total shares or voting rights of the target *and* the acquirer undertakes to resell any shares held in excess of the relevant thresholds within 18 months.

(iv) the increase in shares or voting rights results from a decrease in the total number of shares or voting rights of the target.

(v) the acquirer is already deemed to control the target because it exercises *de facto* control over decisions at shareholders' meetings by virtue of its voting rights.

(vi) the target is already *majority*-controlled by a third party (acting alone or in concert with other parties).

(vii) one or more members of a group of companies that are consolidated for accounting purposes and which already controls the target passes the threshold.

(viii) passing the threshold results from a shift within a shareholders' group already controlling the target that does not significantly change the ownership balance between members of such group.

(ix) passing the threshold results from the execution of an agreement filed with the CBV and published by the SBF that results in an action in concert among its signatories, provided the signatories:
- did not acquire any "significant" amount of voting securities in the year preceding the filing made with the CBV; *and*
- undertake not to "significantly" modify the balance of their holdings within two years thereafter.

The General Regulation does not define the meaning of the term "significant". The determination of whether acquisitions made by the interested parties are significant is made by the CBV on a case-by-case basis.

Even though the General Regulation states that the CBV is not *bound* to grant an exemption when an acquirer falls within one of the above exemptions, it generally does so when one is available. If the CBV grants an exemption to the mandatory offer requirement, it informs the public thereof through a release published by the SBF. The release includes the ground(s) for the exemption granted together with any undertakings given by the acquirer, such as an undertaking to resell part of the shares, or not to change holdings significantly (Article 5-4-7 of the General Regulation).

(iv) The European Take-over Code

French mandatory tender rules anticipate the rules set forth in the proposed Thirteenth Company Law Directive, the so-called "European Take-over Code". This proposal, issued in 1989 by the European Commission, was amended on 14 September 1990. Its basic philosophy is to co-ordinate the rules relating to take-overs of European Union companies listed on a regulated securities market in the European Union and to introduce a Europe-wide mandatory tender rule.

The Directive provides that the acquisition of securities resulting in a total holding by the acquirer exceeding one-third of the voting rights of a listed target triggers an obligation to make a tender offer for all of the target's securities. In calculating its holdings, an acquirer must include:

(i) securities on which it has a right of usufruct;
(ii) securities on which it has a call option;
(iii) securities that are deposited with it and in respect of which it can exercise voting rights (unless the owner of the securities has given specific voting instructions).

The Member States would, however, be able to exempt acquirers that acquire securities:

(i) without consideration;
(ii) through the exercise of pre-emptive rights on the occasion of a capital increase;
(iii) within the framework of a merger by acquisition or a corporate split-up;
(iv) bringing the acquirer beyond the trigger threshold by no more than 3% of the voting rights, provided the acquirer undertakes in writing to divest securities to the extent necessary to return below the threshold within a period not exceeding one year;
(v) if the acquirer already controls the target;
(vi) if the target is controlled by a group unrelated to the acquirer, and the controlling group undertakes in writing not to relinquish control over the target.

The current proposal would also give the supervisory authorities discretionary power to exempt other operations pursuant to a reasoned decision.

It is further provided that each Member State must accept prospectuses that have been approved by the supervisory authorities of the Member State where the first admission to listing was obtained. Under this mutual recognition rule, supervisory authorities may not require the inclusion of any additional information not required by the home Member State or the Member State of first listing, as the case may be.

4. Standing offers ("garanties de cours")

Acquirers acquiring shares from identified vendors and reaching a majority of the voting rights or capital of the target may, with the CBV's approval, launch a simplified offer in the form of a standing offer in lieu of a mandatory offer.

(i) The basic rule

Any acquirer purchasing (or having the right to purchase) shares from one or more other identified parties (as opposed to purchases made on the open market) that result in the acquirer holding more than 50% of the voting rights *or* the capital of a publicly traded company, may apply to the CBV in order to be authorised to carry out a standing offer to purchase all shares that may be tendered for sale by any other shareholder (Article 5-3-5 of the General Regulation). Prior to the enactment of the 1989 Law, the standing offer procedure was mandatory when one acquired a controlling interest (*"bloc de contrôle"*). The concept of a controlling interest was not defined but it was generally thought to mean 40% to 50% since, under French company law, 40% ownership is presumed to constitute control if no other shareholder holds a greater percentage of ownership. In rare instances, the authorities have deemed even smaller percentages to constitute control. For example, in 1985, an acquirer was required to comply with the standing offer procedure even though he controlled only 29% of the capital of the company in question. The rules were a bit unclear and brokers were under an obligation to inform the authorities if they had reason to believe that any transaction of shares by their customers could constitute an unreported transfer of a controlling interest.

The standing offer is governed *inter alia* by the simplified offer rules (see Chapter 8).

The General Regulation also applies the standing offer procedure to the acquisition of a controlling interest in a holding company (whether listed or not) giving the acquirer control of a majority of the voting rights in a publicly traded company, provided that the shares of the publicly traded company represent an "essential part" of the holding company's assets (Article 5-3-7 of the General Regulation).

(ii) Listing of the price for the block of shares

Up to the enactment of the "significant block deal" rule in August 1994 one sensitive issue raised by the use of the standing offer procedure was that of price (see p. 47 *supra*). Indeed, as noted above, subject only to limited exceptions, all purchases and sales of securities listed on the official or second market, including the purchase of a block of shares from an identified seller, had to be effected by brokers at the listed price, generally through an *application* (see price determination rules p. 46 *supra*).

Therefore, at the time the acquirer and the seller entered into agreement concerning a block of shares (the acquisition of which would render the *garantie de cours* applicable), there was always some uncertainty as to whether or not the purchaser would be able to acquire the shares at the contractual price. This was because the transfer of the shares could only occur if and when the agreed price was actually quoted on the exchange.

In the case of a standing offer, acquirers sometimes had recourse to option contracts enabling them to purchase the majority block at a specific price. However, these contracts raised the same issue since the price had to be listed in order for the option contract to be registrable with the SBF. In practice, once an agreement was reached, banking institutions acting on the acquirer's behalf would immediately disclose the proposed transaction to the SBF and try to obtain from the authorities the listing of the desired price in order to be able to register an option contract at this price or register the transaction through an application.

Alternatively, banking institutions acting for the account of the acquirer could try to cause the price for the shares to increase up to the desired level through offers carried out on the open market, a course of action which raised various legal issues since one may not manipulate stock prices.

However, as a result of the significant block trade rule, the CBV may now authorise the majority block to be acquired at any price, whatever the listed price is.

(iii) Approval by the CBV

Since May 1992, the standing offer procedure is no longer mandatory as far as companies listed on the official or the second market are concerned. On the contrary, it may now only be followed with the CBV's approval. If there is no approval, the acquirer has to initiate a mandatory tender offer. In practice, if there are no special circumstances and if the price offered to minority shareholders is fair, the attitude of the CBV is generally co-operative.

The standing offer procedure remains *mandatory* in the case of a purchase of shares from identified parties that results in the acquirer holding more than 50% of the voting rights or the capital of a company whose stock is traded on the over-the-counter market (Article 5-3-6 of the General Regulation).

If a purchaser acquires less than the majority of the voting rights or the capital of a company traded on the over-the-counter market, it is required to file neither a standing offer, since it does not reach the majority level, nor a mandatory offer, since this procedure only applies to companies listed on one of the main markets.

(iv) Same price rule

(a) General

In a standing offer, the acquirer must undertake to purchase all shares tendered by other shareholders during the ten to 15 business day period that runs from the date when the shares of the company first resume trading. The price offered is normally the same price as the price paid for the controlling interest.

In exceptional circumstances, and with the approval of the CBV, the price offered to the other shareholders can be lower if the purchase price payable for the controlling block is not paid in full in cash at the time the transaction is completed. Another exception to the "same price" rule applies in situations where the controlling block changes hands pursuant to an agreement under which the seller agrees to indemnify the purchaser for certain identified undisclosed liabilities. The obtaining of a lower price for minority shareholders is nevertheless not frequent and the stock market authorities generally require evidence that there are one or several *identified* risks guaranteed by the seller. Examples might include the risk of a major tax reassessment within the context of a tax audit in progress or a major liability in relation to an ongoing litigation. In general, one cannot reduce the price offered to minority shareholders by more than 10%.

(b) Indirect acquisitions

In the case of an indirect acquisition of a listed target, one would typically have a separate price or valuation and be able to compute the so-called implicit price (*"prix implicite"*) of the listed company. This price would have to be offered to minority shareholders.

One example of pricing in an indirect acquisition occurred when Genty SA, the parent company of Genty Cathiard, was acquired in 1990. In this case, Genty SA held stock in two other companies and it was possible to value these companies and deduct the value from the total price paid, thus determining the price for the Genty Cathiard shares to be offered to the minority shareholders within the context of the *garantie de cours*.

Another transaction was the Delmas–Vieljeux case (see Chapter 1) where the Bolloré group was required to file a bid, not only on a listed parent company (Compagnie Financière Delmas–Vieljeux), but also on its listed subsidiary, Delmas–Vieljeux. In this case, the acquirer had submitted a valuation of Delmas–Vieljeux independently of the price paid for the parent company through the multicriteria approach normally used for tender offers of the normal category. The CBV had approved Bolloré's offer on 11 July 1991 but a minority shareholder of Delmas–Vieljeux challenged the CBV decision, stating that the price had been computed without reference to the price of the parent company. The Court of Appeals of Paris upheld the CBV's approach, stating that minority shareholders were adequately protected through the multicriteria approach and that the multicriteria analysis

101

could be used in order to assess the price to be offered to minority share-holders in the case of an indirect acquisition.[10]

(v) Press release

Persons proceeding with a standing offer must publish a detailed press release not later than the business day prior to the commencement of such procedure. The press release must conform with certain guidelines issued by the CBV. It must explain how the price was set, how the resulting securities purchases will be financed, the acquirer's intentions in terms of management and whether the target will remain listed or not after the offer. It does not have to include financial statements of the acquirer and is far less detailed than the prospectus required for a tender offer. The release must be submitted to the COB for prior review simultaneously with the filing of the standing offer (Article 20 of COB Regulation No. 89-03).

(vi) Commencement of the offer

When the CBV is satisfied with the acquirer's undertakings, the SBF publishes a notice approving the offer. This notice would also include the price and amount of shares being sold, and the price at which the acquirer is making its standing offer. When the CBV has been provided with evidence of the requisite approvals and when the press release has been approved by the COB, the CBV publishes a notice announcing the commencement of the offer.

Trading normally resumes two business days after publication of the notice and the purchase of the majority block would typically take place upon recommencement of trading. The purchase of all shares tendered by the other shareholders of the target during the ten to 15 business day period would also begin upon recommencement of trading.

In a standing offer procedure, the shares are acquired on the market throughout the term of the offer and purchases and the sales are then final. This is different from the tender offer procedure where shares are only acquired at the end of the tender offer since the SBF centralises all tenders and deliveries of securities. As noted above, in a tender offer, tenders can be revoked up to the last day of the offer and are automatically cancelled if there is a competing bid. In this regard, the standing offer procedure is safer than the tender offer. During the course of a standing offer, the acquirer would not be authorised to purchase any shares on the market at a price other than the price of the standing offer.

(vii) Competing bids

Before the Schaeffer precedent (see discussion *infra*), it was generally said that the standing offer was the safest procedure since the transaction permitted

---

[10] *Maison Antoine Baud* v *Bolloré Technologies and Sofical*, Court of Appeals of Paris, Section CBV, Bull. Joly 1992, p. 69, note Le Cannu.

an acquirer to "secure" the purchase of the majority block before the commencement of the offer, thus rendering a competing bid unlikely. This has proved not to be entirely true since the Schaeffer precedent.

On 24 March 1994, Zuber Laederich, a mid-size French holding company specialising in the take-over of companies in financial trouble, had been granted irrevocable options to acquire 33.5% of the stock of Schaeffer, a listed textile company. Since Zuber Laederich already held 24.8% of the stock of Schaeffer, it now had majority control and consequently filed a standing offer for Schaeffer at FF140 per share on 25 March 1994. Shortly afterwards, and before the exercise of the options, a third-party bidder filed a voluntary tender offer for Schaeffer at a price of FF148 per share, reserving its right not to declare its offer effective if it was not able to hold at least a majority of the stock of Schaeffer. Zuber Laederich's option rendered the competing bid ineffective since Zuber Laederich was certain to acquire majority control, even though the market had been offered a higher price by the new bidder. In an unprecedented move, the CBV demanded that Zuber Laederich either renounce its options and file a voluntary bid or withdraw its offer. The request was made on the basis of the principle of free competition among bidders which has applied in each tender offer battle since the OCP case (see p. 14). Zuber Laederich ultimately renounced its options and filed a voluntary bid, but was over-bid by another third party.

On the basis of this case, once a standing offer is announced, and if a third party bid is launched at a higher price, it seems that the purchase and sale agreement covering the block may be challenged by the authorities as long as the acquisition of the majority block has not closed.

5. **Three procedures for acquiring control over listed companies**

Three procedures are available to investors wishing to acquire "control" of French listed companies. The voluntary tender is the oldest procedure, while the standing offer was created in 1973 to give minority shareholders a way out in case of a change of control. The mandatory tender was introduced in 1989 and it is likely that this procedure will, little by little, replace the standing offer. The pros and cons of the three procedures are as follows:

The standing offer procedure is only available if the acquirer is able to obtain, after the acquisition of blocks of shares from identified sellers, the majority of the voting rights (or capital) of the target. The standing offer procedure is simpler and faster than the tender offer procedure, since it is required to remain open for a shorter period (ten to 15 business days as opposed to 20 business days in the case of a tender offer). It is also a safer procedure, since it permits the acquisition of a majority of the voting rights (and thus control) prior to the initiation of the offer, whose acquisition would in practice eliminate any risk of competing bids (although this might not be entirely true since the Schaeffer case).

The other alternatives (voluntary tender offer or mandatory tender offer) are more complex than the standing offer procedure. They are also more costly since they require the drafting and publication of a prospectus. The tender offer procedure also involves a much greater level of disclosure to the public as compared to the standing offer procedure, since the prospectus must include more detailed information than the press release required in the case of a standing offer.

The voluntary tender procedure is also less sure than the mandatory and the standing offers since, in view of the OCP case and the principle of equality among competing bidders, an acquirer can no longer obtain irrevocable commitments that a key shareholder will tender its shares. The voluntary tender procedure, however, allows the acquirer to make its offer conditional on obtaining at least a minimum amount of shares (more than 50% or at least two-thirds of the voting rights of the company).

Chapter 7
Defensive Measures Against Hostile Tender Offers

Defences available are limited and there is no defence that would totally insulate the management from a successful hostile bidder.

Defences available under French law are limited and there is no defence that would totally insulate either the management or controlling shareholders of a listed company from a hostile bid. One example is the landmark OCP case where the management of a listed company (holding less than 2.5% of the stock) had contributed most of the company's activities to two SCAs controlled by it. In the course of a tender offer battle, the management was finally compelled by the stock market authorities to undertake to sell the SCA's shares to any competing bidders (see Chapter 1).

Also, there are various limitations on anti-take-over devices. The management of French companies must always comply with the corporate interest (*"intérêt social"*) doctrine on the basis of which a company must always act to protect its own interests, which are not necessarily the same as those of controlling shareholders or the management. On the basis of this principle, a target would not be allowed to dispose of a key subsidiary for the sole purpose of annoying a hostile bidder. Moreover, management must always respect the interests of the shareholders, both in the organisation of defences and in its behaviour during a take-over battle.

This being said, there are a great variety of anti-take-over defences in France, and certain devices (such as the creation of double voting rights) are a peculiarity of French law. There are two main categories of anti-take-over device: measures that may be adopted before a tender offer is launched, and those that may be taken in the course of a tender offer, the latter being much more limited than the former.

1. Measures that may be adopted before an offer is launched

Measures that may be adopted before an offer is launched are only available before a notice announcing the filing of the offer is published by the SBF because, once the offer is made public, the target would not be authorised to modify its by-laws, issue securities to friendly parties or generally restructure its activities.

There are three main classifications of anti-take-over devices. The first one requires amendment of the company's by-laws (this merely requires the holding of an extraordinary shareholders' meeting). The second comprises arrangements with friendly parties through agreements, holding structures and issue of shares reserved for specific parties. Finally, a target can restructure its businesses (perhaps by acquiring businesses in a regulated area or changing its corporate form) or issue non-voting securities.

(i) Amendments to by-laws

In France it is common for a company to modify its by-laws in order to establish additional thresholds on voting rights and on shareholdings for which notification is required. Double voting rights and identifiable bearer shares can also be created in this way.

(a) Knowledge of the identity of existing shareholders

A. Additional disclosure thresholds

The by-laws of a publicly traded company may provide that any shareholder holding 0.5% of total voting rights must notify the issuer of its stake within 15 business days. An issuer can also provide that each shareholder (acting alone or in concert with another) who reaches 1%, 1.5%, 2.5%, 3%, 3.5%, 4% and 4.5% of the company's voting rights is to file a threshold notification within 15 days (Article 356-1 of the Company Law).

This technique is widely used in France (*e.g.* La Compagnie de Saint-Gobain (0.5%), Pernod Ricard (0.5%) and Saint-Louis (2.5%)).

B. Registered shares

While most securities traded on the French exchange are in bearer form (*"au porteur"*), the by-laws of a company may provide that its shares be registered. This allows the issuer to have access to the names of all its shareholders (Article 2 of Decree dated 4 August 1949).

This is one of the defences put up by Compagnie Générale des Etablissements Michelin and Lagardère Groupe, two of the few *sociétés en commandite par actions* or ("SCAs") – a corporate form that is similar to a limited partnership – listed in France. Registration is sometimes mandatory for companies active in regulated sectors such as press, television and defence companies.

Another possibility is to provide that shareholders reaching a certain level (*e.g.*, 10%) must immediately register their shares with the issuer.

C. Identifiable bearer shares ("TPIs")

In order to enable listed companies to have some of the benefits of registered shares without resorting to that form of security, it is possible, through a specific provision in the company's by-laws, to provide that the issuer can obtain information from the French securities clearing agency (SICOVAM) relating to the identity of the bearer (Article 263-1 of the Company Law). The technique is referred to as the setting up of *titres au porteur identifiables* ("TPIs"). This measure is only of limited efficiency since requests for identification of shareholders take a certain time and only result in knowledge of the name of the registered holder. Further, foreign shareholders having their shares held through non-resident banks would, in principle, remain unknown, the SICOVAM having access only to the name of the foreign intermediary. Acquirers wanting to be discreet can thus place their shares with an unknown subsidiary or a foreign entity. The TPI mechanism has been adopted by more than 50 French listed companies.

(b) Fidelity premiums

These are two particularities of French corporate law which grant certain additional rights to shareholders who have held shares for a minimum period.

A. Double voting rights

The by-laws of a French company may grant double voting rights to shareholders who have owned registered shares for at least two years, so long as the shares have been paid in full (Article 175 of the Company Law). If desired, the double voting rights can be limited to French and other European nationals (Article 175 *in fine* of the Company Law).

The by-laws may provide for a period of ownership longer than two years. In this situation, the CBV may refuse to list shares of an issuer whose by-laws provide for an ownership period of more than four years in order to grant double voting rights (Article 3-1-13 of the General Regulation). Certain companies nonetheless have longer waiting periods (for example, the by-laws of Pernod Ricard provide that registered shares held by the same shareholder for more than *ten years* are granted double voting rights).

Examples of waiting periods for double voting rights are Valeo (five years), Sibille SA (three years reserved to French and European residents), Essilor International (five years) and BHV (two years).

This device renders the acquisition of control more time-consuming since the acquirer, if faced with a core group of existing shareholders enjoying double voting rights, has to wait before being able to enjoy the same privilege as the existing shareholders. The device also renders more difficult the computation of the actual holdings of voting rights of the target, since it is almost impossible for third parties to know precisely which of the existing shares give rise to these privileges.

Shareholders of companies granting double voting rights can monitor the amounts of voting rights held by them (if they want to avoid being subject to the mandatory offer rules or reaching a level which is subject to disclosures) without having to actually sell or otherwise dispose of their shares. This can be done by deregistering registered shares (and placing them in bearer form) or by transferring them to affiliated companies as was done by the Maus family prior to the acquisition of Au Printemps by Pinault, (see Chapter 1).

B. Financial fidelity premium (*"prime de fidélité"*)

A financial fidelity premium encompasses any granting of a financial advantage to shareholders holding shares for a certain period.

Up to the enactment of Law No. 94-578 of 12 July 1994 (creating new Article 347-2 of the Company Law), financial fidelity premiums were rarely used. The few examples of issuers using the device were SEB, L'Air Liquide and SIPAREX. Mechanisms used at that time included subscribing to additional shares or the granting of increased dividends if a shareholder had held shares for more than a given period. These techniques were possible because Article 269 of the Company Law authorised an issuer to create preferred voting shares.

It is now possible, under Article 347-7, to provide in the by-laws that shareholders who have held registered shares for at least two years will be paid a "preferred" dividend which cannot exceed 110% of the dividends paid to other shareholders. The exact rate of the preferred dividend is laid down in the by-laws. As far as companies listed on the official or second market are concerned, the total amount of shares entitled to receive the preferred dividend held by each shareholder cannot exceed 0.5% of the issuer's capital. Further, the preferred dividend cannot be paid before the close of the second fiscal year following the relative amendment to the by-laws.

On the down side, financial fidelity premiums impose a financial burden on the issuer in that, if the issuer does not want the perceived return (and thus the purchase price) of the already listed stock to decrease, it must increase the aggregate amount of its dividends.

(c) Ceilings on voting rights

The by-laws of a French company may limit the voting rights that can be exercised by any single shareholder (Article 177 of the Company Law). Such a limit must be imposed in a non-discriminatory fashion on all voting shares issued by the target.

This technique has been used by a few issuers. For example:

- Pernod-Ricard imposes a 30% ceiling on each shareholder;
- Total imposes a 10% ceiling (20% in the case of double voting rights);
- Groupe Danone imposes a 6% ceiling (12% for double voting rights), except if a shareholder reaches two-thirds of the capital, in which case the limit no longer applies);

– Alcatel-Alsthom imposes an 8% ceiling (16% in the case of double voting rights);
– Schneider imposes 10% and 15% ceilings;
– Crédit National imposes 20% and 40% ceilings, subject to the same termination provisions as Groupe Danone.

These provisions are strong deterrents for hostile acquirers who may be unable to exercise sole majority control over an acquired target, but at best share joint control if the former key shareholders stay in place. In such cases, however, there might be pressure by the COB on the management to withdraw control, as happened in the OCP case. Further, such a device could lead to major shareholders' disputes temporarily delaying the acquisition of sole control by the bidder.

For these reasons, the COB announced that, in its view, ceilings are acceptable only if they are coupled with a clause removing the ceiling when one shareholder reaches majority control (1992 Bull., page 48, 1993 Bull., page 50). At the same time, the COB announced, in 1985, that it would not disapprove the listing of a company imposing ceilings on the actual ownership of shares (Bull. No. 181, May 1985).

(d) Devices concerning the Board of Directors

The board of directors of a *société anonyme* ("SA") adopts resolutions by a simple majority of directors present or represented at the meeting (Article 100 of the Company Law). The by-laws of an SA may, however, provide that certain decisions require a higher majority vote or a unanimous vote. This type of provision does not have the same effect under French corporate practice as in the United States since (i) French boards of directors are not elected for staggered terms, (*i.e.*, all members of the Board are elected by a majority vote of the shareholders) and (ii) directors may be dismissed by a majority vote of an ordinary meeting of the shareholders at any time and without cause.

The by-laws of a company may, however, require that the directors, in order to be eligible, have special qualifications. For instance, it is possible to provide that the members of the Board be either French or European nationals or have some specific professional credentials.

These measures would only have a limited impact since an acquirer could always modify the by-laws of a listed target if it acquires more than two-thirds of the capital. If, however, someone retains the so-called blocking minority (more than one-third of the company's voting rights), this renders the acquisition by a hostile party of control over the target's board of directors more burdensome.

(e) New shareholders to be approved

The by-laws of a French company may include a provision whereby any acquisition of shares by a third party (a person other than an existing shareholder) is subject to the prior approval of the Board of Directors. This

111

type of clause (called a *"clause d'agrément"*) is frequently used by privately held companies. As far as publicly held companies are concerned, a company cannot be listed on the official market if its by-laws include such a provision (Article 3-1-13 of the General Regulation).

COB Regulation No. 89-03 provides that an approval clause cannot be used by the management of a listed company to refuse the entry of a new shareholder within the context of a tender offer, except if the clause results from a specific provision of French law (Article 3). For example, the by-laws of companies operating in certain regulated sectors (*e.g.* the press) have to include such a provision. For these reasons (and because such a clause would seriously impair market liquidity), this type of clause is rarely used except for a few companies traded on the over-the-counter market.

(ii) Arrangements with friendly parties

Agreements with friendly parties can be of many types and structures.

(a) Main types of agreements

Members of a friendly group may enter into first refusal agreements whereby the parties would not be authorised to sell or otherwise dispose of their shares to a third party without first offering those shares to the other parties. Agreements of this type, when entered into among shareholders of companies listed on either the official or the second markets, have to be disclosed to the CBV for publication by the SBF. They have generally been held to be enforceable within the context of a hostile offer, provided they are entered into before the commencement of the offer.[1]

Another category of agreements establish the rules governing additional acquisitions and dispositions of shares. These agreements would typically include a clause organising a joint response if a hostile bid is launched. The members of the group may also undertake not to sell their shares to the hostile bidder if one member of the group launches a competing bid, or to sell their shares or launch a competing bid only if the majority so decides.

Other agreements are "stand still" agreements, *i.e.*, agreements whereby two parties undertake not to acquire shares (eventually exceeding a certain level) in each other's capital or in a third company. One party can also undertake not to sell or otherwise dispose of its shares. These agreements are valid provided they are for a limited term.

(b) Creation of joint holding companies

Friendly parties can place their shares in a listed company in a private holding company. This technique enhances the enforcement of share-

---

[1] *Peltic, Baizeau and others* v *Schwich*, Commercial Court of Paris, 6 April 1987, Court of Appeals of Paris, 23 June 1987, Bull. Joly 1987, p. 701, Cour de Cassation, Commercial Chamber, 7 March 1989, Bull. Joly, 1989, p. 430; *Sodexho* v *Codec-Una*, Commercial Court of Corbeil-Essonnes, 25 February 1987, Court of Appeals of Paris, 30 March 1989, Bull. Joly, 1989, p. 978.

holders' agreements since all the friendly parties' shares are placed in the same hands. The disposal of the target's shares would generally be subject to various procedures (such as approval by the board of directors of the holding company or by a meeting of its shareholders) which can easily be monitored. Transfers of the target's shares would generally be replaced by transfers of the holding company's shares, which is thus more flexible, since it is a private company and no recourse to a stockbroker is needed. Transfer of shares would also be more discreet. Holding companies are often used by members of a family controlling listed companies. Since January 1994, it is even possible to have recourse to the new *société par actions* ("SAS") form, which enables the establishment of strict rules on management, share transfers and shareholders' exclusion. In an SAS, the shareholders have almost complete discretion in framing the rules governing management and shareholders' rights. The by-laws can even include a provision forcing a shareholder to sell out its shares in certain circumstances.

(c) Issue of securities to friendly parties

A target company may issue to a friendly party either securities which may be converted into equity securities or securities with warrants to buy equity securities.

It is essential that the true purpose of the issue of shares to the friendly party be fully disclosed (*i.e.* to place them in friendly parties' hands) and that no transfer of control of the company holding the warrants be made after an offer is filed. Also, the issue of the securities to the friendly parties should not take place within the context of a *public* offering of securities with cancellation of the existing shareholders' preferential subscription rights (during which the friendly parties would in practice be acquiring most of the offered securities). Rather, it should be a private placement of securities reserved for such parties, the names of which would be disclosed to the other shareholders when waiving their preferential subscription rights for those parties.

It is also vital that the friendly parties be seen as independent from the company's management. If the issue is coupled with options or arrangements as to voting on the securities, it might be considered as a fraud or at least a scheme to avoid the application of mandatory provisions of French law since:

 – a company may not hold its own shares;
 – a company cannot vote shares indirectly controlled (see the regulation of "*auto-contrôle*", *infra*);
 – the management of a listed target cannot invoke a shareholders' approval clause against a bidder (see the regulation of "*clauses d'agrément*", *supra*).

This technique was used in the tender offer initiated by Schneider on Télémécanique Electrique in February 1988. Télémécanique had, prior to the offer, issued warrants to buy shares of COFITEL, a shell company controlled by Télémécanique's management. Following the filing of the offer, the shares in COFITEL had been transferred to Framatome, the "white knight' found by the management. Following summary proceedings initiated by Schneider, the courts decided that the warrants held by COFITEL had to be placed in escrow and could not be exercised.[2] Schneider also commenced an action on the merits in order to have the issue of warrants cancelled on the basis that it had been presented as being made for the sole benefit of employees of Télémécanique, whereas, in fact, it was reserved to the management and friendly parties. Schneider also argued that the sale of the COFITEL shares resulted in an indirect sale of Télémécanique shares, which type of transaction cannot take place in the course of a tender offer. Since Schneider ultimately over-bid Framatome prior to the court's final decision, Schneider withdrew from this legal action.

Another example is the issue of bonds with warrants to buy shares (*obligations avec bons de souscription d'actions* – "OBSA") made by Moët Hennessy in 1987 before its merger with Louis Vuitton. The public issue had been disclosed to the market as a public offering of securities on the international market. It turned out that most of the bonds had been placed with identified French investors with close ties with the issuer in order to place equity securities in friendly hands. The court held that the transaction was not a true public placement but rather an issue reserved to identified persons and that, therefore, the shareholders had been misled when approving the capital increase.[3] The issue was, however, not cancelled for technical reasons (the OBSA had been traded for many years so it was impossible to trace all the deals made, and the plaintiffs had only challenged the issue of warrants, forgetting to challenge the issue of the bonds).

(d) Cross-shareholding

Participation in a friendly party's capital is also a way to signal a potential alliance to the market. Sometimes, the participation can be reciprocal in which case one speaks of cross-shareholding (*"participations croisées"*).

There are numerous examples of cross shareholdings in France; for example, Banque Nationale de Paris indirectly holds 19% of the shares of Union des Assurances de Paris, which in turn owns 15% of BNP.

However, there is a technical obstacle under French law since, under Article 358 of the Company Law, a company may not own any share of another company if it directly owns more than 10% of such other company. A technique for dealing with this issue is for friendly parties to arrange for an indirect subsidiary of each of them to acquire shares (or shares in parent companies). Another technique is to contribute the shares of the relevant companies to a holding company. This technique allows friendly parties to

---

[2] *Schneider* v *Cofitel and others*, Court of Appeals of Paris, 18 March 1988, Gaz. Pal. 1988.2.461; JCP, éd. E, 1988, II, 15248, Note Forschbach; Dalloz 1984, 359.

[3] *ANAF and others* v *LVMH and others*, Court of Appeals of Paris, 1st Chamber, 2 November 1989, Gaz. Pal., Note Marchi et Fontbressin; Bull. Joly 1989, p. 983; JCP, éd. E, 1990, II, 15863.

place shares of several companies for which control protection is sought within the same hands.

(e) Some considerations concerning agreements with friendly parties

Agreements with friendly parties raise three types of issue. They generally need to be disclosed, they can result in an action in concert among the signatories, and they are not always easily enforceable.

A. Disclosure

Agreements with friendly parties are normally subject to disclosure to the CBV under Article 356-1-4 of the Company Law since shareholders of listed companies must report all shareholders' agreements to the CBV. When provided with such an agreement, the CBV decides whether or not the signatories are acting in concert and then publishes its decision, together with the main terms of the agreement, in the SBF bulletin. A proper filing of a shareholders' agreement may also enable the parties to be granted exemptions from the mandatory offer requirement if passing the mandatory offer thresholds (one-third of capital or voting rights) only results from the execution of an agreement *filed* with the CBV and *published* by the SBF. This only applies if the signatories did not acquire any "significant" amount of voting securities in the year preceding the filing and undertake not to "significantly" modify their holdings within two years thereafter.

Similarly when an offer is filed, all agreements with friendly parties have to be disclosed immediately to the target and the public through press releases. They also have to be disclosed in tender offer prospectuses (Article 4 of COB Regulation No. 89-03).

B. Secrecy

In the old days, agreements with friendly parties were sometimes secret and not always made in writing; they took the form of "words of presidents" (*paroles de président*) or "gentlemen's agreements".

These agreements were not easily enforceable before a court since it was difficult to prove their existence. Also, oral agreements were fragile since they usually only bind one individual (who can resign or disappear). Successors would not always have to agree to be bound by a predecessor's word.

One example was that of parking (*"portage"*) transactions in which a third party acquires securities for the account of an undisclosed principal with the right to sell ("put") its shares to the principal, and the right for the latter to purchase ("call") the shares at any time. *Portages* were rather popular prior to the enactment of the 1989 Law, as an acquirer could remain unknown to a target and its shareholders.

Since the 1989 Law, these agreements are no longer permissible since they would almost always constitute a breach of French disclosure requirements relating to threshold notifications, shareholders' agreements and actions in concert.

The most salient example of undisclosed *portages* is the *Ciments Français* case. Ciments Français, one of the main French producers of cement, was a subsidiary of Paribas. Its Chairman, Pierre Conso, had entered into secret *portage* agreements with financial intermediaries whereby the latter were to hold shares in several listed companies for Ciments Français' account, including Guintoli, a French contractor. The portages had apparently been made in order to avoid having to launch public offers on these companies since, had the shares effectively been held by Ciments Français, the latter would have been required to immediately file mandatory tenders. They implied a FF2 billion undisclosed financial liability for Ciments Français (and a potential loss of FF800 million). In 1992, Ciments Français was sold by Paribas to Italcementi, an Italian company, and Paribas, which apparently was not aware of the *portages*, did not disclose them to Italcementi. When the purchaser found out about the *portages*, Conso resigned and Paribas agreed to reimburse Italcementi part of the acquisition price and to bear part of the costs of the public offers that had to be made on the listed subsidiaries of Ciment Français. Pierre Conso was accused of presenting false financial statements as *portages* usually constitute off-balance-sheet items for the undisclosed party and was fined FF400,000 by the COB.[4]

C. Action in concert

Arrangements with friendly parties must also be approached with care since they may easily result in the parties being deemed to be acting in concert (see Chapter 4). This would be serious since parties acting in concert are considered as a single party subject collectively to open-market purchase reporting (threshold notifications and declaration of intent) and mandatory offer requirements.

D. Enforcement

It is difficult to obtain specific performance when one wishes to obtain the enforcement of agreements of this type. For example, it is usually held that non-compliance with first-refusal agreements only results in damages and that securities sales made in violation of contractual undertakings may not be cancelled. Another obstacle is that, generally, *bona fide* acquirers of listed securities hold valid title and beneficiaries of pre-emptive rights are therefore not able to recover the securities transferred by another party to such an agreement.

For these reasons, such agreements are sometimes coupled with enforcement mechanisms, the securities concerned being placed in escrow with a bank or registered with powers granted to the bank to monitor the enforcement of the agreement. Other possibilities are to provide for punitive

---

[4] Decision dated 2 September 1993 upheld by the Court of Appeals of Paris on 7 April 1994, Bull. COB No. 279, April 1994, p. 23.

damages (which are legal under French law, provided they are not grossly excessive) or to place securities, subject to special arrangements, within a holding company.

Other limitations are that agreements to vote on shares are of questionable enforcement and that stand-still agreements must have a limited duration.

(iii) The *société en commandite par actions* ("SCA")

A listed target may, pursuant to a decision of its extraordinary shareholders' meeting, elect to be transformed into an SCA, an entity which is comparable to the US limited partnership.

An SCA is an entity in which there are two types of partner: active ones (*"commandités"*) and passive ones (*"commanditaires"*). Active partners have unlimited liability for the debts of the SCA. Passive ones enjoy limited liability. An SCA is managed by one or several managers (*"gérants"*), who may be legal entities and need not be active partners. The passive partners act through meetings and elect a supervisory board (*"conseil de surveillance"*).

The by-laws of an SCA may provide that its manager is appointed for an indefinite term. In this case, the manager may be removed only for cause pursuant to a court order or by amendment of the by-laws requiring both unanimity of the active partners and a decision of the passive partners. The SCA's by-laws may also provide that the manager will be elected by the active partners alone, without a vote of the passive partners. The SCA's status can thus be used to entrench management even if there is a change of control within the passive partners' organisation.

The SCA status for listed companies is not viewed with favour by the COB, although the authorities have in the past authorised the listing of a few SCAs. Two examples are: Euro Disney (a huge project supported by the French government) and Compagnie Générale des Etablissements Michelin.

From a stock market regulation viewpoint, the transformation of a currently listed company into an SCA results in its majority shareholders being required to launch a public repurchase offer (see Chapter 13).

On the other hand, bidders could be deterred by the transformation of a large and attractive unlisted subsidiary of a potential target into an SCA whose management would be protected from removal if a successful tender offer were made against the parent. This technique was used by the management of OCP which had contributed 80% of its activities to two SCAs controlled by OCP's management. To secure an offer filed by a friendly bidder, (Gehe AG), the management had granted options to Gehe to acquire 75% of the shares of the two SCAs if and when it was successful with its bid. As a result of the granting of these options, the approval of the first bid by the CBV was cancelled by the Court of Appeals of Paris and the management was asked by the stock market authorities to grant equal treatment to all potential bidders. In the case of disputed takeovers, therefore, these defences are less strong than they appear.

(iv) Capital reduction

A French company may not in principle purchase its own shares (Article 217 of the Company Law). Nevertheless, within the context of a capital reduction decided by an extraordinary meeting of shareholders, a company may purchase its own shares for cancellation. This technique enables an issuer to reduce its float and thus increase the relative stake of its key shareholders.

Any such capital reduction programme is subject to a special procedure enabling creditors to oppose the decision within 30 days following the filing of the capital reduction plan with the commercial court. Pending cancellation, the repurchased shares may not be voted upon.

(v) Holding of shares by indirect subsidiaries

Up to July 1991 it was possible, under certain conditions, for an indirect subsidiary of a French company to hold shares in its ultimate parent and thus to control part of the latter's voting rights, subject to an aggregate 10% ceiling on the voting rights that could be exercised by all such indirect subsidiaries under the issuer's control. This technique was referred to as "self control" (*auto-contrôle*). It was frequently used by French issuers to control part of their voting rights and to reserve shares for friendly parties, the shares so held being available to be sold to a friendly party if needed. Consequently, a fair number of French companies indirectly held their own shares.

Since July 1991, however, voting rights on shares held by indirect subsidiaries may no longer be exercised at all and French companies are thus tending to progressively dispose of these shares. The technique can, however, still be used in order to reduce the float available to a potential hostile acquirer or to "reserve" certain shares of the target for a friendly party. The transfer of such shares to the friendly party may not, however, be made after the commencement of a tender offer (see *Perrier* case, p. 13 *supra*).

This technique must be approached with care since, as noted *supra*, a French company may not generally purchase its own shares nor, under Article 217-9 of the Company Law, lend funds or grant security interests in any of its assets in order to allow a third party to purchase its shares. Accordingly, the indirect subsidiary cannot appear to be a mere nominee of the target or of the intermediate subsidiary. The acquiring subsidiary should not be a mere shell, but rather an entity with some holding activities. The financing of the purchase of the shares by the relevant subsidiary cannot involve, in any way, the help of the parent or any direct subsidiary. The transaction should also be compatible with the nature and level of activity of the purchasing company.

(vi) Acquisition of a business or company in a regulated area

A target company can ward off potential acquirers by itself acquiring a business or company in a regulated area. For example, the indirect acquisition of control of a banking institution is subject to the prior approval of the Comité des Etablissements de Crédit (see p. 178 *infra*). Accordingly, the approval of any offer by the CBV against a target controlling a credit institution is contingent on obtaining the CEC's approval and the CEC is said not to like hostile bids by financial raiders.

Another example concerns press enterprises where, under specific statutory prohibitions, non-European capital cannot, in the aggregate, exceed 20% (see p. 179 *infra*).

Other limitations and restrictions concern the weapons industry, the television industry, insurance activities, stockbroking (the acquisition of control over a broker is subject to CBV approval), companies licensed to render public services, mining businesses, and oil businesses where direct or indirect investments are either subject to prior approval or to specific ceilings (sometimes applicable only to foreign investors).

Other limitations exist in other countries. For example, in the United States certain limitations concern the banking, communications, defence, airline and insurance sectors (where investments are subject to federal or state approvals). It is thus possible for a French target to invest in these sectors to deter investors since, under French regulations, the commencement of a bid is subject to the granting of all French and foreign approval.

Investments in regulated sectors must make some sense for the group concerned. One may not diversify in regulated sectors (such as the press or the banking sector) for the sole purpose of creating additional hurdles for unsolicited acquirers without any business logic. By so doing one would take the risk of being criticised on the basis of the corporate interest (*"intérêt social"*) doctrine.

As far as privatised companies are concerned, the French government can retain special rights through the issue of a golden share (*"action spécifique"*). This allows the Minister of the Economy to approve the acquisition of participations exceeding certain thresholds by one or several investors acting in concert (see p. 168 *infra*).

(vii) The equity leverage system

This is one interesting aspect of French securities practice. There is a saying that "French capitalists may effectively control their companies while only owning 5% of the stock". This is the French *"holdings en cascade"* system.

Indeed, most French investors are generally keen on keeping total control over listed targets. When, however, financial needs are great, they have no choice but to float a part of the capital.

In this situation and in order to retain effective majority control over their investment, they place outside investors at various levels within the chain of control of the company. For example, family Y would have the majority of holding 1, itself having the majority of holding 2 in which is allowed the first circle of financiers (banks, managers, close friends, etc). Holding 2 would then own a majority of the industrial target. This structure can include as many intermediate holdings as necessary. Holdings can also be used to collect financings, organise tax planning schemes or to monitor financial transactions in a family context.

This technique has been widely used by family-controlled companies and French tycoons. Examples are the companies controlled by Vincent Bolloré, Bernard Arnault (who controls LVMH, Bon Marché, Dior, etc) and François Pinault.

(viii) Price stabilisation

Maintaining a listed price at a high level is certainly one of the most simple and efficient anti-take-over devices. Thus, companies whose shares are traded on either the official market or the second market may purchase up to 10% of their shares on the market for the purpose of stabilising the price of their shares (Article 217-2 of the Company Law).

The acquisition by a company of its own shares in order to stabilise the market for the shares is subject to a series of requirements and formalities. These are:

- the purchase and sale of the shares must be authorised by an ordinary shareholders' meeting, whose authorisation must establish maximum and minimum price limits and be valid for a maximum period of 18 months;
- the company must have created reserves (in addition to the legal reserve) at least equal to the value of the shares purchased;
- the acquisition must be made on an exchange (*i.e.*, through stockbrokers);
- the acquisition must not result in a decrease in the company's equity to an amount that is less than the company's capital plus its non-distributable reserves; and
- the acquired shares must be fully paid up.

Transactions made by the issuer are subject to certain rules since, under COB Regulation No. 90-04, transactions are presumed to be made in order to stabilise the market of the shares if:

- they are made against the trend of the immediately preceding sales;
- they represent a maximum volume of 25% of the total average daily transactions in the stock over the preceding five business days (with respect to shares listed on the monthly settlement market);
- they are effected by only one intermediary per business day.

When held by the company, the shares may not be voted and no dividends may be paid thereon. In addition, no preferential subscription rights attached to the shares may be exercised in the event of an equity issue.

Shares thus held by the issuer can be sold or transferred by any means (a sale, an exchange or within the context of an exchange). They can also be cancelled if there is a capital reduction. Any such transfer and cancellation must be disclosed to the CBV and the public.

(ix) Issue of non-voting stock

The issue of non-voting stock enables an issuer to obtain equity funds from new investors while retaining voting rights, thus preventing any dilution of existing voting rights.

(a) Issue of investment certificates

The issue of investment certificates (*"certificats d'investissement"*) can, in theory, serve as a defensive device. *Certificats d'investissement* are securities similar to common stock but are issued without voting rights. Voting certificates (*"certificats de droit de vote"*) would be issued separately. They were created in order to allow companies nationalised in 1981 to raise funds without losing State control. *Certificats d'investissement* may be issued up to an amount representing 25% of the capital of the issuer (see Article 283-1 of the Company Law).

If the holder of an investment certificate acquires a voting certificate, both certificates disappear and a new share of stock is created. The market for voting certificates must thus be watched closely by the issuer.

The formalities relating to both the general meetings of investment certificate holders and the anti-dilution rights of investment certificates holders are rather burdensome. This type of security has therefore almost ceased to be used.

(b) Issue of non-voting preferred shares

A similar result can be achieved through the issue of non-voting preferred shares (*actions à dividende prioritaire sans droit de vote* – "ADPV").

The issue of ADPVs is subject to the following conditions:

– the issuer must have been profitable for the past three years;
– the issue is subject to a ceiling of 25% of the company's capital (as in the case of *certificats d'investissement*);
– any dividends must be at least equal to 7.5% of the par value (which dividend is cumulative);
– the issuer's managers (plus spouse and children) cannot subscribe.

Holders of ADPVs automatically recover voting rights if the minimum dividends have not been paid for three years up to the year when all minimum dividends (including cumulative dividends carried forward) are paid. For these reasons, and because they impose a financial burden on issuers, very few listed companies have issued ADPVs.

ADPVs can deter a potential acquirer that wishes to reorganise a target since holders of ADPVs must approve any merger or spin-off in a special shareholders' meeting with a two-thirds majority. The holder of at least one-third of these shares would thus be authorised to effectively veto any such decisions.

(x) Puts and calls on key assets

These techniques (known in the United States as "crown jewel options") consist of the granting by the target of options on key assets exercisable if someone launches a hostile bid. They are not used in France since they would most likely be viewed both as contrary to the French corporate interest (*"intérêt social"*) doctrine, and as obstacles to the principle of normal competition among bidders. Another problem is that they might be seen as a constructive liquidation of the target (or a modification of the company's purpose) requiring prior approval of the extraordinary shareholders' meeting.

A comparable result can conceivably be obtained through clauses inserted in strategic arrangements (joint ventures, licensing or distribution agreements), provided these are entered into before the launching of a bid and are not for the sole purpose of annoying hostile parties. For example, joint venture agreements frequently provide that each partner can terminate the venture if control in its partner changes or if the latter allows a competitor to become a key shareholder.

However, such arrangements raise delicate issues. For instance:

– are the termination clauses material facts to be disclosed to the market and, if so, when?
– if disclosed, will the authorities require the launch of a repurchase offer?
– what price needs to be specified for the options?

Arrangements of this type are not favourably viewed by the COB. One example is a joint venture agreement entered into by Bénédictine that was the subject of a tender offer in 1988. The agreement provided that each of the joint venturers could be required to acquire the other's participation in the joint venture company in the event of a change in control at the request of the Chairman of the venture company. The COB held that this provision was an obstacle to normal competition among bidders and requested that the Chairman should waive this provision. The Chairman did so (COB 1988 Report, p. 81).

(xi) Issue of shares to employees

French companies may issue shares to, or organise stock option plans for, their employees.

Under some such plans, employees transferring their shares to third parties before the expiration of a designated period (typically, five years) forfeit certain tax advantages.

2. **Defensive measures that may be adopted during a hostile tender offer**

As soon as the tender offer has been made public by the SBF, most of the defensive measures discussed above are no longer available and management of the target must act with special care in its transactions on the exchange, in all transactions leading to the sale or encumbrance of any key corporate assets, and in all other transactions outside the ordinary course of business.

There only are a few defensive measures available once an offer has been filed.

(i) Competing tender offer

In the case of a hostile tender offer, a friendly party (a "white knight") or the target's shareholders or management may initiate a competing bid up to five business days before the end of any pending offer. In fact, the COB has repeatedly stated that the proper way to contest a tender offer is a competing tender offer, because it alone ensures equal treatment of all shareholders desirous of tendering their shares.

As already discussed, if the offer is for cash, the competing bid must be at least 2% higher than the initial tender offer although, if the initial tender offer is subject to a minimum number of shares being tendered, the new bidder may elect to offer the same price so long as it does not impose any minimum share requirement. The increased bid requirement does not apply to an exchange offer. All responses to a tender offer from the target's shareholders become null and void if a competing offer is announced, and persons having made the preceding offer must declare their intentions not later than five business days after the date when the competing offer is launched (Article 5-2-15 of the General Regulation).

Notwithstanding the search for a "white knight", the target's management may not transmit any insider information to the friendly bidder, nor can the target finance, whether directly or indirectly, the friendly party's offer. Also, management is not allowed to reserve a securities issue or to sell shares placed with an indirect subsidiary to the friendly party.

(ii) Litigation

"The minute an offer is filed, you must sue everybody, the acquirer, its bankers, its advisers and all authorities concerned" one used to say on Wall Street in the "golden eighties". This is becoming increasingly true in France.

The target (or its shareholders) can try to challenge the terms of the initial offer, as approved by the CBV, before the Court of Appeals of Paris (see 33 *supra*). A challenge is an efficient way to gain time for the target since proceedings before the Court of Appeals usually take a month, during which the initial offer remains open.

A challenge to the CBV's decision can be made on the basis that the acquirer has been granted an unfair advantage (as in the OCP case), or that the price of the offer is too low (in general, challenges of this type are not successful since the Court considers that the CBV is sufficiently close to the market to deal with this issue). If the CBV's decision is upheld (as is generally the case), it usually decides that the offer will be closed within five business days after the date on which the Court of Appeals renders its decision.

If the CBV's decision is overruled, the initial bid is cancelled and the first acquirer can decide to file a new bid or back out from the transaction (if it is acting within the context of a voluntary offer). In the case of a mandatory bid (or a *garantie de cours*), the acquirer would be required to file an amended bid.

Other litigation can be based on the grounds that the acquirer did not properly disclose material items, is an insider, did not properly file for required administrative approvals (*e.g.* for antitrust purposes), or did not grant equal treatment to all shareholders.

(iii) Actions by employees

A target may attempt to use its workforce to organise labour demonstrations or strikes against a hostile acquirer. For example, the employees of Télémécanique Electrique organised various demonstrations against the tender offer initiated by Schneider SA in 1987 (see Chapter 1). The same situation occurred in the tender offer launched by Bolloré Technologies on Rhin-Rhône in 1988.

The management of the target should not appear to be the organiser of these demonstrations or strikes, which instead should be triggered by the unions or the employees themselves.

(iv) Public relations campaigns

Companies involved in a tender offer frequently engage in public relations campaigns and enrol the help of PR agencies for this purpose. All advertisements connected with the offer, however, must be filed with the COB for approval before publication and managers of the acquirer and of the target must act with special care in their statements.[5] The board of directors of the target is required to include in its prospectus an opinion on the advantages and disadvantages of the offer. This affords management an opportunity to publicly present its arguments against the tender offer. Management can, for example, criticise the price, the acquirer's strategy, or the financing of the offer. If the acquirer has incurred huge borrowings, the management can argue that the target will be dismantled or, at least, no funds will be available for investments.

---

[5] See *Framatome* v *Schneider*, Order of the President of the Commercial Court of Paris, 29 February 1988, Gaz. Pal., 1988, 2, 470.

(v) Use of certain French regulatory constraints

(a) The use of antitrust law

French law provides that any industrial concentration reaching certain levels that may affect competition may be submitted for examination to the Competition Council (see p. 176 *infra*).

Even when no filing is made by an offering party, the Competition Council may be used by any other interested party to attempt to block or challenge a hostile tender offer through the filing of a claim with the Minister of the Economy. This was done in 1993 in the case of the tender offer filed by UFISUSE, an affiliate of the Saint-Louis group, for Sucreries de Chalon-sur-Saône. Chalon's management claimed that Saint-Louis already held a significant market share in the sugar business and that the offer resulted in the increase of a dominant position. Nevertheless, Saint-Louis' bid was a success and Sucreries' management withdrew from its legal action.[6]

(b) The use of foreign investment regulations

In the case of a listed company, ownership or control of 20% or more of its capital or voting rights by a non-French resident (33.33% in the case of a company traded on the over-the-counter market) requires the prior approval of, or a prior declaration to, the Treasury.

The Treasury has discretionary powers to grant or withhold its authorisation without explanation with non-European bidders and the target's management can thus attempt to put discreet pressure on well-chosen persons. This is even truer when a French competing bidder is involved, since French administrations usually prefer (by culture or nationalism) a "French solution".

(vi) Capital increase during offers

Under French law, capital increases must be decided upon by the extraordinary shareholders' meeting. The meeting may also delegate to the board of directors the authority to proceed to capital increases or to generally decide upon the issue of equity securities. Since Law No. 94-679 of 8 August 1994, the board of directors of listed companies can sub-delegate to the chairman the right to proceed to a capital increase or the issue of equity securities. Prior to the enactment of the 1989 Law, two landmark cases decided that the board of directors could not use these authorisations while an offer was pending.[7]

---

[6] See *Ballard et autres* v *La Sucrerie Raffinerie de Chalon-sur-Saones et autres*, Court of Appeals of Paris, 27 October 1993, Section CBV, RJDA 94 No 422.
[7] Commercial Court of Paris, 25 January 1988, rendered within the context of the Bénédictine offer; and, in Belgium, *Société Générale de Belgique* v *CERUS*, Court of Appeals of Brussels on 1 March 1988 Rev. Sociétés 1988, 245.

Article 180 of the Company Law specifically allows shareholders to give advance authorisation to the board of directors to issue additional capital once an offer has been made. The law expressly grants such authorisation for the period during which an offer is open, so long as:

- the shareholders have expressly authorised it prior to such offer;
- the delegation of authority is for the period up to the next annual meeting; and
- the issue is not reserved to any specifically identified beneficiaries.

In practice, this option is rarely used.

(vii) Acquisition of shares on the market

While an exchange offer is pending, the General Regulation bars open-market purchases by the acquirer (or any persons acting in concert with it) of any of the target's securities and of the securities offered in exchange therefor. On the other hand, if the offer is for cash, the acquirer may make open-market purchases so long as it has not based its offer on tender of a specified minimum number of shares.

Also, the target company is strictly prohibited from causing indirect subsidiaries to acquire the target's securities (Article 3 of COB Regulation No. 89-03). Further, no purchase of the target's securities may be made outside the regulated market without recourse to a stockbroker (Article 5-2-18).

An interesting question concerns whether a third party or a minority shareholder can substantially increase its stake during an offer without filing a competing bid. This was the issue raised in the CSEE transactions.

CSEE is a medium-sized company active in the signal and defence electronics business that, in 1989, had contributed its industrial activities to two subsidiaries. In 1990, CSEE entered into a joint venture agreement with Finmeccania (a subsidiary of the Italian state industrial holding IRI) and transferred to its Italian partner a 49% interest in both of the subsidiaries. CSEE also granted co-management rights to Finmeccania, as well as options to buy CSEE's stake in case of deadlock among the partners.

One year later, Quadral (the main shareholder of CSEE), began increasing its stake in CSEE, arguing that it did not know about the Finmeccania transactions. Finmeccania also began acquiring shares on the market but, on 15 May 1991, Quadral disclosed that it held, together with Banque SAGA, more than 20% of CSEE voting rights. One month later, Finmeccania reached the 10% level. Finmeccania then applied to the Treasury Department for approval to acquire up to 33.33% of the votes. In the meantime, Quadral was able to cause CSEE to increase its capital and, by subscription on 6 September, crossed the one-third threshold of CSEE's voting rights and held (in concert with Saga) 37.39% of the votes. Quadral subsequently filed a mandatory bid for all the outstanding stock of CSEE but was only able to acquire shares to enable it to hold 3.63% of additional voting rights. Finmeccania was buying shares at a higher price. Quadral was thus not able to reach majority control after its offer. In the meantime, Finmeccania had reached one-third of the voting rights, but disclosed that it did not intend to acquire more.

The issue was that Finmeccania, with one-third of the votes, 49% in CSEE's key subsidiaries and co-management rights, was in practice able to control most of CSEE's activities. Quadral thus asked the CBV to force Finmeccania to file a competing bid for CSEE on the basis that the proper challenge to a bid is a competing bid. Finmeccania declined, stating that it wished to remain below one-third of the votes. The CBV chose not to force Finmeccania to bid and the CBV's decision was upheld by the Court of Appeals of Paris.[8] The COB disagreed and announced that normal market operations should have forced Finmeccania to file an offer since, according to the COB's policies,[9] the company would not be allowed to increase its shareholdings substantially through this process.

(viii) Increase of the stock price above the offer price

The target's shareholders (or friendly parties) can acquire stock on the market in order to increase the stock price while an offer is pending. In such a case, other shareholders might be tempted to sell the shares to the acquiring party instead of tendering their shares in the context of the offer.

One example is the tender offer launched by Paribas for Compagnie de Navigation Mixte in 1989 (see Chapter 1). Paribas' offer failed since several shareholders and friendly third parties acquired Mixte shares on the market at a price higher than the tender price. The acquirers were asked by the market authorities to certify that they were not acting in concert with the target and they did so. The stock market authorities were embarrassed by these transactions but were unable to demonstrate the existence of an action in concert. This approach can, however, be dangerous if the acquirer has no valid purpose for increasing stock prices, since manipulating the stock price is proscribed. In this regard, COB Regulation No. 90-04 of 5 July 1990 provides that trade orders must be consistent with the goals pursued by acquirers and the COB may request any party to publicly explain the purpose of a transaction (Article 4).

Open-market purchases (including purchases made by parties acting in concert) can also be made by the acquirer. However, if they are made at a price above the offer price, the offer price is automatically increased to 102% of the offer price or, if the price of the open-market purchases is higher than 102% of the offer price, the offer price is automatically increased to the same price as the price paid on the market.

---

[8] *Quadral* v *Finmeccania*, Court of Appeals of Paris, 20 November 1991, Section CBV, Dalloz 1992, 193, Note Guyon, Bull. Joly, 1992, p. 76, note Jeantin.
[9] See the COB position stated in *Printemps* v *Radar*, Ordinance of the President of the Commercial Court of Paris of 19 October 1979, unpublished.

(ix) A leveraged buy-out

The management of the target can attempt to structure a leveraged buy-out ("LBO") to maintain control over the target.

The only successful LBO made in response to an offer took place in 1988 when Valeo initiated a hostile bid for Epeda-Bertrand-Faure ("EBF"). A syndicate of banks, led by Banque Worms, then proposed Chargeurs SA as "white knight". Unfortunately, Chargeurs changed its mind and reached an agreement with Valeo, and these two companies filed a joint bid.

EBF then tried to find an alternative solution that took the form of an LBO organised by Crédit Commercial de France. A competing bid was launched through a holding company called Gefina (the shareholders of which were several industrial companies) and Gefina took over a series of loans arranged by the Crédit Commercial de France. Key shareholders and the management of EBF retained their shares (which had double voting rights) and GEFINA's bid was a success. Through the LBO structure, the management was able to retain control without recourse to a "white knight".

One of the issues raised with this defence is that the organisation of an LBO must be completed within a rather short time period since the deadline for the filing of a competing bid can be as short as four weeks (five business days of waiting period plus 15 business days). It may, however, be possible for the target to gain time through litigation proceedings.

(x) Sale of assets

The sale by the management of key assets is not a defence available in France on the basis of the *intérêt social* doctrine. Furthermore, managers of listed companies may not, without the approval of the extraordinary shareholders' meeting, modify the corporate purpose or constructively liquidate the company's businesses.

Further, as noted above, actions not made in the ordinary course of business are subject to COB scrutiny. For example, in the Perrier takeover battle, the Commercial Court of Paris cancelled the sale of Perrier shares held by an indirect subsidiary of the target.[10] Such a sale was, however, surrounded by suspicious facts (the transaction had been done in haste without the required corporate formalities).[11]

(xi) Pacman defence

The "pacman defence" is a tender offer launched by the target on the acquirer's shares. This defence has never been used in France since it would be subject to various regulatory obstacles *i.e.*:

---

[10] *Nestlé* v *Société de Participation et de Gestion*, Commercial Court of Paris, 16 March 1992; Bull. Joly 1992, p. 526.

[11] See also *Compagnie Financière de Suez* v *Compagnie Industrielle*, Order of the President of the Paris Commercial Court, 30 August 1989; Bull. Joly 1989, p. 818.

- a company may not hold shares of its parent if the latter holds at least 10% of the former (Article 358 of the Company Law);
- the initial offer would in theory be terminated before the end of the "pacman" offer unless the CBV adjusts the calendar of the first bid (Article 5-2-10 of the General Regulation);
- such an offer would require notification and the prior advice of the COB under Article 3 of COB Regulation No. 89-03.

3. **Conclusion on defences**

(i) Criteria for choosing defences

(a) Cost

The most expensive measures are the holding of shares of the target by indirect subsidiaries, the purchase of shares through a capital reduction and, in the case of a tender offer battle, the filing of a competing tender offer.

The establishment of a financial fidelity premium imposes a certain financial burden on the issuer since the issuer has to increase dividends in order to keep stock prices high. The issue of shares to employees or to a friendly party may have the same effect since it results in dilution of the existing shareholders.

Modification of the company's by-laws (including the establishment of additional ceilings on shareholdings for which notification to the issuer is required, double voting rights and requirements as to board members) can be made at almost no cost as no more than an extraordinary shareholders' meeting would be required and can be held at the same time as the annual meeting.

(b) Complexity

Both the purchase of a target's shares by indirect subsidiaries and cross shareholding may be organised by the legal representatives of concerned companies with the approval of the board of directors. Arrangements with friendly parties may also be carried out by the legal representatives of the target. On the other hand, the negotiation of arrangements with friendly parties may be a complex exercise and one must carefully consider whether the parties involved will be deemed to be acting in concert.

Most of the restructuring measures discussed above would involve the holding of an extraordinary shareholders' meeting and disclosure to the market. The same applies to *certificats d'investissement* and ADPVs which, because of their complexity, are almost never used.

(c) Discretion

Since the 1989 Law, there is almost no anti-take-over device that can be kept secret by the management of a listed target who wishes to play by the rules. In fact, as a practical matter, most of the companies organising defences are keen to publicise their devices.

The entering into of agreements with friendly parties and the holding of shares by indirect subsidiaries or by friendly parties almost always needs to be publicised since the friendly parties would otherwise be deemed to be acting in concert with the controlling shareholders of the target and one would rapidly reach the statutory levels, *i.e.*, 5%, which is the lowest statutory ceiling. Further, if these transactions were carried out on the exchange, they would result in a stock price variation that could be analysed by the market. Also, most agreements with friendly parties would be disclosable to the CBV under Article 356-1-4 of the Company Law and made public by the SBF.

The transformation of a key subsidiary into an unlisted SCA would be subject to certain publicity through the legal notices and the filing of the by-laws of the subsidiary, and the management would be under a duty to disclose it to the market under the continuous reporting requirements laid down in COB Regulation No. 90-02.

The other defences (low threshold notification requirements and double voting rights) can be more discreet, since they would only have to be disclosed in the agenda of the shareholders' meetings published in the BALO, in the report of the board to the meeting and, after adoption by the shareholders' meetings, in the by-laws of the company. No press release would generally be required since these devices are quite common in France.

(e) Efficiency

Limitation of voting rights is a rather efficient device since the acquirer would have to make a public offer for substantially all of the shares of the target (and would be unable to acquire control through *ramassage*). Also, the bidder could, at best, acquire the same amount of voting rights as the existing key shareholders and discussions would have to take place.

The purchase of a press company (publishing papers in the French language) is an absolute deterrent for non-European acquirers. Use of the SCA status would not withstand a contrary desire of a majority shareholder of the parent for very long since such shareholder could go to court to apply for an order dismissing the manager of the SCA. Also, in view of the OCP case, such a defence would not hold up for very long in the event of a change of control in the listed parent.

Financial fidelity premiums, double voting rights and restructuring measures only have a deterrent effect on the acquirer since they increase the cost of the offer (in the latter case, the cost of reorganising the target after the offer). Double voting rights would also lengthen the period necessary for the acquisition of control by the acquirer but this would not really count since a bidder would generally bid for all the target's stock and provide that its offer is conditional on acquiring a majority.

The efficiency of the holding of shares of the target by indirect subsidiaries is debatable. On the one hand, the target acquires control over the voting rights so acquired (that are no longer on the market). These shares can be transferred to a friendly party if need be prior to the filing of an offer. On the other hand, in the case of a tender offer, the acquirer would automatically gain control over shares thus held without having to pay for them.

(ii) General principles in tender offer battles

Whatever defences are ultimately chosen, it is essential that the target's management and advisers comply with the following general principles which result both from COB regulations and general principles of French law. These principles, if not complied with during a pending tender offer, can be enforced by suspension of the target's listing or a lengthening of the duration of the offer, as well as by the COB fines or injunctive relief. Further, criticisms by the COB can trigger civil actions for injunctive relief or damages by any interested party. A breach of these general rules can even result in a bid being cancelled, as appeared in the OCP case.

(a) Equality and free competition among bidders

As a result of the OCP case, it is critical in every tender offer, both as a practical and legal matter, to respect the principle of equality of treatment among bidders during tender offer battles. This is the cornerstone of the current French tender offer rules. Under this principle, options granted by the management of a target over key assets can result in a bid not being valid. The granting of irrevocable rights to acquire a substantial amount of the target shares may also have the same result.

The competition among the parties involved must be exercised through tender offers, competing bids and increased bids.

Also, management cannot use approval clauses (*clauses d'agrément*) to oppose acquisitions by one bidder versus another.

(b) Equality of treatment among all shareholders and respect of shareholders' interests

COB regulations emphasise that it is critical in every tender offer to respect the principle of equality of treatment and provision of information to all shareholders. This principle is the key to understanding the French authorities' behaviour. It is the reason why all shareholders are to be paid the same price in a standing offer and why no special benefit may be granted to the controlling shareholders in a tender offer. Under this rule, no special benefit may be granted to one shareholder in the form of a special premium or a consideration different than the one offered to other shareholders (*e.g.* the main shareholder gets cash while the others get securities).

The application of this principle resulted in absurd situations in the OCP case. The CBV, still shocked by the cancellation by the Paris Court of Appeals of its approval of Gehe AG's offer, required the second bidder (AURA Expansion) to invite the public either to tender its shares immediately for FF865 or to be granted an option to sell the shares during a two-year term at FF865 plus interest at market rate. The rationale for the CBV's decision was that one of the key shareholders of OCP had been granted this option. The CBV considered that the principle of equality of treatment had to be applied strictly and that all shareholders had to have the same option. This would have required the SBF (and other intermediaries) to centralise the names of all tendering shareholders. Shortly after the approval of the second bid, Gehe filed an increased bid and eventually won the battle.

(c) True and fair disclosure

All material facts must be truly, fairly and promptly disclosed by all interested parties. Under this principle, any agreement that may affect the evaluation or the outcome of the offer and entered into by the shareholders of the target (or any persons acting in concert with them) must be disclosed to the companies involved, the CBV and the COB. These agreements must also be disclosed to the public through press releases (Article 4 of COB Regulation No. 89-03).

All information disclosed must be accurate, precise and sincere. The disclosure of inaccurate, imprecise or false information constitutes a breach of COB regulations and can result in the imposition of injunctions and fines by the COB.

(d) Respect of the corporate interest

In general, the management of French companies must always act in compliance with the corporate interest, even in the absence of a tender offer. The corporate interest can be defined as "the sole interest of a group of companies" as an economic institution.

The corporate interest does not always coincide with the interests of:

- shareholders (whether controlling or minority holders);
- employees (who may be dismissed if the economic situation so requires);
- the State, including the tax and social security administration (or other public institutions) – a group may generally try to minimise taxes and social security contributions or transfer businesses elsewhere if the best interests of the group so provide;
- creditors; and
- clients.

The corporate interest is generally said to be a mix of the interests of the foregoing persons (whether financial or strategic), or more exactly, consists in optimising such interests. The key case in this area concerned a French subsidiary of Fruehauf, an American trailer manufacturer. Fruehauf-France, a 70% subsidiary of the American Fruehauf group, became subject to a US regulation declaring an embargo over China in 1964. Fruehauf-France had entered into agreements for the delivery of parts to Berliet (a French truck manufacturer affiliated with Régie Nationale des Usines Renault), to be exported to China. The parent company of Fruehauf-France ordered its subsidiary to cease the deliveries to Berliet, to the great displeasure of its French 30% minority shareholder, who initiated legal proceedings. The court decided that the termination of the deliveries was contrary to the corporate interest doctrine and ordered Fruehauf-France to resume delivery.[12]

Although the corporate interest doctrine is obscure and poorly defined, it must be a real concern of managers in the course of an offer since COB Regulation No. 89-03 explicitly states that this doctrine must be complied with throughout the pendency of an offer (Article 3, paragraph 1). It is of great importance for listed companies which have minority shareholders, the interests of which are not always consistent with the management's (or main shareholders') interests.

On the basis of this doctrine, a target would not be allowed to dispose of one of its key subsidiaries for the sole purpose of annoying a hostile acquirer or to transform key subsidiaries into an SCA controlled by the management. The same would be true for diversifications made in regulated sectors (such as the press and the banking sector) for the sole purpose of creating additional hurdles for unsolicited acquirers.

(e) The abuse of majority doctrine

Another doctrine is the abuse of majority doctrine (see Chapter 12). Under this doctrine, decisions taken in the sole interest of a majority (or controlling) shareholder can be voided if they are detrimental to minority shareholders. This doctrine might also result in certain defences not being available (such as transforming an existing listed company into an anti-take-over bastion for the sole interest of the majority shareholder as was the case in the OCP transaction).

(f) The European Take-over Code guidelines

The proposed European Take-over Code lays down certain principles to guide the supervisory authorities in scrutinising offer documentation, most of which are consistent with the French rules. These are:

(i) equal treatment of target shareholders;
(ii) provision of sufficient time and information to allow addressees of a bid to reach a properly informed decision;
(iii) the board of the target is to act in the interest of all shareholders and observe a careful balance in taking defensive action against a bid;
(iv) avoidance of speculative trading; and
(v) the offer is not to unduly impede the regular conduct of business of the target beyond a reasonable time.

It is also provided that the board of the target may call a general meeting of shareholders before the expiry of the acceptance period of a bid with a view to obtaining shareholders' approval of defensive action.

---

[12] Court of Appeals of Paris, 22 May 1965. 14th ch. JCP 1965, II, 14274 *bis* with opinion of Advocate General Nepveu; Dalloz 1968, 147, note Contin.

4. **The "Debate"**

These are the rules governing tender offers, acquisitions and disposition of listed securities. The current French regulatory frame is now mature, fair and sophisticated. Nevertheless, as is the case in other countries, tender offers in France, are the subject of much debate. The arguments can be summarised as follows:

(i) Pros

Acquirers, raiders and investment bankers say that tender offers are good for the market. Through them, shareholders are given the opportunity of realising huge capital gains and this is one of the reasons why people invest in listed companies. Also, the constant threat of a hostile bid invites the management of listed companies to stay attentive to its shareholders by keeping stock prices high, paying substantial dividends, carrying out true and fair disclosure, etc. The more hostile the bid, the higher the price gets for everyone's benefit.

Further, investors (industrial groups, multinational companies) need to be able to invest in attractive targets to develop synergies. Tender offers are needed for the external growth of industrial companies.

They are a good way to restructure companies. They are the only means to quickly solve the disputes among key shareholders which can ruin a company.

Finally, tender offers are a fair way to acquire companies. Since the 1989 Law and the introduction of the bid on all equity securities rule – the tender offer rules have guaranteed an equal treatment among all shareholders. All offers are strictly reviewed by the stock market authorities who ensure equal treatment among shareholders. Without tender offers, minority shareholders would be stuck indefinitely in companies where there was a change of control.

(ii) Cons

Key shareholders, families controlling companies and unions say that acquirers of listed companies are only interested in the financial component of their investment. As soon as a target is acquired, the new shareholders dismantle the company in order to make financial gains (and/or reimburse part of the acquisition costs).

Offers tend to disorganise listed companies. Following an offer, companies are frequently subject to lay-offs and restructuring. They are also sometimes subject to blackmail (called "green mail") by raiders who are only interested in financial gains.

Tender offers are frequently the occasion of criminal behaviour, insider trading and stock price manipulation.

As a result, the management of a potential target spends its time watching stock prices and trading volumes instead of taking care of strategic and industrial issues or managing the company. Management is frequently the first victim of a tender offer since the acquirer often cleans out the management after it wins its target.

There is also a "France for sale" argument which goes something like this: "Anyone can come into this country and buy out any French listed company, provided they have the financial capability"; and "Soon, all France will be owned by US and Japanese investors". Indeed, since not many French companies are among the top Fortune 500 companies, they are easy targets for foreign giants. The argument has gained even greater credence since the 1989 Law, since when no investor can buy more than one-third of a listed target (or even act in concert with a shareholder holding more than one-third of a listed target) without being required to buy all of the outstanding equity securities. This represents a huge financial commitment which French groups can seldom afford.

Finally, it is argued that the French regulatory scheme is complex, unclear and incomprehensible except to some polished lawyers and investment bankers. The sanctions are out of proportion to the aims of the regulations.

(iii) A market?

The debate on the pros and cons of tender offers is a never-ending story and depends on the mood of the market. Pros and cons can be weighed indefinitely. The bottom line is that tender offers are a natural component of the financial market and the public cannot be expected to invest in stock without being given a chance to withdraw in the event of a change of control or strategy in the companies concerned. This "aspect" of the stock exchange market surely exists in France where take-overs, whether friendly or not, are common, as this is the case in the United Kingdom and the United States. Certain countries, including Germany, Switzerland, and The Netherlands, however, are generally excluded from the take-over game.

CONTENTS OF CHAPTER 8

Chapter 8
Simplified Tender Offer Procedure

In certain limited cases, the CBV can authorise the use of a "simplified offer procedure".

The rules applicable to simplified offers are the same as those applicable to normal offers, except for certain specific rules discussed below. In general, simplified offers are shorter and involve less disclosure than standard tender offers. Standing offers (*"garanties de cours"*), which are described in Chapter 6 *supra*, are also classified as simplified offers.

1. Limited number of cases

Cases where the CBV can authorise an acquirer to carry out a simplified offer are limited and are laid down in Chapter 3 (Title 5) of the General Regulation. They are as follows:

(i) Offers made on 10% or less of the target's securities

Offers on no more than 10% of the voting shares (or voting rights) of the target that result in the acquirer owning no more than 10% of the target's voting shares (or voting rights), pre-offer holdings included, are the first category of simplified offer. These offers would cover situations where an acquirer wishes to acquire a minority stake in a listed target. These transactions are not very frequent since acquirers in this situation generally prefer to buy shares on the open market or do a block deal.

(ii) Offer made by majority holders

A simplified offer can also be filed by a shareholder (or a group of shareholders acting in concert) already holding at least one-half of the capital *and* the voting rights of the target, in order to increase its control or with a view to reinforcing its control. This type of offer usually takes place when a majority holder wishes to acquire at least 95% of the company's voting rights in order to be able to delist the company through the subsequent filing of a repurchase offer or squeeze-out (see Chapter 13).

(iii) Offers made on securities other than common stock

Offers made exclusively on shares with preferred dividends, investment certificates or voting certificates (see p. 121 *supra*) or debt securities are also governed by the simplified offer procedure.

(iv) Capital reduction programme

Repurchase offers made by an issuer in order to redeem its own shares can also be made through the simplified offer procedure. A company may purchase its own shares for cancellation. This technique enables the issuer to reduce its float and thus increase the relative stake of key shareholders. It must be decided by an extraordinary meeting of shareholders.

2. Term

The term of a simplified offer may be limited to ten business days in the case of a cash offer or 15 business days in the case of an exchange offer (or a combined or alternative offer). Repurchase offers made by an issuer in order to redeem its own shares must, however, be made for at least 30 calendar days (Article 5-2-3 of the General Regulation).

3. Price

As in the case of a normal tender offer, when there is a cash offer, the price of the offer (as well as the other terms of the offer) are to be approved by the CBV.

In the case of a cash offer made by a shareholder (or a group of shareholders) already holding at least one-half of the capital and the voting rights of the target (referred to in paragraph 1(ii) *supra*), the price of the offer may not be less than the average listed prices (weighted by trading volume) over the 60 business days preceding the date of filing of the offer. Exemptions to this rule may be granted by the CBV (Article 5-3-4 of the General Regulation).

Chapter 9
Audit of Listed Targets

It is possible to gather documents and information available from public sources to determine the identity of key shareholders of listed targets, anti-take-over devices organised by the target's management and possible regulatory obstacles.

Should a potential acquirer take any precautionary measures prior to investing in a listing company? On the one hand, this is not at all the French habit and is a burdensome exercise. Also, it is a very delicate technique with regard to listed companies since one must ensure that the audit will remain strictly confidential in order to avoid unnecessary price increases and insider trading. It is also said that, since listed companies are subject to many disclosure rules, requirements and sanctions, they are a safer investment than privately-held companies. On the other hand, a tender offer can be a very large project that can validly justify some caution, and a fair amount of information exists that is publicly available with regard to listed companies.

It may thus be useful for an investor to gather some of the documents available from public sources (commercial courts and stock market authorities) to determine the identity of key shareholders, anti-take-over devices organised by the target's management and possible regulatory obstacles (antitrust regulations, press law and banking regulations).

The following is a summary of documents publicly available.

1. Documents available from administrations

It is not universally known that a fair amount of information concerning listed companies is available through the French administrative bodies.

(i) French courts

Documents to review carefully are the annual reports of the target and key subsidiaries, which are filed with the courts annually by each French company. The report states the names of shareholders holding more than

5%, 10%, 20%, 33.33%, 50% and 66.66% of the company's voting rights as well as key business and financial data. Access is also possible to financial statements that have to be filed on an annual basis. Further, it is valuable to investigate filed shareholders' and board of directors' minutes in order to explore whether the management is authorised by the extraordinary shareholders' meetings to issue equity securities (the shareholders' meeting of French companies can delegate to the management the right to do this).

Acquirers should also investigate the target's (and key subsidiaries') by-laws ("*statuts*"), which are available through the local Commercial Courts on a no-name basis. This allows investigation of whether the management has organised anti-take-over devices. One particularly common device re-quires shareholders reaching the 0.5% level to file a notification of their holdings with the company within two weeks. Failure to do so may result in automatic loss of voting rights exceeding 0.5%. Further, the by-laws can impose a cap on any shareholders' aggregate voting rights or grant double voting rights to registered shares held by the same shareholder for more than two years, thus watering down the buyer's stake. Through a specific provision in the company's by-laws, the target may also obtain the name of holders of bearer shares from financial intermediaries (see the TPI mechanism, p. 109 *supra*).

(ii) Documents available from the stock market authorities

Official notices ("*décisions et avis*") published by the SBF concerning listed companies are public documents available at the SBF and the COB, as well as by subscription. These documents concern threshold notifications, secur-ities listings, public offers and declarations of intent. The SBF also publishes the main terms of all shareholders' agreements transmitted to the CBV (see p. 55 *supra*). The stock market authorities also keep extracts from the *Bulletin des Annonces Légales Obligatoires* ("BALO"), all prospectuses registered with the COB and fairly complete files of press articles concern-ing French listed companies.

(iii) Other sources

Other sources of information are the French Intellectual Property Agency (Institut National de la Propriété Industrielle – "INPI"), where trademarks and patents are registered, and the tax administrations, through which an acquirer can verify the location and actual ownership of key pieces of real estate.

An acquirer can also check press articles (through databases or other-wise) as well as the COB's monthly and annual reports. There are also databases available through the French "*Minitel*" service.

It is sometimes possible to obtain information on litigation (whether civil or criminal) involving the company and its shareholders through the French judicial system, which is, in principle, public.

2. **Documents available to shareholders**

The acquirer or a discreet subsidiary can acquire some shares and thus gain access to the shareholders' attendance sheet for all the shareholders' meetings held during the last three fiscal years (Article 170 of the Company Law). Shareholders also have access to the current shareholders' list 15 days before each shareholders' meeting (Article 169 of the Company Law). These lists can be invaluable for computing the respective holdings of key shareholders as well as the number of voting rights held. However, they only include the names and addresses of the holders of registered shares, since holders of bearer shares are unknown to the target.

3. **Bankers, managers and advisers**

It is valuable to gather information on the banks and advisers of any potential target in order to avoid conflicts of interest and leaks of confidential information. Similar information concerning key managers, officers and shareholders (and affiliates) is precious. For this reason, the early selection of a French financial adviser, taking into account potential conflicts of interest and financial backing (a take-over can be a very large project), is advisable.

Chapter 10
Public Offerings of Securities, Listing and Privatisations

In this chapter, we will discuss certain characteristics of public offerings and listing of securities in France, as well as French privatisations that have resulted in key innovations in this area.

1. Public offerings of securities

Both a prospectus and a special notice need to be published prior to any public offering of securities. Also, foreign issuers may be required to obtain Treasury approval and file certain documents with Commercial Courts prior to such an offering.

Public offerings of securities by French companies can either take the form of a capital increase and/or the issue of securities, or result from a sale of existing securities by key shareholders. In the case of an issue of new securities, the offering usually involves the holding of an extraordinary meeting of shareholders at which authority is granted to the board of directors (who can, in turn, delegate authority to the chairman) to realise the issue of new securities. Most of the time, public offerings are coupled with a listing of the securities on the exchange.

(i) COB disclosure rules: the prospectus

(a) General

The principal requirement regarding a public offering is that a prospectus needs to be prepared (Article 6 of the 1967 Ordonnance). The prospectus must be approved by the COB, which may require that additional information be included. It must contain all information necessary for investors to establish a judgement in respect of the assets, activities and financial situation of, and future developments relating to, the issuer, as well as in respect of the rights granted to the issued securities.

The prospectus may not be circulated or made available to the public prior to COB approval. It must, however, be made available to the public before any public offering of the securities. The prospectus may be split into several documents, a master prospectus (*"document de référence"*) and an offering prospectus (*"note d'opération"*). The offering prospectus can, in turn, be made in two stages, a preliminary offering prospectus and a final offering prospectus, as was the case in the 1993/1994 privatisations.

Prior to listing, any material modification in the information disclosed in the prospectus must be immediately communicated to the public through a press release. Any such press release is also subject to the prior approval of the COB.

Rules concerning prospectuses differ, depending on whether the securities are being listed on either the official or the second market, or publicly offered without an official listing.

(b) Rules applicable in case of a listing on the official market

Any issuer, whether French or foreign (other than the French State), intending to list securities on the official market must register a prospectus with the COB (Article 1 of COB Regulation No. 91-02). French issuers already listed on the French official market offering securities outside France must do the same. COB Regulation No. 91-02 implements in France the EC Council Directive Co-ordinating the Requirements for Drawing Up, Scrutiny and Distribution of Prospectuses to be Published for the Admission of Securities to Official Stock Exchange Listing of 17 March 1980. French rules are thus similar to rules applicable in other European countries which have implemented the Directive.

A. Content

Each prospectus is divided into three main parts:

(i) a description of the issuer, including its shareholding, activities, management, recent events and possible evolution, together with the issuer's consolidated financial statements;

(ii) a description of the offering (securities offered, price, purposes, etc); and

(iii) the signature page, the main part of which is the chairman's acknowledgment that all information included in the prospectus is accurate; that the prospectus includes all information necessary to investors; and that it does not include any material omissions (the signature page also includes a certification of the issuer's financial statements by its auditors).

B. Registration procedure

The prospectus must be submitted to the COB, in the French language, at least 15 days prior to the anticipated date of listing or beginning of the offering period (Article 4-1 of COB Regulation No. 91-02). In practice, issuers usually send to the COB drafts of the prospectus well in advance to avoid unanticipated delays.

As far as foreign issuers are concerned, its listing agent is to designate, with the approval of the COB, a French audit firm that will review the issuers' financial statements, together with a French translation.

In its review, the COB's primary function is to check whether information contained in the prospectus conforms to regulatory requirements and is adequate to inform the public. In this connection, the COB may request the publication of any additional information it deems necessary.

The COB may also make comments on the prospectuses through a warning (*"avertissement"*) on the first page of the prospectus or elsewhere. There are some examples where the COB granted registration of a prospectus but suggested that the market for the securities offered was not liquid enough or that the issuer's financial situation was not sound. The COB also uses warnings to insist on particular points already disclosed in the prospectus.

The COB may also order the issuer's auditors to carry out additional investigations or, with the issuer's approval, mandate an outside audit firm to do so. In practice, the COB can be rather pushy on issuers and advisers if it wishes information to be disclosed or the terms of the offering to be amended. The COB enjoys broad discretion in this regard and may refuse to grant its *visa*.

Once approved, the prospectus must be published either in a financial newspaper having national circulation in France (*e.g.*, *Les Echos*, *La Tribune* or *l'AGEFI*) or made publicly available at the time of listing of the securities or, in case of a stock issue, on the first day of the subscription period (Article 11 of COB Regulation No. 91-02).

C. Exemptions

Certain offerings may be exempted from the registration requirement: (i) issues reserved to a limited number of investors; (ii) issues of free shares (capitalisation of reserves etc); (iii) issues representing less than 10% of the issuer's capital, provided the concerned securities are already listed; or (iv) issues reserved to employees (Article 13 of COB Regulation No. 91-02).

D. Shelf registration

Issuers listed on the official market can prepare, each year, a master prospectus, the French equivalent to the US shelf registration. The master prospectus is a general disclosure document that contains detailed legal and financial data on the issuer (shareholding, activities, management, recent events, possible evolution and other financial informations), but no information concerning a particular securities issue. In practice, the annual report and the master prospectus can be merged in one single document since the information contained in the annual report is usually valid for at least one year. The master prospectus must be registered with the COB and, once registered, made available to the public (Article 6 of COB Regulation No. 91-02).

151

Issuers who have registered a master prospectus only need register an offering prospectus when publicly offering new securities. The offering prospectus gives details about the offering (tranches, structure, securities offered, offering syndicate and the price) but does not give information concerning the issuer. The master prospectus is deemed to be incorporated in the offering prospectus, although information updating the master prospectus can be included in the offering prospectus.

The draft offering prospectus need only be filed with the COB two business days prior to the listing or the issue, whereas the filing of a "normal" prospectus must be made at least two weeks in advance. In fact, the COB is usually able to register offering prospectuses within one business day.

E. Reference to a recent prospectus

If a prospectus has been registered with the COB less than a year earlier, and the prior issue concerned securities of the same category as those proposed to be issued, an offering prospectus can also be registered (even if no master prospectus has been registered). In such a case, the prior prospectus needs to include the last certified annual accounts and all information required to adequately inform the public (Article 7 of COB Regulation No. 91-02).

F. Recognition of European prospectuses

In accordance with Article 19 *et seq* of Regulation No. 91-02, any offeror located in a Member State of either the European Union or the European Economic Area can request recognition by the COB of a prospectus prepared for the purpose of an offering of the same securities in another Member State provided that such prospectus:

(i) is translated in French;

(ii) has been approved by another Member State within the past three months; and

(iii) was prepared in accordance with European Council Directive Coordinating the Requirements for Drawing Up, Scrutiny and Distribution of Prospectuses to be Published for the Admission of Securities to Official Stock Exchange Listing of 17 March 1980.

The COB is only required to approve such prospectus if the other relevant Member State has enacted legislation implementing the Directive.

The COB may not impose any form of separate approval or require any additional information to be included in the prospectus except for information specific to the French market, such as information relating to the tax treatment of income derived from the securities, to the financial institutions acting as fiscal agents in France, and to the publication of mandatory notices to investors.

The application for recognition by the COB of a foreign prospectus must contain:

(i) the foreign prospectus;
(ii) a French translation thereof, when applicable;
(iii) a certificate of approval by the regulatory authorities of the other relevant Member State; and
(iv) additional information specific to the French market.

With respect to prospectuses drawn up more than three months prior to the request to the COB but relating to securities which have been listed in another European Union Member State within six months prior to such request, the COB may consult the authorities of the other Member State and decide to exempt the issuer from the obligation of preparing a new prospectus, subject to the updating of the prior prospectus.

In the event that securities are publicly offered or listing is requested in several Member States simultaneously, the conformity of the prospectus with applicable regulation must be verified by the national regulatory authorities of the Member State where the issuer has its registered office.

(c) Rules applicable in case of a listing on the second market

An issuer intending to list securities on the second market must also register a prospectus (*"note de présentation"*), with the COB under COB Regulation No. 88-04 (Article 24 *et seq*). The prospectus must include similar information to that required in the case of listing on the official market.

There is no *per se* registration procedure with the COB, although the prospectus must be filed with the COB at least three months in advance and "informally" approved. If the offering takes place nine months after the close of the preceding fiscal year, interim bi-annual accounts (in the form of statement of results) must be prepared.

(d) Rules applicable to other public offerings

A simplified prospectus (*"prospectus simplifié"*) is to be prepared in connection with other public offerings (*"offres au public"*) of securities, *i.e.*, offers which are not coupled with a listing on the official or the second market. Most of these offerings would cover situations where the securities are being offered for sale on the over-the-counter market.

A. The notion of public offerings

Article 1 of Regulation No. 92-02 of the COB lays down five criteria for establishing a "public offering" in France:

(i) the "diffusion" of securities among more than 300 persons;
(ii) the use of financial institutions for the placement of securities;
(iii) the use of advertisements or other means of publicity in connection with the placement of securities; and
(iv) solicitation of the public in connection with the placement of securities.

153

The concept of public offering is thus extremely broad since the mere use of a financial institution technically results in an offering being deemed public. Further, the mere solicitation of investors by mail or telephone may have the same results. Investment solicitation activities (*"démarchage"*) are governed by Law No. 72-6, dated 3 January 1972 if the following three conditions are met: (i) the solicitation takes place at the residence or place of business of the purchaser or in so-called "public places" (this criterion is also met when solicitation is done by mail or telephone); (ii) the solicitation concerns the sale, purchase, exchange or subscription of securities; and (iii) the solicitation activities are conducted on a regular basis. Solicitation activities may only be carried out by credit institutions, stockbrokers and insurance companies.

Since the concept of public offering is so broad, the exemptions provided for in Article 4 of the Regulation are essential (see Section C, *infra*).

B. The simplified prospectus

A simplified prospectus only needs to be registered with the COB if the offering concerns the issue of new securities. The registration procedure is similar to the one concerning securities listed on the official market, except that there is no shelf registration programme. The prospectus only needs to be filed with the COB if the offering concerns a sale of securities.

C. Exemption

According to Article 4 of Regulation No. 92-02, no prospectus need be prepared in the following cases:

(i) The offering is made to persons in connection with their professional activities;

(ii) The aggregate amount of the offering is less than FF250,000 or an equivalent amount in a foreign currency;

(iii) The offering concerns securities that may be subscribed or acquired for a minimum investment of FF1 million or an equivalent amount in a foreign currency;

(iv) The unit purchase price of the securities offered is greater than FF1 million or equivalent in a foreign currency;

(v) The offering concerns shares or units of an Undertaking for Collective Investment in Transferable Securities ("UCITs") (*i.e.*, investments funds or trusts) other than a closed UCITs.

(vi) The securities are offered in connection with an exchange offer, a merger or a partial transfer of assets;

(vii) The offering concerns equity securities that are issued without consideration as a dividend payment or in connection with a capitalisation of reserves;

(viii) The securities are offered as a result of the exercise of a right attached to securities, the issue of which earlier gave rise to the publication of a prospectus;

(ix) The securities are offered in exchange for shares of the same issuer and their issue does not result in an increase in the issuer's capital;

(x) The subscription or acquisition of securities is a condition to receiving services rendered by *organismes de caractère mutualiste* (such as certain insurance companies);

(xi) The offer concerns euro-securities.

These exceptions do not apply to offerings for subscription or purchase of equity securities reserved to the employees of the issuer or of the issuer's group.

(ii) BALO notice

A second requirement is that any public offering of securities must be coupled with the publication of a notice in the BALO. The BALO is a peculiarity of French securities practice. It is a section of the French official journal that nobody reads with the exception of bankers, lawyers and COB officials. French listed companies are required to publish information in the BALO such as notices of shareholders' meetings and financial statements (see Section 3 *infra*). Under the Law of 30 January 1907 all offerings must be recorded in the BALO; such offerings being defined as "the issue, the exhibition, the offer for sale, the introduction on the market" of securities.

The BALO notice is to include certain specific information concerning the issuer, including: (i) the name of the issuer; (ii) its nationality; (iii) its registered office; (iv) the corporate purpose; (v) the duration of the issuer; (vi) its share capital; (vii) the issuer's balance sheet; and (viii) prior securities issues. Certain additional items apply to foreign issuers and the BALO notice must inform the public of where the prospectus registered by the COB is made available and, if applicable, financial newspapers in which the prospectus was published. Any advertisement made in connection with the offering must refer to the BALO notice.

(iii) Registration by foreign issuers with the Registry of Commerce

A foreign company without a branch in France that wishes to publicly issue securities in France must file certain documents with the *Greffe* (clerk) of the Paris Commercial Court prior to listing. The documents must include a French translation of its by-laws and a special administrative form (Article 57 of Decree No. 84-406 of 30 May 1984). The issuer must keep the file updated as long as its securities are publicly held in France.

(iv) Exchange control filing for foreign issuers

Public offerings in France of securities issued by foreign issuers are, in principle, subject to the prior approval of the Treasury. Article 9 of Decree No. 89-938 of 29 December 1989 relating to exchange control regulations provides, however, that securities issued by entities located in OECD countries may be offered in France without such prior authorisation. Securities issued by Member States of the OECD benefit from the same exemption.

As far as non-European foreign investment funds and trusts are concerned, non-exempted securities (including securities issued by non-EC investment funds), cannot be issued or sold in France, whether privately or publicly, without the prior authorisation of the Ministry of Economy. Since, in practice, this authorisation is almost never granted, whether in the context of a public offering or in the context of a private offering, as far as shares of non-European UCITs (or funds) are concerned, only shares of funds incorporated in European Union Member States may be sold in France.

2. **Listing procedure**

Listing involves a two-step procedure; first, the CBV must approve the principle of a listing, second, the securities must be effectively offered on the market.

(i) Prior approval of the CBV

(a) General

Whereas listing on either the official market or the second market requires the prior approval by the CBV, securities may be traded on the over-the-counter market merely on the request of a prospective seller or buyer.

Under CBV General Decisions No. 88-4 and 88-7, an application for the listing on either the official or the second market must be submitted directly by the issuer, which may be assisted by one or more authorised financial institutions. The CBV may, however, decide to list a security on the official market on its own and without any request from the issuer (Article 3-1-5 of the General Regulation).

The issuer must file with the SBF an application containing certain detailed information and must indicate the name of the stockbroker that it has selected to act as primary dealer for its securities.

The CBV may request to be provided with any complementary information. It can also make a listing conditional on specific requirements and may refuse a listing altogether in the interest of the market. It enjoys broad powers in this regard.

According to Article 3-1-7 of the General Regulation, the CBV must make a listing decision within six months of its receipt of an application or, if it requests further information, within six months of its receipt of such additional information. In practice, however, the CBV usually makes its decision more promptly.

Once the CBV's decision has been made, and unless the COB has opposed the CBV's admission to listing, the listing is announced through the publication of an SBF notice indicating the date of the first price quotation and the method of offering of the securities that has been selected (see Section (ii) *infra*).

The General Regulation establishes different listing regimes applicable to equity securities issued by French issuers, debt securities issued in France by French issuers, securities (whether equity securities or debt securities issued in France) issued by foreign issuers, securities issued outside France, and securities to be listed on the second market. Because of their practical importance, we will limit our discussion to listings of equity securities.

(b) Official market

The official market is reserved for companies which have published financial statements for at least three years and at least 25% of the total capital stock of which is held by the public as of the date of the listing or immediately thereafter, unless the CBV grants an exemption to the 25% requirement (Article 3-1-10 *et seq.* of the General Regulation).

(c) Second market

Listing on the second market is usually reserved for middle-sized French companies which are not large enough to be listed on the official market or for expanding companies which prefer to be listed on the second market before being listed on the official market. The second market is reserved for companies having published financial statements for at least two years and at least 10% of the total capital stock of which is floated (Article 3-1-27 of the General Regulation).

At the end of a three-year period on the second market, the CBV decides whether to transfer the securities to the official market or delist them for trading on the over-the-counter market (Article 3-1-33 of the General Regulation). The CBV may also decide to keep a company listed on the second market.

Also, on the second market, the banks and brokers involved in the offering often participate in pools (*"contrats de liquidité"*) which are organised to provide counterparts and to achieve a liquid market (Article 6-4-2 of the General Regulation).

(ii) The actual offering – the "introduction"

The *"introduction"* is the actual offering of securities on the exchange that takes place once the CBV has approved the listing. There are three methods of offering securities on a French stock exchange:

(i) the sales procedure with a minimum price (*"procédure de mise en vente à un prix minimal"*);
(ii) the OPV (*"offre publique de vente"*); and
(iii) the ordinary procedure (*"procédure ordinaire"*).

These procedures are described in Articles 3-2-1 *et seq* of the General Regulation and in the CBV General Decision No. 88-9.

The offering is announced to the market through an SBF release that discloses the offering procedure followed before the first price quotation.

(a) Offerings with a minimum price

This offering procedure consists of a prior public notice to the market five business days in advance of the listing indicating the number of offered securities and their minimum unit price. With the approval of the SBF, the offerer may reserve its right to modify the price offered at least two business days before the first listing (Article 3-2-12 of the General Regulation). If there is a change in the offering price, the SBF publishes a new release announcing the change and the way the purchase orders can be confirmed or withdrawn.

The SBF then collects orders from investors and determines the first quotation price. It may reject orders for a price it considers manifestly excessive. It may also allocate the offered securities in lots and obtain bids per lot.

(b) Public offers of sale ("OPVs")

An OPV requires a prior public notice five business days in advance of the listing indicating the number of offered securities and their firm unit price. The SBF centralises purchase orders. The first quoted price is that indicated in the offer.

With the approval of the SBF, the sellers may, however, elect to modify the price offered at least two business days before the first price quotation (Article 3-2-14 of the General Regulation). In the case of a change in the offering price, the SBF publishes a new release announcing the change and the way the purchase orders can be confirmed or withdrawn.

(c) The ordinary procedure

The ordinary procedure allows trading in the securities to commence as of the date of introduction without any further requirements. The offering is announced to the market through an SBF release published at least two business days before the first price quotation. The release announces the minimum price that the offeror is willing to accept.

On the offering date, purchase orders are placed with stockbrokers who communicate such orders to the stockbroker acting as the primary dealer for the securities, in accordance with standard market procedures for purchases of securities.

The SBF also indicates the maximum variation in the share price.

3. Continuous disclosure requirements for listed companies

French listed companies must disclose financial statements and notices of shareholders' meetings in the BALO. Parallel rules apply to foreign issuers. All issuers must also promptly disclose price-sensitive information.

(i) Financial statements and shareholders' meetings

(a) French companies

Subject to criminal penalties, companies listed on the official market are required to publish both preliminary and final financial statements in the BALO (Article 294 *et seq* of Decree No. 67-236 of 23 March 1967 ("the 1967 Decree"). In addition, the COB generally requires that companies listed on the second market undertake to carry out the same publications upon listing.

The COB also requires that a press release disclosing the main figures of the draft annual financial statements be published by listed companies the next business day after the meeting of the board of directors that approves such accounts. This requirement exists in order to avoid improper transactions on the concerned securities since, at this stage, the results for the previous fiscal year are generally final.

Companies listed on the official market must also prepare and publish in the BALO certain financial figures on a semi-annual and quarterly basis.

Direct and indirect subsidiaries of companies listed on the official market exceeding certain thresholds (even if they are not listed) must also publish their own financial statements in a legal announcement newspaper and a special notice must be inserted in the BALO.

Further, publicly held companies are required to publish notices of shareholders' meetings in the BALO prior to any shareholders' meeting, such information to include draft resolutions submitted to said meetings as well as specific information relating to mergers, securities issues and spin-off.

(b) Foreign companies

The disclosure requirements governing foreign companies are subject to the requirements laid down in COB Regulation No. 88-04.

Under this Regulation any foreign issuer listed on the official market generally must publish in France periodical information equivalent to that given to other stock exchanges where its securities are listed. A foreign issuer must at least inform the French shareholders of: (i) the date of the shareholders' meetings (and make it possible for shareholders to exercise their voting rights); and (ii) the declaration and payment of dividends, issue of new shares, and transactions involving the subscription, attribution, withdrawal and/or conversion of securities.

The COB must be informed of: (i) any proposed modification of an issuer's deed of incorporation and by-laws; (ii) any changes in the composition of shareholders' equity in comparison to previously published information; and (iii) as soon as possible, any modification in the rights attached to the different categories of shares. Also, the COB considers that information regarding material changes in shareholdings must also be disclosed to the CBV.

Under the COB rules, a foreign issuer must make available to the public its financial statements and management report within six months following the end of the fiscal year together with a French translation of these documents (or the most significant excerpts thereof). The excerpts must include the balance sheet and other elements permitting the shareholders to appreciate the general prospects and key decisions relating to the future of the company. Within four months from the end of the first half-year period of each fiscal year, semi-annual financial statements (including commentary) must be published. The semi-annual information must show revenue and net pre-tax profits (including consolidated information when available).

(ii) Prompt disclosure of price-sensitive events

(a) What needs to be disclosed?

These rules are the mirror image of the ones applicable to parties involved in an M&A transaction, which are discussed in Chapter 3.

Under COB Regulation No. 90-02, listed companies must provide the public with information regarding price-sensitive events, facts or circumstances (Article 4). Any disclosure that provides information that is not accurate, precise and true subjects the issuer to COB's reliefs.

Disclosure must be made in respect of any material fact that, if it were known to the public, might have a "significant" impact on the price of a listed security; any element of a financial transaction that might have a significant impact on the price of a listed security; any modification of a company project previously disclosed; and, upon request, any information that the COB deems useful for the protection of the investors and the good performance of the market.

The COB considers that events to be disclosed to the public should include a material change in senior management, material negotiations that can no longer be kept confidential, the loss of an important customer, or the prospect of material litigation.

In the event of failure by the issuer effectively to comply with disclosure requirements, the COB may publish such information itself and request suspension of the trading of the shares of the company.

An issuer must generally ensure that it provides information equivalent to that given to other stock exchanges where its securities are listed.

(b) How must events be disclosed?

The disclosure of information is normally made through a press release which must be made available to the COB at the latest upon publication (Article 8 of COB Regulation No. 90-02).

The mere publication of information by third parties does not release the issuer from its disclosure duties. The issuer must make sure that the information is complete and actually reaches the public. In other words, the issuer is liable if a press release (or any equivalent method of disclosure) does not accurately reproduce the information disclosed by the issuer and if such disclosure provides the public with an inaccurate or misleading information.

160

(c) When must events be disclosed?

All necessary disclosure must be made as quickly as possible, although disclosure during the hours of trading of a listed security should be avoided. In addition, when the security is traded in several markets, the issuer should take into account the time difference between such markets and make disclosure simultaneously. When timely disclosure cannot take place in respect of potentially market-disruptive information, the issuer should request the SBF to suspend trading and prepare an official release.

Regulation No. 90-02 provides some exceptions to the principle of prompt disclosure (Article 4). In fact, when disclosure could harm the interests of the issuer or the success of a financial transaction, it may be postponed, provided that the issuer is capable of keeping the information confidential.

In addition, when an official press release cannot be issued before a meeting with journalists or financial analysts and the suspension of trading is not justified, the issuer may request those attending the meeting to keep the information confidential until the official disclosure following the meeting. In general, the COB discourages such embargo procedure since it is difficult to control improper use of the privileged information.

The publication of a press release should precede any press conference or any meeting with financial analysts when the information provided on such occasions might lead to a material variation of the price of the relevant shares.

The COB considers that as soon as a price-sensitive matter is discussed during the meeting of the board of directors of a listed target, a press release relating to the matter must be promptly issued (subject to the exception discussed *supra*). The rationale for this rule is that a board of directors often comprises outsiders (bankers, shareholders and friendly parties), and members of the workers' committee also attend the meeting. It is thus considered that once an issue has been officially discussed there, it can no longer be kept confidential.

(iii) The CBV's filings

Upon listing, and as long as its securities are listed, the issuer is required to undertake to:

(i) provide the CBV with the minutes of all shareholders' meetings;
(ii) notify the CBV of any modifications in the by-laws and of any decisions of the corporate bodies relating to shares of the company;
(iii) request approval from the CBV prior to establishing the timetable for any financial transaction involving pre-emptive or priority rights of existing shareholders;
(iv) notify the CBV of any new event which, because of its impact on the financial situation of the company, could lead to material variations of the price of the shares on the stock exchange;

(v) provide the CBV with all communications or publications to securities holders disseminated by the issuer, as well as any financial or economic reports that the company may publish;

(vi) arrange on the French stock exchange for the delivery of the shares and the payment of dividends without charge to the holders, and notify the CBV of any modification in the designation of the financial intermediaries acting as transfer and/or financial agents with respect to the shares (this mainly applies to foreign issuers);

(vii) if the shares are listed abroad, keep the CBV informed in a manner that is equivalent to, and as complete as, the disclosure made to the relevant foreign authorities with respect to the foreign listing (Article 3-1-2 of the General Regulation).

(iv) European Directives

EC Council Directive 79/279 of 5 March 1979 sets minimum standards of disclosure for issuers of securities admitted to official listing on European Union securities exchanges. Although the Member States may adopt more stringent rules than the ones imposed by the EU's harmonisation Directive, the EU rules afford some guidance in interpreting and assessing the French rules. The key rules of the Directive are as follows:

(i) Issuers whose shares are admitted to listing on EU stock exchanges must ensure equal treatment for all shareholders who are in the same position;

(ii) Issuers must also ensure that all holders of debt securities ranking *pari passu* are treated equally;

(iii) Issuers must ensure that the necessary facilities and information are available to enable shareholders to exercise voting and financial rights;

(iv) Issuers must inform the public as soon as possible of any major new developments in their sphere of activity which are not public knowledge and which may, by virtue of their effect on their assets and liabilities or financial position or on the general course of their business, lead to substantial movements in the price of their shares or, as regards listed debt securities, affect their ability to meet the contractual obligations in connection therewith;

(v) Issuers whose shares are listed on the stock exchanges of different Member States must ensure that equivalent information is made available to the market at each of these exchanges; issuers whose shares are listed outside the EU must also respect an equivalence-of-information obligation but only to the extent that the information disclosed outside the EU may be of importance for the valuation of the securities listed in the EU;

(vi) Under the Directive, disclosure must be effected through publication in one or more newspapers distributed throughout the country where the securities are listed, or by making available the disclosure documents within that country at a place made public by means of an advertisement in the press. Disclosure information must be sent simultaneously to the regulatory authorities.

4. **Privatisations**

Privatisations involve a combined public offering, private sales to key shareholders and an employees' offering. Privatisations must be authorised by Decree, following statutory approval, and prices must be blessed by an independent commission.

Privatisations are the most dramatic type of public offerings. They involve much larger amounts than offerings made by issuers of the private sector in Europe. For example, the privatisation of Elf Aquitaine in March 1993 was a FF100 billion offering. Privatisations also attract public attention since they are surrounded by intense advertising campaigns that include TV advertisements, posters and toll-free numbers.

Privatisations in France are managed by the Treasury Department of the Ministry of Economy which, through a steering committee (*"comité de pilotage"*), oversees the whole privatisation process. The committee is composed of representatives of the Treasury (and the financial adviser to the French State), the issuer (and its financial adviser and lawyers), the SBF (acting on behalf of the CBV) and the COB.

(i) Nationalisation v privatisation

The history of French privatisation is worth a short note. It all started in 1982 when the Socialist Government decided to nationalise almost all of the banking sector and the largest French industrial companies (Nationalisation Law No. 82-155 of 11 February 1982).

When, in 1986, the Right came back into power, one of the very first steps of the Chirac Government was to announce that it would undo what had been done by the socialists. Consequently, in between 1986–88, 29 key financial institutions and industrial companies were privatised, including certain gems of the French economy such as Compagnie Saint Gobain, Compagnie Financière Paribas, Crédit Commercial de France, Compagnie Générale d'Electricité, Agence Havas, Société Générale, Compagnie Financière de Suez and Société Matra.

Against all odds, the Socialists regained power in 1988. However, they took a lower profile than before and announced that they would maintain the status quo (this was Mitterand's *"ni ni"* – *ni privatisation, ni nationalisation*). The Government, however, quickly discovered that it was unable to provide the companies it owned with the capital they needed and several state-owned groups were allowed to sell activities to private investors, while others were authorised to publicly offer minority stakes. For example, Caisse des Dépôts et Consignations publicly sold 49% of the stock of its subsidiary Crédit Local de France; Péchiney contributed key assets to a subsidiary, the capital of which was thereafter partially sold to the public; and part of the capital of Total was floated.

In a surprising move, the French Government also tried discreetly to re-nationalise certain of its former gems. For example, in 1990, the Minister of Economy, with the help of the very respectable state-owned Caisse des Dépôts et Consignations, tried to organise a financial raid on Société Générale, France's financial giant privatised in 1986. This turned out to be a total failure and a nation-wide scandal, particularly as some of the participants were suspected of insider trading.

In 1993, the Right was back in power and the new government made privatisation of the industrial and financial sector a priority. The second wave of privatisation began. It is still going on and remains a key component on the French scene.

(ii) Legal framework

(a) A statutory blessing

According to French constitutional laws, both privatisations and nationalisations must be authorised by statute.

The general framework of French privatisations is based on Law No. 86-912 of 6 August 1986 (the "1986 Law"), a statute originally enacted to lay down the implementing terms of privatisation transactions carried out by the French State in 1986. This statute was amended by Law No. 93-923 of 19 July 1993 (the "1993 Law") that authorised the government "to transfer to the private sector" (*i.e.*, privatise) several public sector companies listed in the law.

Subsidiaries of state-owned companies were allowed to be transferred to the private sector without any requirement for further legislative action. On the contrary, subsidiaries of companies that had joined the public sector under a statutory provision (*i.e.*, through nationalisation) could only be privatised in two ways: (i) together with their parent company, or (ii) separately in accordance with an express legal provision.

The 1993 Law resulted in several amendments to the 1986 Law aimed at giving more flexibility to the government. In particular, the provisions relating to transfers to the private sector of public sector companies indirectly owned by the State were amended with a view to facilitating such transfers. The threshold under which such transfers may be authorised by decree was increased from FF500 million to FF1 billion. Likewise, "small' transactions relating to companies with less than fifty employees or the turnover of which is less than FF50 million, were exempted from any notification requirement.

(b) Approval by decree

Each privatisation exceeding certain levels must be authorised by a specific decree followed, in certain cases, by a second decree appointing the chairman of the board of directors or the members of the management committee of the privatised company. The privatisation can be made through a public offering and/or through private sales entered into by the State (or any entity controlled by it) and one or several purchasers.

(c) The Privatisation Commission

Under Article 3 of the 1986 Law (as modified by the 1993 Law), a Privatisation Commission (*"Commission de la Privatisation"*) replaced the former Commission for the Valuation of Public Sector Companies set up by the 1986 Law.

The powers of the new Commission are:

(i) the assessment of the value of the privatised companies; and

(ii) a right of veto with respect to the purchasers of securities chosen by the government in the case of an off-market purchase.

In conducting its appraisal, the Commission is to take into account criteria commonly used in M&A transactions: listed prices, net asset value, profits, the existence of subsidiaries and financial prospects.

In addition, with respect to allotment of securities for consideration other than cash, the Commission sets the exchange ratio on the basis of which the number of securities issued will be determined, and clarifies the way in which benefits conferred on certain categories of purchasers are taken into account in determining the sale price of the offered securities.

The Privatisation Commission is composed of seven independent members appointed by decree who serve for a term of five years and who are selected on the basis of their "economic, financial and legal expertise".

The prices (or exchange ratio) for the privatised assets cannot be lower than the determination made by the Commission, subject to the specific benefits to which employees and certain individuals may be entitled to by law (such as price discounts, instalment payments, bonus securities).

(iii) Several tranches

Each privatisation made (in whole or in part) through a public offering is generally divided into several tranches involving three parallel transactions; a combined public offering with several tranches, a private sale to a group of stable shareholders, and an employees' offering.

The "combined offering" generally includes four tranches:

- a public tranche underwritten by a syndicate of banks and reserved to European residents and nationals taking the form of an OPV (see p. 170 *infra*);
- an institutional offering reserved for French institutional investors;
- several foreign offerings made outside France, generally in the United States and in the United Kingdom; and
- a true "international" offering made outside France and the other jurisdictions where the securities are officially placed.

In order to ease the transaction, all four tranches are generally arranged by the same lead managers. Usually, the French public offering takes the form of an OPV with a fixed price. For the other tranches, customary placing techniques are used and prices are set by the underwriting syndicate.

(a) The employee offering

In the case of a public offering, 10% of the securities offered must be reserved for current and former employees of the privatised company. If the purchase orders issued by persons of this category exceed 10%, the conditions for reduction of the orders are determined by the Minister of Economy. If, on the other hand, orders are less than 10% the Minister may, within six months following the offering, offer the unsold securities to the employees again in the form of a public offering with the same preferential conditions.

Preferential conditions are granted to employees, provided that they keep the securities for a minimum period of time (thus preventing a flow back of the securities on the market, as had sometimes happened in previous privatisations when the offering price was particularly attractive). Preferential conditions include:

(i) payments deferred for up to three years;

(ii) discounts of up to 20% on the lowest price offered to other subscribers;

(iii) the issue of bonus securities up to a maximum of one bonus share for every share acquired directly from the state and held for at least one year from the date the share is fully paid in and freely transferable. These securities may not be sold for two years regardless of the level of discount granted, or before payment has been made in full.

(b) The French public offering

Priority rights may be granted to individuals (as opposed to legal entities) who are French citizens, French residents or nationals of the European Union, upon decision by the Minister of Economy.

Where the purchase orders cannot be fully met, they must be reduced, usually on a proportional basis or by drawing lots. For example, in the BNP privatisation, priority purchase orders that were originally for 40 shares per individual had to be reduced to 18 shares per individual.

Preferential conditions may also be granted in the form of payment deferral for up to three years and the allotment of bonus securities up to a counter-value of FF30,000 subject to a maximum of one security for every ten securities acquired directly from the State and held for at least 18 months after they have been paid in full. It should be noted that partly paid securities are freely negotiable, unlike those purchased by employees. In the case of payment default, the State may automatically recover title to the securities concerned and sell them on the market.

Privatised securities may be exchanged for the 6% 1997 bonds issued by the Government in 1993 (known as the "*Emprunt Balladur*"). In order to encourage payment with the bonds (and subscription thereof), additional priority rights may be given to bond-holders within the limits laid down by the Minister of Economy.

(c) The French institutional offering

French and European Union legal entities, including investment funds, cannot be granted the priority rights mentioned above. This has led to the creation of a specific tranche reserved to French institutional investors to ensure that they have access to a minimum number of securities. This technique was used in the BNP privatisation. More recently, the institutional offering has been merged with the foreign offerings.

(d) Foreign offerings

The 1986 Law limits direct transfers of shares to non-EC foreign investors to 20% of any privatised company's share capital.

The securities offered in the foreign tranches are sold through an international placement, fully guaranteed by a bank syndicate. In the case of BNP, the international placement was divided into three zones (the United Kingdom, the United States and the rest of the world). A portion of the foreign placement may be subject to a "claw-back" provision for the benefit of the French public offering. In the case of BNP, 20% of the shares initially allotted to foreign investors were re-allocated to the French public offering.

(e) Sale to stable shareholders

During the 1986–1987 privatisations, sales of shares to core groups (*"noyaux durs"*) of shareholders were criticised for lack of clarity and openness. It was said that only groups with close links with the government had been selected as key shareholders. The rules were changed in 1993 to ensure the openness of selection of the key shareholders, now named "groups of stable shareholders" or *groupes d'actionnaires stables* ("GAS"). The Privatisation Commission now plays a key role in the formation of the stable shareholders, while in 1986–87 the selection of the core groups rested exclusively with the Minister of Economy.

Stable shareholders must agree to be bound by limitations laid down in a shareholders' agreement (*"cahier des charges"*) defined by the Minister of Economy. They are generally required to purchase a substantial stake (*e.g.* 0.5% or more in the case of BNP) of the issuer's capital and are generally asked to grant to each other rights of first refusal. In the case of BNP, each purchaser was restricted from disposing of any of its shares for three months and 80% of those shares were restricted for a further 21 months.

The choice of the stable shareholders and the terms of the sale are subject to the decision of the Privatisation Commission. Stable shareholders usually consist mainly of French multinational groups although, in recent privatisations, several foreign groups were allowed as shareholders.

(f) Exchange offers for non-voting securities

In order to simplify the shareholding structure of privatised companies, preferred securities previously issued by State-owned companies, such as certificats d'investissement (stock certificates without voting rights), *certificats pétroliers* (petroleum certificates) or participating securities (*titres participatifs*), are generally cancelled via a public exchange offer. *Certificats d'investissement* are discussed on p. 121 *supra*. *Certificats pétroliers* are securities issued by nationalised oil companies which are similar to a *certificat d'investissement*, except that the voting right associated with the certificate is held by a State-controlled institution, the Caisse des Dépôts et Consignations, rather than the State itself. A *titre participatif* is a non-voting security issued by a nationalised company which entitles the holder to remuneration which consists of a fixed interest portion and a variable portion. This remuneration is generally greater than that provided by ordinary shares.

The exchange ratio must take into account the value of the voting rights as well as the elimination of any dividend priority rights attached to such certificates. In the case of *certificats d'investissement*, the cancellation of the securities can also be made by way of a sale of voting certificates to holders of investment certificates, resulting in the automatic creation of ordinary shares. In any event, the government must sell all unsold voting certificates to the company one year after its privatisation at a price set by an expert appraiser.

(iv) The golden share

For fear of seeing French gems taken over by foreign raiders, it was provided that the French State could retain special rights through a golden share (*"action spécifique"*) in the newly privatised companies. This share is not subject to any time limit whereas under the 1986 Law such rights expired at the end of a five-year period. Prior to the 1993 amendments, the golden share enabled the Minister to veto investments in excess of 10% of a privatised company's equity made by one person or by several persons acting in concert. This technique had been used in the context of the privatisation of Havas, Matra, Elf Aquitaine and Bull. The golden share was automatically converted into an ordinary share five years after its creation.

Under Article 10 of the 1986 Law a decree can determine, for each of the companies concerned and prior to its privatisation, whether the protection of national interests requires that a common share held by the State be transformed into a golden share bearing certain specific rights.

The rights that may be attached to the golden share are the following:

(i) the right for the Minister of Economy to approve one or several shareholders acting in concert to exceed one or several thresholds laid down by decree;
(ii) the right to appoint one or two directors (or members of the Supervisory Board) representing the State but with no voting powers;
(iii) the right to veto certain decisions regarding the transfer of assets adversely affecting French national interests.

A decree pronounces the transformation of the share of common stock into a golden share and this transformation is automatically effective. Apart from instances where national independence is at stake, the golden share may, at any time, be definitively transformed by decree into common stock.

In the case of companies or groups active in the health industry, national defence and security, investments exceeding 5% made by foreign individuals or legal entities under foreign control are subject to the approval of the Minister of Economy.

Investments carried out in violation of the preceding provisions result in the holders of such interest not being entitled to exercise their voting rights and being required to transfer their shares within three months. The Minister informs the chairman of the company concerned of any such violation and this information is communicated to the shareholders at the next general meeting. At the end of the three-month period, a forced sale of the shares is initiated under terms provided by decree.

(v) Prospectuses

In a privatisation, the COB and market players have created innovative disclosure techniques requiring the registration of three successive sets of prospectuses.

(a) The master prospectus

First, the issuer must register with the COB a master prospectus (the *document de référence*, see p. 151 *supra*) which includes detailed legal and financial data (shareholding, activities, management, recent events, possible evolution and financial statements). Generally, the master prospectus must be prepared and filed with the COB at least 20 days prior to the beginning of the OPV. A summary of the master prospectus is prepared and registered with the COB at the same time.

The master prospectus is aimed at institutional investors, analysts and intermediaries, while the summary is targeted at the public at large.

(b) The preliminary offering prospectus

Before the beginning of the pre-marketing campaign, a preliminary offering prospectus (*"note d'opération préliminaire"*) is drawn up and registered with the COB. This prospectus gives details about the transaction (tranches, structure, securities offered, offering syndicate, etc) but does not state the price, or the actual date of the offering. The preliminary offering prospectus does not contain any information on the issuer since the master prospectus is deemed incorporated in it.

(c) The final offering prospectus

Once the price and date of the offering are set, the final offering prospectus (*"note d'opération définitive"*) is prepared and registered with the COB.

(vi) Other advertising materials

The COB also verifies, on an informal, non-registration basis, all other advertising materials, including advertisements in the press, radio and by television messages. It also verifies, on an informal basis, prospectuses prepared for foreign markets and the international market. In this case, the COB merely verifies that disclosures made in France are at least as complete as the disclosures made outside France. Often a single international prospectus is used for all foreign offerings, supplemented, for some jurisdictions, by local addenda.

(vii) Pre-marketing

Pre-marketing is a key innovation in French securities practice since, in principle, no solicitation of the public can occur prior to the final registration of a single prospectus (or an offering prospectus when a master prospectus had been previously registered).

The pre-marketing campaign involves the following steps. Ten days prior to the beginning of the OPV (but after publication of the preliminary offering prospectus), revocable purchase order forms (*"mandats révocables"*), together with a summary of the general prospectus are sent via the French banking network to prospective purchasers. The revocable purchase orders include a maximum subscription figure in French francs but no figure for securities.

At the same time, institutional investors are also solicited and begin submitting indications of interests to be included in the so-called *livre d'ordre* (this is the so-called "book building").

Thereafter, on the first day of the OPV, the price is set and the final offering prospectus is published in the press. Up to four days after the beginning of the OPV, persons having issued revocable purchase orders may withdraw their orders. In practice, very few revocations take place.

The period during which the securities of the privatised companies are offered to the public is generally six business days (which is shorter than the offering periods for the 1986 privatisations for which a 15-day period was used).

The placement of securities with institutional investors is longer than the OPV and usually lasts ten business days while the price of the offering is generally higher than the price of the OPV.

The pre-marketing technique has also been used in public offerings made by companies of the private sector (see, for example, the initial public offering of Compagnie des Alpes, SBF release No. 94-3286).

5. Secondary public offerings

Another category of public offerings covers public offers of sale (*offres publiques de vente* – "OPV") of already listed securities, a secondary public offering in the US sense. Such an OPV is available to an investor in a listed company (including companies whose stock is traded on the over-the-counter market) provided that the investor publicly offers securities representing at least:

- 10% of the securities of the same type issued by the company; or
- 20 times the daily average of the trading volume in such securities on the exchange over the six-month period immediately preceding the offer (Article 7-3-2 of the General Regulation).

To launch an OPV, the offering shareholder needs to obtain the prior approval of the CBV. An OPV also requires the publication of a press release approved by the COB, or, if the offer is for 15% or more of the capital of the issuer, the registration of a prospectus with the COB. An OPV may also require, upon request by the CBV, the guarantee of the undertakings of the offerer by a financial institution or the deposit of the securities offered into the custody of the SBF.

With the approval of the SBF, the offerer can make its offer conditional on being able to sell at least a certain percentage (not to exceed 25%) of the amount of securities offered (Article 7-1-4 of the General Regulation).

Public offers of sale must be open for at least three business days.

Chapter 11
Administrative Approvals and Filings

When reaching specified levels of ownership, an acquirer may be required to carry out certain filings with French (and/or foreign or European) authorities. In addition, certain restrictions apply to foreign investors in France.

1. Filing with the Treasury

If the acquirer is a non-resident (or a French company under foreign control) reaching, alone or in concert with others, directly or indirectly, more than *20%* of the capital or voting rights of a French company listed on either the official or the second market, it is required to make an exchange control filing with the Treasury (Articles 1-5°-b) and 12 of Decree No. 89-938 of 29 December 1989). In the case of both companies traded on the over-the-counter market and privately-owned companies, the triggering level is 33.33% of the capital or voting rights (Article 123 of Circular dated 15 January 1990).

The Treasury is one of the most prestigious administrations in France. Its decisions in relation to foreign investments are governed by the general interest of the Nation (*"intérêt national"*), a French concept that basically allows the Treasury to allow or disallow any foreign investment, with the exception of European investments.

Notification to the Treasury is normally made by letter outlining the proposed transaction and setting out its purpose, its financing and a description of the investor and the company being invested into. In the case of a major acquisition, the process usually involves a canvas behind the scenes of administrative agencies and perhaps others interested in the industry concerned. There is, however, an increasing liberalisation on matters of substance together with an easing of the formalities of application and a reduction in the time required to obtain approvals. As far as listed companies are concerned, the Treasury is usually accommodating in the context of friendly acquisitions.

175

As far as European investors are concerned, the Treasury must respond within two weeks. An entity is deemed to be a "European Union investor" if more than one-half of its capital and voting rights are held by European residents or other European investors. In general, the Treasury cannot disallow the transaction and its role is only to verify that the investor is a "true European". However, if the Treasury considers that the transaction has an impact on public order, public health (excluding pharmaceuticals), or public safety, it has the discretionary power to approve or disapprove the transaction. The same rule applies to investments in the armaments and military industries, as well as to investments in entities participating, even occasionally, in the administrative or political authority of the State (or municipalities or regions).

European investors of a certain size may also be "recognised" as such on a permanent basis by the Treasury either in the context of a particular transaction or independently from any transaction. Such recognition is very useful prior to the launching of a tender offer in order to avoid pressures on the Treasury by the target (and friendly parties) in the course of the reviewing of an offer. In such a case, the offer is no longer subject to the prior declaration or authorisation requirements but only to the filing of *post facto* reports (Article 343 *et seq* of Circular dated 15 January 1990).

As far as non-European investors are concerned, the Treasury must respond within one month (for sizable investments). As already noted, the approval is essentially wholly discretionary and a refusal of approval need not be explained.

If the Treasury requests additional information during the two-week (or one-month) period mentioned *supra*, a new review period would begin to run upon the delivery of the information requested.

Certain areas may be regarded as sensitive for foreign investments, such as the defence industry, the media sector, the press (where a statute prohibits non-European ownership exceeding 20% of the capital, see p. 179 *infra*) and the acquisition of certain Franco-French symbols (such as internationally known *Bordeaux Châteaux*).

2. Antitrust filing with the French Ministry of Economy

Once an acquirer acquires a "determining commercial influence" over a target's business behaviour, the acquisition qualifies under French law as a business "concentration" (Article 39 of Ordinance 86-1243 of 1 December 1986). There is no simple test to determine whether or not such determining influence has actually been acquired since a majority stake is not a prerequisite. In fact, it could be concluded that a simple blocking minority (33.33%) of the target's voting rights, in the context of other commercial or contractual links, can give an acquirer the necessary influence over a target.

There is no mandatory notification requirement under French merger control rules (unlike in certain other European jurisdictions). Notification may be made by the acquirer either before the transaction or within three months thereafter. In such a case, the Ministry must decide whether or not it will object to the acquisition within two months of the notification. If it decides to object (or if it has serious misgivings), the Ministry must refer the file to the Competition Council (Conseil de la Concurrence) (Article 40 *et seq.* of Ordinance No. 86-1243 of 1 December 1986). The Council must then render its advisory opinion within four months so that the Ministry can decide whether and under what conditions to authorise the transaction. If no notification is made, the transaction may be investigated at any time. In practice, the Treasury often consults the antitrust division of the French Ministry of Economy before authorising a foreign investment.

Under French merger control rules, the Ministry of Economy may prohibit or impose certain conditions on mergers and acquisitions if:

– the parties to the transactions together have more than a 25% market share within France; or
– they have a total French turnover of more than FF7 billion and at least two of them have a French turnover of at least FF2 billion.

If there is no ministerial decision within the aforementioned period, and assuming that the parties have properly filed the optional notification, the Minister is prevented from challenging the transaction following expiration of the period.

The criterion for examining the transaction is whether the transaction creates or reinforces a dominant position in a manner that would be detrimental to competition. Past experience tends to indicate that public interest is also taken into consideration by the Ministry in issuing its decision, in particular where foreign investors are concerned.

3. European merger control

Notification of a concentration with a Community dimension must be made to the European Commission within one week of either the execution of the purchase agreement or the announcement of the tender offer or the acquisition of a controlling interest (whichever is the earlier). The acquisition may not be completed prior to the notification or within the first three weeks thereafter. In the case of a tender offer, however, the acquirer may go forward with its offer, provided it does not exercise the voting rights acquired in the course of the offer. This means that the acquirer may not vote at shareholders' meetings as long as the Commission has not blessed the transaction, but can take over *de facto* management control.

A concentration has a "Community dimension" if:

(i) the aggregate turnover of all companies or groups of companies involved is more than ECU5 billion, worldwide; and

177

(ii) at least two of the companies or groups of companies involved each have a total turnover within the Community, in all product lines, of more than ECU250 million;

unless:

(iii) each of the companies or groups of companies involved has more than two-thirds of its European turnover in one and the same Member State (Article 1 of Council Regulation (EEC) No. 4064/89).

The above thresholds are calculated on the basis of the aggregate turnover of the parties directly involved in the transaction plus the turnover of all parents and affiliates of such parties (except that only the turnover of the entity or group that is sold is taken into account with respect to the seller). If the transaction is of a Community dimension, no filing needs to be made with the French Ministry of Economy (see Section 2 above) or any other national authorities for merger control purposes.

The Commission has one month to examine a concentration notification and decide whether to open proceedings. Proceedings may last up to a further four (or in certain cases five) months if the Commission determines that the transaction raises serious doubts requiring an investigation and must end with a decision of compatibility or incompatibility with European antitrust rules, subject to the review of the European Court of Justice. Failure by the Commission to act within these deadlines is treated as a finding of compatibility with such rules.

The criterion for assessing the compatibility of a transaction with the European rules is essentially whether it would result in the creation or the strengthening of a dominant position on a European market.

If the transaction is not deemed to constitute a concentration with a Community dimension, and therefore does not fall under the European Merger Regulation, the procedural rules under national law are applicable.

4. Other filings

(i) French Comité des Etablissements de Crédit

Other filings include application for prior approval by the Comité des Etablissements de Crédit ("CEC") if the target, or any of its direct or indirect subsidiaries, is a credit institution. A prior declaration with (or prior approval of) the CEC is needed as soon as someone acquires, alone or in concert with others, (whether directly or indirectly)[1] 5%, 10%, 20% or 33.33% of (or effective control over) one or several credit institutions (Articles 5 et seq. of Regulation No. 90-11 of the Comité de la Réglementation Bancaire).

The CEC filing involves a very detailed and burdensome application,

---

[1] See *Compagnie du Midi* v *Generali and others*, Order by the President of the Commercial Court of Paris, 21 June 1988, Gaz. Pal. 1989.2.678, Note Marchi; Dalloz 1989, 419, Note Vasseur, Bull. July, 1989, p. 908.

together with mainly informal visits by officials of the Bank of France. There is a meeting of the CEC on the third Thursday of each month and, in general, applications must be made within three weeks preceding the relevant CEC meeting. In the case of acquisitions of listed companies the CEC can be expected to react quite promptly. In order to speed the process and as a matter of courtesy, it is sometimes worth visiting the Head of the Credit Institution Department at the Bank of France as well as the General Secretary of the CEC prior to the announcement of the transaction.

(ii) The US FTC and Department of Justice

If both the target and the acquirer conduct business in the United States, whether directly or indirectly, a filing with the Federal Trade Commission and the Department of Justice might also be necessary under the Hart-Scott-Rodino Antitrust Improvements Act.

(iii) The German FCO

Another sensitive country for antitrust purposes is Germany. If both the target and the acquirer conduct business in Germany, whether directly or indirectly, it should be ascertained whether a filing with the German Federal Cartel Office ("FCO") or *Bundeskartellamt* is necessary.

An acquisition of listed shares may constitute a "merger" within the meaning of the German Law Against Restraints on Competition when an acquirer reaches 25% of the issuer's capital, depending on the turnover of the parties. In such a case, the transaction has to be notified to the FCO and cannot be completed without prior clearance by the FCO. The FCO must determine within one month from the receipt of a complete notification whether it will enter into an extended investigation of the transaction. If it decides to do so, it must normally issue a decision within three months.

5. Statutory prohibitions

(i) The press

Where the investment directly or indirectly concerns a "press publication", limitations are imposed on the permitted extent of foreign ownership by Law No. 86-897 of 1 August 1986. Article 7 of the law prohibits any acquisition that has the effect of bringing foreign ownership, directly or indirectly, to more than 20% of a company publishing in the French language. No exception exists to this restriction, which is subject to criminal sanctions, but the limitation is subject to international treaties to which France is a signatory that provide either for so-called "national treatment," or for reciprocity, "in the domain of the press". This provision is, for the time being, only construed as excluding European residents from the scope of the limitation.

(ii) Others

Other limitations and restrictions concern the armaments industry, the television industry, insurance activities, stock market brokerage, companies licensed to render public services, mining and oil businesses.[2]

For example, under Article 39 of Law No. 86-1067 of 30 September 1986, a person, acting alone or in concert with others, may not hold, directly or indirectly, more than 49% of the capital or voting rights of a company licensed to broadcast a national television network. This restriction applies without distinction to both French and foreign investors.

---

[2] See for example Decree-Law of 18 April 1939 relating to the legal regime of war equipments, weapons and munitions and implementing Decree No. 73-364 of 12 March 1973; Decree-Law of 12 November 1938 and Decree No. 70-410 of 15 April 1970 concerning the nationality of providers of public services; Articles 25 to 30 of the Mining Code, Law of 30 March 1928 relating to oil importation and implementing Decrees No. 82-1109 and 82-1110 of 23 December 1982; Article 2-1-2 of the General Regulation relating to change of control of stockbrokers; Article R 322-11-1 of the Insurance Code and Article L 596 of the Health Code concerning the management of pharmaceutical companies.

Chapter 12
Rights of Minority Shareholders

Minority shareholders only have limited rights and have no say in the management of companies.

A minority shareholder investing in a French company only has limited rights and, in the absence of specific contractual arrangements with the majority shareholders, a minority shareholder has no say in the management of the company. The Company Law provides that a company is managed by a board of directors which is elected by the ordinary shareholders' meeting on a mere majority basis. Thus, the main shareholder can generally control the management of the company and its subsidiaries. This is particularly likely as there is no "staggered" board in France and minority shareholders cannot obtain board seats except with the agreement of the controlling shareholders; again, there is no such thing as "fiduciary duties" of board members in France. In addition, French key shareholders are generally keen on keeping sole control of their companies which they think is essential *vis-à-vis* their clients, bankers and suppliers.

Being a minority shareholder in a French company is thus not always easy if one does not go along with the main shareholder. Minority shareholders can have recourse to the few shareholders' associations that exist in France (Association pour la Défense des Actionnaires Minoritaires ("ADAM") or Association Nationale des Actionnaires de France ("ANAF"). However, although these institutions have frequently challenged decisions made by key shareholders supposedly against the interest of minority shareholders, they have mostly been successful in gaining press attention. They have not yet been able to cancel decisions already made.

Minority shareholders' rights are discussed below.

1. Attendance at shareholders' meetings and related rights

(i) Attendance

Each shareholder has the right to attend, and to participate in, shareholders' meetings. A company may nonetheless provide in its by-laws that shareholders holding ten or fewer shares cannot attend ordinary share-.holders' meetings (Article 165 of the Company Law). Several shareholders can satisfy this threshold requirement by combining their holdings and by appointing one of them as their common representative.

In practice, only main shareholders show up at shareholders' meetings. Meetings are also often attended by members of the press (who acquire some shares in order to be able to attend the meeting) and a few others. It is possible to vote by mail or by proxy in shareholders' meetings.

(ii) Right to ask questions

Any shareholder (irrespective of the size of its holding) may submit written questions to the board of directors prior to any shareholders' meeting. The directors are required to answer such questions at the meeting. For this reason, a meeting of the board of directors is always held prior to each shareholders' meeting.

(iii) Right to obtain certain documents and information

Prior to shareholders' meetings, shareholders may request copies of, or access to, the following documents and information related to the agenda for the meeting:

- yearly financial statements;
- consolidated accounts;
- reports of the board of directors and the statutory auditors;
- the names of the directors and the general manager(s); and
- the list of shareholders (very useful information if one is preparing a bid) (Articles 168 *et seq* of the Company Law).

A company's failure to respond to requests for information or documents may result in a court holding that the shareholders' meeting is null and void.

(iv) Right to submit draft resolutions

Holders of shares exceeding specified thresholds (the applicable threshold depending upon the size of the company's capital and ranging from 5% to 50% of the capital) have the right to propose resolutions at shareholders' meetings. Several shareholders, who individually would not qualify, can satisfy this threshold requirement by combining their shareholdings. Share-holders' associations can also do this in certain situations (see Section 8(ii) *infra*) (Article 160 of the Company Law).

(v) Court-ordered shareholders' meetings

Shareholders may petition competent courts to order that a shareholders' meeting be held. This request must be supported by some evidence of necessity. In fact, in the case of listed companies this measure would only be applicable in extreme cases.

By contrast, shareholders holding individually or collectively at least 10% of the capital may petition the court to appoint a representative and to require such representative to call a shareholders' meeting (Article 158 of the Company Law). This request does not need to be supported by evidence of necessity, but there must be evidence that the request is filed in the interest of the corporation; this interest has been held to exist, for example, where there is a conflict between majority and minority shareholders about the sale of the company's interest in a subsidiary. Shareholders' associations can also do this in the circumstances described in Section 9(ii) *infra*.

2. Right to obtain certain information

Any shareholder has the right, at any time, to obtain access to certain documents connected with the shareholders' meetings held during the last three fiscal years, including financial statements, consolidated accounts, a roster of directors, reports from the board of directors and the statutory auditors, the aggregate amount of compensation paid to the five or ten highest-paid employees (depending on the number of employees of the company), and minutes of the shareholders' meetings and related attendance sheets (Article 170 of the Company Law). Also, as noted above, prior to any shareholders' meeting, shareholders may request information and documents related to the agenda for the meeting.

3. Questions

Shareholders holding individually or collectively at least 10% of the capital may submit written questions twice a year to the chairman of the board about any matter which may jeopardise the company's operations. Answers to these questions must be given in writing within one month, and copies must be sent by the company to its statutory auditor. This procedure is intended to draw the attention of the statutory auditor to the company's financial difficulties. Also, as noted above, any shareholder (irrespective of the size of its holding) may submit written questions to the board of directors prior to a shareholders' meeting. Shareholders' associations are also entitled to ask questions.

4. Management expertise

There are two ways in which shareholders can obtain the appointment of an expert in order to investigate a particular transaction made by the company. They are provided by Article 226 of the Company Law and general French civil procedure rules.

(i) Article 226 of the Company Law

Article 226 of the Company Law allows shareholders holding individually or collectively 10% of the capital (or shareholders' associations) to petition the court to appoint one or several experts to report on one or more management decisions. A similar petition may be made by the workers' council, the public prosecutor (*"Ministère Public"*) and the COB (which has, so far, not used this option).

This mechanism enables a minority shareholder to investigate a particular transaction, since shareholders usually do not have access to management information. Subject to criminal penalties, the company is bound to grant the expert access to any relevant documentation and the court may decide that the expert's fees will be paid by the company. The report issued by the expert must be disclosed to the auditors of the company and included in their annual reports to the annual shareholders' meeting. The report must also be discussed by the board of directors and sent to the COB when a listed company is in play.

The scope of the management expertise is, nonetheless, limited since it only permits investigation of transactions made by the company itself and not by other companies of the group. Therefore, through this procedure a shareholder cannot investigate transactions made by subsidiaries. Further, no investigation may be made under Article 226 for transactions that require a shareholders' meeting (mergers, spin-off or sale of substantial assets).

(ii) Article 145 of the French New Code of Civil Procedure

Shareholders therefore frequently have recourse to the general expertise procedure set forth in Article 145 of the French New Code of Civil Procedure that allows any interested party to petition the court for the appointment of an expert for a "legitimate purpose" or in order to investigate facts in view of a litigation. This procedure is more frequently used than the one outlined above since it generally allows shareholders to investigate transactions made at the subsidiaries' level, as well as key transactions requiring shareholders' approval. There is no need for the plaintiff to show that there is urgency and the courts are rather flexible in allowing the expertise to proceed.

Investigations of this type are, however, less likely to raise public attention, since the expert's report does not need to be disclosed to the board, the auditors, the shareholders or the COB.

5. Blocking minority

Shareholders holding more than one-third of the company's voting rights can effectively veto any decision made by the extraordinary shareholders' meeting which requires a two-thirds majority vote (Article 153 of the Company Law). This would cover any merger, change in the company purpose, modification to the by-laws, issue of equity securities and sale of a key asset.

Although a one-third stake does not give management control, it effectively grants substantial powers *vis-à-vis* majority holders in the case of corporate reorganisations.

6. Litigation

Shareholders may sue directly, or derivatively, in the company's name.

Direct suits may be brought by shareholders who have suffered damage, as shareholders, as a result of faulty behaviour or action by one or several directors, the statutory auditors, the company or majority shareholders. This would be the case, for example, if the board of directors approved false or misleading financial statements. Direct suits can be brought before both civil and criminal courts. Directors may be held jointly liable for non-compliance with laws and regulations, as well as for negligence (Article 244 of the Company Law).

In general, derivative suits are brought by the legal representatives of the company, for example when the new directors sue the former ones following a take-over. Derivative suits may also be brought by any shareholders (this is the so-called *ut singuli* legal action) or by shareholders' associations. All damages collected in the course of a derivative action must be paid to the company.

Collective action procedures that allow several shareholders to appoint a common representative to commence an action in their names are available for both direct and derivative suits. However, collective action procedures for derivative suits are only available to holders of at least the same percentage of the company's capital as is necessary to be able to submit draft resolutions at shareholders' meetings (see Section 1(iv) *supra*).

7. Removal of auditors

Shareholders holding individually or collectively at least 10% of the capital (or shareholders' associations) may petition a competent court to order the dismissal of the statutory auditors; this request, which must be for cause, must be filed within 30 days of the appointment of the statutory auditors by the shareholders' meeting.

8. Associations

(i) Investors' associations

Individual shareholders can form non-profit associations (*"associations d'investisseurs"*). These were created by Law No. 89-421 of 23 June 1989 (amending Law No. 88-14 of January 1988) and were inspired by the already existing consumers' associations. These associations may initiate civil or criminal litigations in connection with any facts causing harm to the collective interest of investors or to specified categories of them. Since August 1994, the associations can claim damages on behalf of members provided they have received a proxy from at least two members (Law No. 94-679 of 8 August 1994). Investors' associations need to be registered with the Ministry of Economy, following advice from the COB and the Prosecutor. At this stage, there are only a few of them, such as "ADAM". The ADAM is an association whose goal is to protect the interests of individual shareholders. It frequently takes part in legal actions initiated in the tender offer area when the interests of minority shareholders are at stake. Another example is the ANAF which challenged the public issue of bonds with warrants made on the international market by LVMH in 1987. The basis for the claim was that the issue that had been disclosed as public and aimed at institutional investors, was in fact mostly reserved for targeted French investors that were close with the Arnault group. Still another example is the investment club federation (Fédération Nationale des Clubs d'Investissement).

(ii) Shareholders' associations

The newly created shareholders' associations (*associations d'actionnaires*) enable shareholders of companies listed on either the official or the second market to exercise collectively certain minority rights (Law No. 94-679 of 8 August 1994 adding a new Article 172-1 in the Company Law).

Membership of these associations is restricted to shareholders holding registered shares (and not bearer shares) for at least two years with the following minimum percentages of the voting rights:

- 5% for companies with a capital of less than FF3 million;
- 4% for companies with a capital from FF3–5 million;
- 3% for companies with a capital of less than FF50 million;
- 2% for companies with a capital of less than FF100 million;
- 1% for companies having a capital of FF100 million or more.

Associations of this type can exercise most of the rights previously reserved to 10% shareholders; they can petition the court in order to convene shareholders' meetings, propose resolutions at shareholders' meetings, submit written questions twice a year to the chairman of the board about any matter which may jeopardise the company's operations, petition the court to appoint one or several experts to report on one or more management decisions under Article 226 of the Company Law, petition a competent court to order the dismissal of the statutory auditors, and initiate derivative suits against the directors.

The associations do not need to be licensed or registered in any way; however, the by-laws need to be communicated to the COB.

A few consulting firms exist which specialise in minority shareholders' rights. One example is Deminor, a Belgian consulting firm that specialises in advising minority shareholders. Unlike the ANAF or ADAM, it is a commercial company.

9. **Appointment of a court-designated manager (administrateur judicaire)**

In the event of serious difficulties preventing normal operations, an administrateur judiciaire can be appointed by a competent court to manage the company temporarily. However, minority shareholders may have difficulty in requesting this remedy because the mere fact that an open conflict develops between majority and minority shareholders is not normally a sufficient ground to justify appointment of an administrateur judiciaire. This type of measure, as far as listed companies are concerned, would only cover extreme cases.

10. **Abuse of position by the majority shareholders**

Under French corporate law, the basic rule of the corporate game is that "the majority decides" and the minority must comply with decisions made by the majority shareholders. There is, however, a general principle of French law which states that no right can be used in an abusive way. Cases of abuse of law ("*abus de droit*") have been held to exist in situations where an entity exercised its rights unreasonably, with the sole purpose of harming a third party while receiving no benefit itself.

This notion has been used in corporate law in situations where the decision made by the majority shareholder:

- was contrary to the "corporate interest" of the company (see discussion on p. 132 *supra*);
- concerned a key aspect of the corporate life (a merger, a reorganisation, etc);
- was made for the sole purpose of being detrimental to the minority shareholders.

The following decisions have also been held to be abusive: continuous refusal to distribute dividends over many years when the substantial profits earned by the company were not reinvested in the company's operations but merely held in bank accounts; and transfer of the company's assets or activities to another company indirectly controlled by the majority shareholders. While the principle has been used to nullify a decision of the board of directors or a shareholders' meeting in privately held companies, it has never resulted in the cancellation of decisions taken by listed companies.

A similar theory is applicable to minority shareholders; one example being a case where a minority shareholder systematically opposed a capital increase or a corporate reorganisation that was in the best interest of the company.

11. **Right not to be diluted**

Minority shareholders generally have the right not to be diluted in the case of a new issue of equity securities, unless the new issue is 'reserved' to a particular subscriber. This rule is applied rigorously by the COB in the case of listed companies.

In order to protect existing shareholders' rights, listed companies must issue equity securities with shareholders' preferential subscription rights (*droits préférentiels de souscription* – ("DPS"), unless the shareholders' preferential subscription rights have been explicitly cancelled by an extraordinary meeting of the shareholders. These rights are negotiable instruments listed on the exchange. Existing shareholders are entitled to subscribe to the newly issued shares with DPS for a minimum period of ten business days (Article 188 of the Company Law). Alternatively, they may sell their preferential subscription rights at market price on the exchange.

Another possibility, frequently used by French issuers, is to create a non-negotiable "right of priority" (*droit de priorité*) which allows existing shareholders to subscribe to the new shares, on a preferential basis, for the same period. In such a case, the issue price for the new shares cannot be less than the average listed price over ten consecutive business days chosen among the 20 business days preceding the issue (Article 186-1-2° of the Company Law).

12. **Tag-along and similar rights**

Minority shareholders of listed companies are generally offered an "out" where there is a change of control (through a standing or a public offer) or drastic change in the company's activities (through a repurchase offer). Also, if a company does not have a sufficient public market or "float" for its securities and is 95% controlled by one or several shareholders, any minority shareholder can be bought out through a repurchase offer procedure (see Chapters 6 and 8).

13. **Summary**

The foregoing suggests that the rights of minority shareholders holding one-third or less of the voting rights in a French *société anonyme* may be a source of nuisance to majority shareholders of the company, but do not entitle the minority shareholders to become directly involved in, or to obstruct, the management of the company. Decisions at ordinary shareholders' meetings (including appointment of directors, approval of yearly accounts and issue of bonds) require a simple majority vote, while resolutions at extraordinary shareholders' meetings (including those relating to a merger, issue of equity securities or securities exchangeable or convertible into equity securities, liquidation and any amendment of the company's by-laws) require a two-thirds majority.

Chapter 13
Public Repurchase Offers

Public repurchase offers may be initiated by either:
- *95% shareholders to delist the company;*
- *minority shareholders, if one or several shareholders acting in concert hold at least 95% of the voting rights; or*
- *at the request of the CBV if the company undergoes significant legal changes or substantially modifies its activities.*

Public repurchase offers (*Offres publiques de retrait* – "OPRs") were created by the 1989 Law. Since the enactment of Law No. 93-1444 of 31 December 1993, amending the Stock Exchange Law, repurchase offers relate not only to companies traded on the official market or the second market, but also to companies traded on the over-the-counter market that were previously traded on either the official or the second market. Repurchase offers are widely used and there have already been more than one hundred OPRs resulting in the delisting of companies. The creation of the new squeeze-out procedure has increased the number of OPRs since there are many listed companies with no real market for their shares. Public repurchase offers are governed by the simplified offer rules (see Chapter 8). Public repurchase offers can also be coupled with a new squeeze-out procedure (see Chapter 14).

1. Four categories of repurchase offers

(i) Repurchase offers initiated by minority shareholders

If any person (or group of persons acting in concert) owns 95% or more of a listed company's voting rights, *any* minority shareholder of the company may ask the CBV to require the majority shareholders to purchase the remaining shares of the company. The CBV is required to consult with the company before ordering that the repurchase offer for the minority's shares go forward (Article 5-5-2 of the General Regulation).

This type of offer is aimed at allowing minority shareholders to withdraw from companies with no real market for the securities in situations where the float (the amount of stock publicly held) is not sufficient. Whereas there is a strict requirement that companies listed on the official market have a minimum 25% float upon listing (10% float for companies listed on the second market), no such requirements exist once listing is obtained.

Prior to the enactment of the 1989 Law, shareholders of listed companies could thus be left with no real market for their securities and no hope of being bought out. At best, the stock market authorities could threaten the company with delisting because of insufficient trade. The shares would then trade on the over-the-counter market which would usually make things worse for minority shareholders since the over-the-counter market is mostly unregulated and generally less active than the other markets.

This procedure has been used several times in the past and the CBV tends to accept most requests made by minority shareholders. It is, nevertheless, possible for the CBV to refuse such a request if the market for the securities concerned proves to be sufficiently active. This repurchase offer can precede a squeeze-out procedure, if the target's majority shareholders so decide.

(ii) Repurchase offers initiated by 95% shareholders

This category of repurchase offer, which is the counterpart of the preceding one, is more frequently used. It enables holders of at least 95% of the voting rights of any listed company to propose a public repurchase offer on their own initiative if they wish the company to be delisted (Article 5-5-3 of the General Regulation). This offer can also precede a squeeze-out procedure enabling the acquirer to gain total control over the target.

The CBV, if it approves the terms of the repurchase offer, informs the public that, on conclusion of the offer, it will delist the company from the official market or the second market, as the case may be, at the outcome of the offer. In practice, in the absence of a squeeze-out procedure, the target's securities will be traded on the over-the-counter market.

This is the most frequently used category of repurchase offers since there are many listed companies with no active trading. The new squeeze-out procedure has increased the interest of investors in this procedure.

(iii) Repurchase offers resulting from the change of an SA into an SCA

Shareholders holding at least two-thirds of the voting rights of an SA that is changed into an SCA must file a public repurchase offer with the CBV upon adoption of the resolution acting on such a change by the extraordinary shareholders' meeting. In such a case, the majority shareholder is bound to file a repurchase offer and the CBV cannot grant exemptions (it is in fact one of the few cases where the CBV is bound by a strict rule and has no flexibility for its decision) (Article 5-5-4 of the General Regulation).

This procedure is not frequently used since transformations of listed SAs into SCAs are rather rare.

(iv) Repurchase offers resulting from a reorganisation of the company

The last category of repurchase offers is similar to the preceding one but covers a wider range of changes that can affect a listed company (Article 5-5-5 of the General Regulation).

The rule is that a report has to be made to the CBV for the purpose of considering the advisability of a public repurchase offer when the persons controlling such a company intend to:

– propose a change in the legal form of the company or make significant changes to the by-laws, in particular, those affecting transfers of shares and voting rights;
– contribute or sell most or all of the company's assets to another company;
– substantially change the company's activities; or
– suspend distributions of dividends for several fiscal years.

This category of repurchase offers is the most controversial one since the wording of Article 6 *bis* of the 1988 Law does not explicitly authorise the CBV to request the controlling shareholder of the concerned company to launch a repurchase offer.

First, such a repurchase offer must be filed when a listed company is merged into a non-listed company, on the principle that non-listed shares cannot be exchanged for listed shares (see SBF release No. 94-1289 of 2 May 1994 concerning Crédit Agricole Côte-d'Or and SBF release No. 94-583 of 21 February 1994 concerning AGE Développement).

Second, these provisions also apply if a listed company sells or contributes most of its activities to a third party.

Third, a repurchase offer of that type can also be launched to allow minority shareholders a way out in cases of reorganisation of companies in financial trouble (see SBF release No. 94-156 of 14 January 1994 concerning Bail Equipement).

It is, however, uncertain whether the creation of a maximum threshold above which shares may not be voted (as was done by Groupe Danone in 1994), would trigger the repurchase offer obligation (see p. 110 *supra*).

Another interesting issue is whether the repurchase offer obligation would apply in the case of a merger of listed companies. Up to now, this has not been required when the surviving company had a float at least as large as the one of the absorbed company. One example is the Pinault-Printemps/La Redoute merger: in February 1994, François Pinault, the controlling shareholder of both Pinault-Printemps and La Redoute SA, announced that he would merge both companies. La Redoute SA was a listed company, the largest mail ordering company in France and a subsidiary of Pinault-Printemps. Since Pinault-Printemps held more than two-thirds of the votes of La Redoute and the Pinault group owned a majority of Pinault-Printemps, minority shareholders had little to say. The result of the transaction was that La Redoute shareholders were not given any choice but to receive

Printemps shares. The ADAM initiated legal proceedings on the basis that, since Pinault-Printemps was granted some specific advantages (in particular it was gaining ownership of La Redoute assets while the other shareholders were only receiving Printemps shares), a specific procedure was to be followed. The ADAM also argued that the principle of equality of treatment among shareholders had not been complied with. The purpose of the litigation was to force Pinault-Printemps to buy out for cash La Redoute minority shareholders through a repurchase offer or otherwise. The Court of Appeals of Douai disagreed.[1]

2. Terms of the repurchase offer

A repurchase offer may be made for a combination of securities and cash (a "combined offer") or for either cash or securities (an "alternative offer"). It must be made on *all* equity securities and voting rights (including all securities convertible, exchangeable or giving the right to subscribe or purchase equity securities or voting rights).

The price of repurchase offers is often the subject of disputes with minority shareholders. On such occasions, as in the case of normal tender offers, the CBV uses the so-called multicriteria approach. The price element is a key aspect for offers of this category since repurchase offers are usually the last chance for minority shareholders to sell their shares, in particular when the repurchase offer is coupled with a squeeze out.

3. Unavailability of the repurchase offer procedure

The repurchase offer procedure is not available when, in the course of a preceding public tender, the acquirer announces that it intends the target to remain listed following its offer.

In such a case, no repurchase offer may be initiated by minority shareholders (nor by its controlling shareholder) during the period granted by the CBV to the target (or shareholders) to reissue securities to the public (Article 5-5-6 of the General Regulation).

---

[1] *ADAM and others* v *La Redoute*; Court of Appeals of Douai, 1994; Bull. July 1994, p. 994.

CONTENTS OF CHAPTER 14

Chapter 14
Squeeze-out, Delisting and Going Private

This chapter describes what happens when a listed company ceases to be listed and goes private. This usually takes place after a change of control when the acquirer wants to reorganise the target or gain flexibility in its management decisions. Investors in French listed companies are now able to take advantage of the new "squeeze-out" procedure that enables 95% shareholders to acquire total control over listed targets by excluding minority shareholders.

1. The advantages of delisting for majority shareholders

The advantages of delisting a company are substantial since listed companies are subject to numerous disclosure requirements and restrictions.

(i) General advantages

The squeeze-out corresponds to a great need felt by market players. Indeed, following a tender offer (and even repurchase offers) acquirers are frequently left with hundreds of minority shareholders with no interest in the life of the company. These are usually individuals or estates that did not become aware of the offer or were otherwise unable to sell their shares in the course of the offer. They can even be shareholders with unclear intentions that sometimes try to obtain additional financial benefits by being a nuisance to majority shareholders. At any rate, the presence of minority shareholders is often a source of problems for the main shareholder since it does not provide the flexibility linked with sole control. A majority shareholder always has the duty to take into account the interests of other shareholders when making strategic decisions (major investments or disvestments), reorganisation, intercompany pricing and dividend payments (see Chapter 12). In addition, each shareholder generally has the right to attend shareholders' meetings and obtain, on a regular basis, financial documents and information relating to shareholding and management, all of which create costs and administrative burdens as well as posing confidentiality concerns.

The majority shareholder is also subject to a number of requirements applicable to listed companies. These are dealt with next.

(ii) Disclosures

Companies listed on the official market are required to publish final financial statements in the BALO and to publish their financial figures on a semi-annual and quarterly basis. Direct and indirect subsidiaries of companies listed on the official market exceeding certain thresholds (even if they are not listed) must also publish certain financial information. Other companies only need to file their annual accounts with the Registry of Commerce and Companies.

Listed companies must promptly disclose to the public price-sensitive information. They must also prepare prospectuses and detailed reports to their shareholders when undertaking an issue of securities, merger, spin-off or similar transaction. Such information must be provided to the COB and, in certain instances, approved prior to publication. Private companies must merely prepare reports to their shareholders before each shareholders' meeting; such reports are not reviewed by the COB, but are simply filed with the Commercial Courts (Registry of Commerce and Companies).

Listed companies whose voting rights do not equal the total number of their shares, must disclose the total number of their voting rights to the CBV and to the public after each annual shareholders' meeting and whenever the total number of voting rights changes by 5% or more. In addition, acquisitions or dispositions of shares of such companies, when exceeding certain thresholds (5%, 10%, 20%, 33.33%, 50% or 66.66%), must be disclosed to the company in question and to the CBV which in turn publishes such purchases or sales. Non-disclosure is subject to substantial sanctions.

Further, agreements creating a right of first refusal or similar rights concerning the shares of listed companies must be disclosed to the CBV for publication.

Finally, public companies are required to publish notices of shareholders' meetings in the BALO. Private companies are required to send to their shareholders only one notice by ordinary mail.

(iii) Mandatory offers

When an acquirer reaches more than 33.33% of the capital or the voting rights of a listed company (or acts in concert with others and they together reach this level), or increases its holding by 2% or more in less than a one-year period (while holding between one-third and one-half of the stock or voting rights), it is generally required to launch an offer.

Where a face-to-face transfer of shares results in a party acquiring the majority of the voting rights or capital of a listed company, the acquirer may be required to launch a standing offer. Such procedure may be burdensome and costly.

Further, when one or several shareholders of a listed company (or a company whose shares are traded on the *marché hors-cote*) hold 95% or more of the voting rights, they may be required by the CBV, upon the request of any minority shareholder, to carry out a repurchase offer which may represent a substantial financial burden for the majority shareholder.

(iv) Trading

Securities listed on either the official market or the second market must be transferred through stockbrokers. Stockbrokers charge a brokerage fee and a special stamp tax (ranging from 0.15% to 0.3% but subject to a FF4,000 ceiling), payable both by the seller and purchaser, which assessed upon each transfer (certain exemptions apply). Transfers of non-listed securities require only the execution of a one page stock transfer form (*"ordre de mouvement"*) by the transferor. No stamp tax is assessed on the purchase and sale and no stockbroker fee is payable.

Another constraint applicable to listed shares is that the sale of such securities must, with only limited exceptions, be made at a price equal to the listed price and the parties to a sale may not agree on a price other than a listed price. This can be a major constraint for reorganisations and acquisitions.

Finally, trading in securities issued by listed companies, as well as securities listed on the *marché hors-cote*, is subject to significant insider trading regulations that may substantially restrict the ability of a majority shareholder to trade such securities.

2. Delisting

(i) Securities listed on the official or second markets

The CBV usually requires that delistings of French equity securities be coupled with a repurchase offer (see Chapter 13). In certain cases, however, the CBV may decide, upon the request of an issuer or on its own initiative, to delist securities for lack of trading without recourse to an OPR. This would cover cases where an issuer has a minimal float (less than 1%) and almost no trading. Once delisted, the securities would then trade on the over-the-counter market for an indefinite term unless the main shareholders acquire all or substantially all of the stock through a squeeze-out procedure or otherwise (see *infra*).

As regards foreign securities, the situation is different since no repurchase offer or squeeze-out can be made on foreign securities. The CBV thus generally requires that the French public be offered an "out" either through a purchase by a shareholder or, where the securities are listed outside France, through an offer on the main market where the issuer is listed. In the latter case, additional foreign stock exchange fees (brokers' fees and stock exchange taxes) exceeding those that would have been payable in the case of a public offer in France cannot be charged to the securities' holders (see, for example, the delisting of the shares of Pirelli Spa (CBV decision dated 26 October 1994, SBF release No. 94-3280)). In deciding whether or not to delist foreign securities, the CBV is to take into account trading volumes, dividend payments, the size of the float and compliance with stockmarket regulations (Article 3-3-4 of the General Regulation).

(ii) Securities traded on the over-the-counter market

There is no delisting decision on the over-the-counter market since securities can be listed on this market at the request of any prospective seller or buyer. Securities are listed for each calendar month during which a given security has been offered for sale or for purchase, or when a trade has been made. Securities remain listed during the following month but, if no offer or trade occurs during such month, they do not appear on the over-the-counter listing the next month (Article 3-3-8 of the General Regulation).

3. Squeezing-out minority shareholders

Following a repurchase offer, securities not tendered by minority share-holders in the course of the offer can be automatically transferred to the majority shareholder against payment of an indemnity.

Since June 1994, investors in French companies are able to take advantage of a new "squeeze-out" procedure that enables 95% shareholders to acquire total control over listed targets by buying out minority shareholders. In fact, the squeeze-out technique is now widely used in France.

The legal basis for the procedure was laid down in Article 16 of Law No. 93-1444 of 31 December 1993, amending the Stock Exchange Law. The amendment authorised the CBV to modify its General Regulation to set the conditions in which, following a public takeover bid, securities not tendered by minority shareholders in the course of the offer could be transferred to the majority shareholder. The relevant amendments to the General Regulation were adopted on 9 June 1994 and followed by an implementing regulation of the CBV (General Decision No. 94-04 dated 23 June 1994).

The squeeze-out procedure (*"retrait obligatoire"*) concerns only companies whose securities are listed on either the official market or the second market and companies whose securities are traded on the over-the-counter market, provided these latter companies have been previously traded on either the official or the second market.

(i) Preceding repurchase offers

The squeeze-out may follow a repurchase offer initiated either by a 95% shareholder (or several persons acting in concert) for the purpose of delisting the company, or by a repurchase offer initiated by minority shareholders of companies in which one shareholder (or several acting in concert) owns at least 95% of the voting rights (Articles 5-6-1 of the General Regulation).

Consequently, the squeeze-out is only available when one shareholder holds (alone or in concert with others) at least 95% of the issuer's voting rights prior to the launching of the repurchase offer. Persons holding less than 95% of such rights cannot take advantage of the procedure and would normally have to file a voluntary bid prior to the launching of a squeeze-out.

The other categories of repurchase offers are not eligible as "preceding" offers for these purposes. They consist of repurchase offers required in the case of transformation of a *société anonyme* into a *société en commandite par actions* and repurchase offers required in the case of major reorganisation of an issuer (contribution or sale of most of the company's assets, change in the company's activities or by-laws, etc).

When filing its repurchase offer with the CBV, the acquirer must disclose whether it intends to initiate a squeeze-out. The acquirer may either irrevocably undertake to begin a squeeze-out following the repurchase offer or reserve its decision depending on the results of the offer (Article 5-6-2 of the General Regulation). In this latter case, the acquirer would be free to decide whether or not it wishes to carry out a squeeze-out on the basis of the amount of securities effectively acquired in the course of the offer (Article 5-6-3 of the General Regulation).

Upon approval of the offer, the acquirer must then publish a release announcing the squeeze-out in a "legal announcement newspaper" published in the area where the issuer's head office is located.

(ii) Valuation of the target

When filing the repurchase offer, the acquirer must file with the CBV a valuation of the target's securities. According to Article 5-6-1 of the General Regulation and Article 16 of Law No. 93-1444, the valuation is to be made pursuant to "objective methods used in the case of a sale of assets" and the valuation is "to take into account, in adequate proportions, the asset value of the concerned company, its profitability, the average trading prices of the concerned securities, the value of subsidiaries and the company's prospects".

In practice, however, this requirement only restates the existing common practice in the tender offer area where acquirers are always required to justify offer price through the so-called "multicriteria" approach. The multicriteria approach takes into account (i) the listed prices (last listed price, average over one month, six months and one year, weighted by trading volume); (ii) net asset value (reassessed to take into account undervalued assets) of the target; and (iii) price earning ratio (or PER). Frequently, of course, a premium is offered to the market.

(iii) Fairness opinion

A key innovation of the squeeze-out regulation is that the valuation made by the acquirer must be confirmed by a "fairness opinion" (*appréciation*) issued by an "independent expert". This is the first time French stock-market regulations have required that a fairness opinion be issued.

The regulations do not state whether the expert issuing the opinion is required to have a special status or be a licensed institution. In practice, however, experts are mostly financial analysts or auditors.

Further, the regulations do not specify the meaning of the term "independent". Experts having an economic interest in the transaction (such as a bank that is also a shareholder of the target or the bank filing the offer with the CBV on behalf of the acquirer) would probably not be deemed to be independent. As a matter of practice, the stockmarket authorities seem generally to require an "independent" expert who has not been paid for services rendered to the concerned issuer within two years preceding the transaction.

In order to try to resolve these issues in advance, the CBV insists on approving the appointment of the expert before any repurchase offer which is to be coupled with a squeeze-out is filed (Article 1 of the General Decision). The COB has the right to veto the appointment of any expert within five business days after the CBV's approval.

The opinion has to include comments as to the valuation made by the acquirer and an opinion as to the "fairness" of the valuation made.

(iv) Effective date

If the acquirer has undertaken to initiate a squeeze-out regardless of the results of the repurchase offer, the SBF's notice approving the offer will immediately disclose the date on which the squeeze-out will be "effective" ("*date de prise d'effet*"). On the effective date, any securities still held by the public are transferred to the acquirer by the financial institutions holding securities for the accounts of clients (this will be made through appropriate book entries since securities are no longer certificated in France). On the same date, the target's securities are delisted from their respective market by the CBV.

If the acquirer has reserved its decision, depending on the results of the repurchase offer, it must inform the CBV of its decision within ten business days after the termination of the offer. The acquirer's decision is published in the SBF's release that discloses the results of the offer. Such a release also discloses the date on which the squeeze-out is effective. In this case, the period between the publication of this release and the effective date of the squeeze-out cannot be less than ten days, a period that corresponds to the statute of limitations for legal actions initiated for the purposes of challenging the CBV's decisions in the tender offer area.

(v) Indemnity to be paid to minority shareholders

The SBF release approving the squeeze-out must also disclose the amount of the indemnity to be paid to minority shareholders. According to Article 16 of Law No. 93-1444 of 31 December 1993, the indemnity to be paid to minority shareholders must equal either the valuation made by the acquirer or the price offered during the preceding repurchase offer (whichever is the higher). The meaning of this provision is unclear since one does not see how the CBV can approve a repurchase offer price at a level lower than the valuation made by the acquirer. Also, in the case of events taking place in-between the valuation made by the acquirer and the squeeze-out, the indemnity may be subject to an increase.

The acquirer must appoint a bank to be in charge of centralising the indemnification payments to be paid to minority shareholders (Article 3 of the General Decision). If the acquirer has irrevocably undertaken to launch a squeeze-out following the offer, the funds corresponding to the indemnification are transferred to the centralising bank one day after the termination of the offer and, on the same day, the bank credits accounts for the benefit of securities holders. If the acquirer has reserved its decision depending on the results of the repurchase offer, the acquirer is required to transfer the aggregate amount of the indemnification on the date on which the squeeze-out is effective.

In order to inform former minority shareholders of the target (and heirs and assigns), the centralising bank must, each year and for a ten-year period after the end of the offer, issue a press release in a newspaper with national circulation to call the attention of the public to the fact that it holds funds which are available for indemnified parties. The funds are kept by the centralising bank for ten years and thereafter transferred to the Caisse des Dépôts et Consignations, a major state-owned financial institution in charge of public interest banking services. After the initial ten-year period, the funds can be claimed from the Caisse by any former minority shareholder (and heirs and assigns) for an additional twenty-year period. After that, unclaimed funds automatically become the property of the French State.

The General Regulations

Editor's note

Attached is the English translation of the General Regulations of the *Conseil des Bourses de Valeurs* or *CBV*, the so-called *Règlement Général*. This translation was prepared by the staff of the *Société des Bourses Françaises* or SBF for the convenience of English readers and practitioners.

Certain terms included in the translation differ from terms used in the book.

Following is a table showing (i) the French term, (ii) the corresponding term used in the book and (iii) the English translation prepared by the SBF.

French term	Term used in the book	Translation by the SBF
Application	Registered sale	Put-through
Cote Officielle	Official Market	Official list
Hors-cote	Over-the-counter market	Hors-cote
Décision générale	General Decision	Implementing Decision
Garantie de cours	Tending offer	Price guarantee procedure
Ministère de l'économie	Minister of Economy	Economy Minister
Offre publique de retrait	Repurchase offer	Public buy-out offer
Réglement générale	General Regulation	General Regulations
Retrait obligatoire	Squeeze-out	Compulsory buy-out
Société de Bourse	Stockbroker	Bourse member firm

Also, the attached translation is based on the General Regulation as of 28 July 1994, which was up to date as of the date of printing of this book, *i.e.* 13 March 1995. The General Regulation is, however, subject to amendments from time to time.

THE PARIS BOURSE
General Regulations
as of August 1994

Unofficial translation
for information purposes only

An Introduction

The basic rules governing stockmarket activity in France are set forth in the *Règlement Général du Conseil des Bourses de Valeurs* (CBV), or General Regulations of the Stock Exchange Council. These rules are detailed further in *Décisions Générales*, or Implementing Regulations, which are also issued by the CBV.

The following English translation of the General Regulations has been prepared for the convenience of English readers. Only the original French text, however, has any legal value. Consequently, the translation may not be relied upon to sustain any legal claim, nor should it be used as the basis of any legal opinion. In addition, the CBV and the SBF–Paris Bourse expressly disclaim all liability for any inaccuracy herein.

The translation is that of the General Regulations subsequent to amendments adopted in August 1994. At the time of going to press in March 1995, the Regulations had not been modified further.

By way of introduction, there follows a brief presentation of the chief French regulatory bodies, as well as a short explanation of certain French terms.

- The body of rules called the *Règlement Général* or General Regulations, as well as the *Décisions Générales* or Implementing Regulations, are enacted by the market's self-regulatory authority, the CBV. Ten of the twelve members of this authority are elected by Bourse member firms (licensed broker/dealer firms called *sociétés de bourse*).
- The *Commission des Opérations de Bourse* (COB) is patterned after the US Securities and Exchange Commission and is the market's external regulatory authority. The COB's mission consists essentially of protecting investors and ensuring the integrity of the markets, in particular through proper disclosure. In addition, the COB, along with the Banque de France, must issue an opinion on each amendment to the General Regulations of the CBV prior to their approval by the French Economy Minister which brings them into force.
- The *Société des Bourses Françaises* (SBF) prepares and implements regulations and rulings issued by the CBV. It also organises and supervises the market on a day-to-day basis. Its other activities include development and maintenance of the market's central computer systems, acting as clearing house for all trades performed on the regulated central market, and the provision of both corporate action information and market trading data. It is a business corporation whose shareholders are mainly broker/dealer firms. In short, the SBF is the Paris Bourse.
- The *sociétés de bourse* or Bourse members firms enjoy, for the time being, an

exclusive right to trade listed equity securities in France. They are licensed by the CBV. At the end of 1994, 52 were in operation, of which 17 were controlled by non-French interests.

- Three markets, from a regulatory perspective, co-exist in France: the *Cote officielle* or Official List, the *Second marché* or Second Market, and the *hors-cote* ('unlisted') market where securities not quoted on one of the other two markets may be traded. The Official List is the most regulated of the three, the *hors-cote* market the least. The Second Market, only slightly less regulated than the Official List, is designed for small and medium-size companies. It should be added that the *hors-cote* market, while being largely unregulated as regards the companies traded thereon and illiquid for most issues, is nevertheless – unlike "over-the-counter" markets in other jurisdictions – a transparent, centralised market whose intermediaries are the same as those who operate on the regulated markets.

From a trading – rather than regulatory – perspective, two markets must be distinguished. Trades on the *Marché à règlement mensuel* or Monthly Settlement Market are settled – delivered and paid for – at the end of the calendar month; this market, commonly called the RM market, is an account system similar to those which exist in other countries. Trades on the *Marché au comptant* or Cash Market are settled on the third trading day after the transaction. The most liquid equity issues are traded on the Monthly Settlement Market, which is the main French equity market.

- The *Société de Compensation des Marchés Conditionnels* (SCMC) is a wholly-owned subsidiary of the SBF. By delegation of the SBF, it is responsible for market surveillance and clearing procedures, and more generally the organisation of the market for traded options dealt on the MONEP (*Marché des Options Négociables de Paris*). Most options are now floor-traded, but it is planned to move to computerised trading for all MONEP options in the near future, using a screen-based public orderbook.
- The *Société Interprofessionnelle pour la Compensation des Valeurs Mobilières* (SICOVAM) is the French central depository/registry for securities. It is a business corporation whose shareholders are members of the French financial community. It is recalled that French securities were "dematerial-ised" in 1984. Therefore, French securities, with very few exceptions (such as those circulating outside France) are no longer certificated.
- CAC (*Cotation assistée en continu*) is the Paris Bourse's screen-based, computerised trading system which may be used to trade all negotiable securities (except, most notably, some short-term interest rate instruments subject to Banque de France oversight). The CAC system is access-ible from any Bourse member firm, and trading may take place from 10 a.m. to 5 p.m.

The Paris Bourse may be characterised as a centralised, order-driven, automated continuous auction market. A new, more flexible trading system will be progressively introduced during 1995, but these basic characteristics of the French market will not change.

- RELIT (*Règlement/Livraison de Titres*) is the fully automated delivery vs. payment system operated by the SBF and the SICOVAM. This system is fully integrated with the CAC trading system. As pointed out above, monthly account trades are settled at the end of the month and cash trades are settled at T + 3. Furthermore, off-exchange trades may give rise to same-day settlement under the wholesale trade sub-system called SLAB.
- The *Bulletin Officiel de la Cote* (BOC) is the daily official gazette of the Paris Bourse and now contains mainly information on prices, dividends, redemption dates and the like for securities on the Official List or Second Market (the daily statement covering securities traded on the *hors cote* market is also included). The official statements and announcements (*avis*) of the *Conseil des Bourses de Valeurs* and the *Société des Bourses Françaises*, including corporate action notices, which formerly appeared in this publication, are now available either in the form of a weekly booklet, or through a daily post subscription, or by real-time telecopy.
- The *Bulletin des Annonces Légales Obligatoires* (BALO) is the official gazette of legal notices.

The aforementioned acronyms will be used hereinafter to designate the corresponding authorities, bodies, systems and publications: CBV, COB, SBF, SICOVAM, SCMC, RELIT, CAC, BOC, BALO.

CONSEIL DES BOURSES DE VALEURS

Contents

Title 1
Market institutions

Chapter 1
Conseil des Bourses de Valeurs (CBV) (Stock Exchange Council)

Article 1–1–1

The CBV, headquartered in Paris, meets at least eight times a year. Meetings are called by its Chairman. Minutes of each meeting are drawn up and submitted for CBV approval at a later meeting.

Article 1–1–2

For the application of its General Regulations, the CBV specifies conditions relating to market organisation and operation in Implementing Regulations published in the BOC.

Article 1–1–3

By means of Implementing Regulations, the CBV may empower its Chairman to act in the name of the CBV under given circumstances.

Article 1–1–4

The CBV empowers its Chairman to take, in urgent circumstances and in the name of the CBV, any decisions required for proper market operation.

At the following meeting, the Chairman reports to the CBV on any decisions he has made in its name and, where applicable, on any direct prior consultations he has held with CBV members.

Article 1–1–5

Decisions of an individual nature made by the CBV or in its name are enforceable as soon as the interested parties have been informed of such decisions.

Chapter 2
Société des Bourses Françaises (SBF)

Article 1–2–1

The specialised financial institution in-stituted by Law No. 88–70 of 22 January 1988 pertaining to stock exchanges and called the SBF carries out the assignments set forth in the law and in its articles of association. The SBF assists in the preparation and implementation of CBV decisions, in compliance with the prerogatives of the Chairman of the CBV.

Article 1–2–2

After receiving the advice of the CBV, the SBF determines the fees to be charged for the services of general interest that it provides.

Article 1–2–3

The SBF may specify the technical conditions for application of the present Regulations or the Implementing Regulations issued by the CBV by means of notices published in the BOC or by means of instructions sent to the Bourse member firms.

Article 1–2–4

The SBF monitors the activities of Bourse member firms, of their subsidiaries, and of companies over which Bourse member firms exercise legal or de facto control, or considerable influence, as well as the regularity of their operations and their solvency. Such monitoring is ensured in particular by means of on-the-spot verifications and by means of documents filed by Bourse member firms.

The SBF is empowered to ask Bourse member firms to produce regular information, with respect to which it determines the contents and the notification procedures. In particular, the SBF is empowered to set the accounting standards applicable to Bourse member firms and to require them to file regularly the accounting information needed for auditing their activities.

Should the inspection of a Bourse member firm reveal a situation for which

217

additional information is required beyond the normal scope of action of the SBF, the on-the-spot investigations may be extended to the legal entities that control the Bourse member firm, directly or indirectly, as well as to the subsidiaries of the Bourse member firm, in conjunction, where applicable, with the regulatory authorities supervising such legal entities.

Article 1–2–5

An institution that does not have the status of a Bourse member firm and is admitted as a member of the MONEP clearing house or is authorised to act as principal enters into an agreement providing for inspection and monitoring by the SBF.

Article 1–2–6

The SBF monitors all persons under the authority of Bourse member firms or acting on their behalf, and all persons under the authority of the SBF or acting on its behalf, with respect to compliance with their professionnal obligations.

Article 1–2–7

The requirement to hold the professional licence provided for in Articles 6 and 9 of Law No. 88–70 of 22 January 1988 is related to the field of activity of the person concerned, whatever such person's responsibilities may be in this field.

The list of functions to be performed within the SBF or its subsidiaries and requiring a professional licence is set out in an Implementing Regulation issued by the CBV.

The conditions for granting professional licences to the persons concerned are in accordance with the conditions provided for in Articles 2–2–2 to 2–2–6 of the present Regulations for persons under the authority of Bourse member firms or acting on their behalf.

Article 1–2–8

All activities exercised at the SBF or its subsidiaries and related to the operation of the markets are to be carried out with diligence, fairness, neutrality and impartiality.

These activites must be carried out in accordance with market integrity.

Article 1–2–9

Any person acting on behalf of the SBF or of any of its subsidiaries is bound by professional secrecy.

Article 1–2–10

Any person acting on behalf of the SBF and authorised to carry out market transactions for his own account may hold a securities account for carrying out such transactions only at an institution recognised by the SBF. Such recognition implies access by the SBF to any information concerning the relevant transactions and the issue by such institution of statements at required intervals.

Article 1–2–11

Market transactions effected on own account by any person acting in connection with his duties on behalf of the SBF or of any of its subsidiaries cannot be carried out under privileged conditions by comparison with the conditions under which the transactions of customers of Bourse member firms are effected. To this end, orders must be transmitted, executed and recorded in the books in a form and pursuant to rules allowing verification of the observance of the principles set forth in Article 1–2–8.

These provisions apply to transactions effected in connection with any account which can be activated by such person acting privately.

Article 1–2–12

The persons responsible for quotations or market supervision may not trade on their own account in connection with the securities for which they are responsible.

Article 1–2–13

The management of the SBF and of its subsidiaries ensures compliance with the rules set forth in Articles 1–2–8 to 1–2–12.

Article 1–2–14

The SBF establishes internal rules, including an ethical code of conduct applicable to its employees. These rules specify conditions for compliance with the principles set forth in Articles 1–2–8 to 1–2–13, and compliance with any other related rule issued by the CBV. The SBF may adopt additional restrictions with respect to the transactions effected on their own account by its employees.

Subsidiaries of the SBF who are involved in market operation are also subject to the same provisions.

Chapter 3
Association Française des Sociétés de Bourse (AFSB)

Article 1–3–1

An association is hereby created for the purpose of representing collectively Bourse member firms and the SBF, ensuring the defence of their rights and common interests, and preventing or attempting to resolve through conciliation any disputes that the Bourse member firms may have among themselves or with the SBF.

This association is named Association Française des Sociétés de Bourse (AFSB).

Chapter 4
Guarantee fund

Article 1–4–1

Pursuant to Article 6, as amended, of Law No. 88–70 of 22 January 1988, a guarantee fund is established, with the purpose of guaranteeing the commitments of Bourse member firms in favour of clients operating on markets placed under the authority of the CBV.

Article 1–4–2

Holders of accounts opened in their name with a Bourse member firm are covered by the guarantee.

The commitments covered by the guarantee concern the return of securities and cash deposited with Bourse member firms or due from them to their clients as a result of market trades. The guarantee that is applicable following market trades concerns the delivery of or payment for the securities or rights covered by an order placed under proper conditions.

The deposits of securities and cash covered by the guarantee are those made by clients with Bourse member firms in order to carry out market transactions, excluding all other categories of financial transactions. Securities, either French or foreign, including shares or units in collective investment schemes, which are placed in custody, are also covered by the guarantee. Deposits of precious metals are not covered by the guarantee.

Article 1–4–3

The intervention of the guarantee fund is subject to the SBF acknowledging that a Bourse member firm is in default, whatever the cause of the default may be.

Such intervention is published in a notice in the BOC, requesting clients of the defaulting Bourse member firm to file their claims with the SBF with respect to shortfalls in meeting their rights to the securities recorded in their accounts and their cash claims.

Requests for compensation are accepted during a period of three months from the date of publication of the above-mentioned notice.

Article 1–4–4

As soon as the SBF has issued its decision confirming the default of a Bourse member, the SBF has an inventory drawn up comparing on the one hand the actual assets in the form of securities in the custody of the Bourse member firm and on the other the rights of clients in terms of securities recorded in their accounts. In the event of a shortfall in such actual assets, the securities found are divided among the clients proportionately to their rights, and the accounts are released with respect to the securities available in this way.

The guarantee fund reconstitutes the missing rights in terms of securities by priority assignment of an amount equal to two-thirds of its intervention ceiling, with a maximum amount of 2.5 million French francs per account holder. To allow such reconstitution, the guarantee fund may provide its guarantee or advance funds or securities within the limits mentioned above. As the inventory is settled and the securities reconstituted, the release is extended to those securities.

Within the limit of the ceiling mentioned in Article 1-4-5, and to the extent of the amounts remaining available further to the commitment to reconstitute rights with respect to securities, the guarantee fund indemnifies cash claims up to a limit of 0.5 million French francs per account holder.

Article 1-4-5

The overall intervention of the guarantee fund resulting from the default of a Bourse member firm, as of the close of books at the end of the fifth month following publication of the notice provided for in Article 1-4-3, may not exceed 200 million French francs. The indemnity amounts provided for in Article 1-4-4 are reduced, if need be, in due proportion.

Should the fund's resources be insufficient given the required amount of indemnities, the CBV would call for an exceptional contribution from Bourse member firms and the SBF. The SBF contribution in such instance may not exceed 100 million French francs.

The CBV then determines the procedures for reconstituting the guarantee fund.

Article 1-4-6

The intervention of the guarantee fund entails its subrogation in the rights of the claimholders benefiting from the guarantee in connection with the defaulting Bourse member firm, up to the extent of the rights actually covered by the guarantee.

Article 1-4-7

All Bourse member firms contribute to the guarantee fund by means of contributions treated as a mandatory expenditure.

The regular or exceptional contribution of each Bourse member firm is set by a CBV decision, determining the rules for the base and the calculation of such due amounts. Such calculation may take into account, where applicable, not only the data relevant to the firm itself, but also data regarding affiliated companies, where the Bourse member firm may be exposed to a risk due to such companies which could affect the guarantee fund.

Article 1-4-8

The guarantee fund is established in the form of an association recognised by the CBV.

This association enjoys full ownership of the amounts paid in by Bourse member firms by way of the contributions provided for by Article 1-4-7. These amounts become the property of the guarantee fund as remuneration for the services it provides in guaranteeing the market.

The Bourse member firms have no entitlement to the fund. The association's articles exclude the Bourse member firms from membership of the association and from the benefit of any payments made by the association.

An Implementing Regulation issued by the CBV specifies the prudential rules to be observed in managing the available funds.

The board of the association is responsible for the choice of depositaries who are to hold the amounts deposited in the guarantee fund and for the terms of the instructions given to those depositaries or to third parties for the management of such funds. The board of the association monitors compliance with those instructions.

The board of the association shall rule with respect to the intervention of the guarantee fund, after examination by the SBF of all claims.

Title 2
Bourse member firms (Sociétés de Bourse)

Chapter 1
Authorisation and suspension of Bourse member firms

Article 2-1-1

The CBV grants authorisation to Bourse member firms.

The application for authorisation to be filed by a candidate Bourse member firm shall include the following:

- The firm's articles of association (*statuts*) and those of its subsidiaries, if any.
- The amount, composition and distribution of its capital, and of the capital of its subsidiaries, if any.
- The nature of the activities contemplated and plans, if any, for establishing branch offices abroad or for acquiring seats on foreign exchanges.
- A description of the business of shareholders in the firm holding more than 10% of the firm's capital, together, where applicable, with their latest published financial reports.
- Guarantees, if any, provided by the shareholders.
- The composition of the board of directors or other corporate organs, and, where applicable, of the firm's subsidiaries.
- A list of the firm's senior executives, and, where applicable, of those of its subsidiaries.
- A description of the firm's technical resources.
- A list of the firm's holdings representing more than 10% of the capital of the relevant companies.
- An undertaking to acquire shares in the capital of the SBF within the limits established by current regulations.
- A copy of the draft Bourse membership agreement initialled by the SBF, including the identification of any subcontractor to which the candidate Bourse member firm plans to entrust all or part of its responsibilities.

- An undertaking to request the CBV to authorise a compliance officer, responsible for ensuring observance of ethical standards and of prudential provisions.
- An undertaking to apply to the AFSB for membership.
- An undertaking to send the CBV a copy of the firm's internal regulations.
- An undertaking to abide by the provisions of the present Regulations.

The CBV may request any further information.

The CBV shall appraise the guarantees provided in the application for authorisation and notify the applicants of its decision, giving reasons in case of rejection.

The CBV reserves the right to limit the activities that it authorises a Bourse member firm and its subsidiaries to conduct, particularly in view of their technical and financial resources and of the guarantees provided.

Article 2-1-2

Any subsequent modification made to the elements filed with respect to the application for authorisation shall be notified to the SBF.

The following modifications are subject to the prior authorisation by the CBV:

- Modification of the Bourse member firm's legal form.
- Modification of the distribution of the Bourse member firm's capital or of the capital of one of its subsidiaries, where such modification is substantial by comparison with the situation covered by the previous authorisation and may have an effect on the control of the company or of its subsidiary.
- The appointment of the Chairman of the Bourse member firm's board of directors or supervisory board, or of a subsidiary engaging in financial market activities.

– The appointment of a senior executive of the Bourse member firm.
– The acquisition of a seat on a foreign exchange.

The CBV may delegate power to its Chairman to authorise such modifications.

Article 2–1–3

The CBV may limit the use of subcontracting in connection with trading.

Article 2–1–4

Should the CBV or its Chairman, by delegation, consider that the actions of a Bourse member firm are of such nature as to jeopardise market security or integrity, they may decide on total or partial suspension of the Bourse member firm.

The decision shall give the reasons for such suspension.

Article 2–1–5

The authorisation or the total or partial suspension of a Bourse member firm is published in the BOC.

Chapter 2
Issuance and withdrawal of professional licences

Article 2–2–1

The requirement to hold the professional licence provided for in Articles 6 and 9 of Law No. 88–70 of 22 January 1988 is related to the field of activity of the person concerned, whatever such person's responsibilities may be in this field.

The list of functions the performance of which within a Bourse member firm requires a professional licence is set out in an Implementing Regulation issued by the CBV.

Each Bourse member firm shall keep the SBF informed of the list of persons under its authority or acting on its behalf who perform functions requiring the holding of a professional licence. Any failure by a Bourse member firm to abide by the obligation for one or several of such persons to hold a professional licence may

result in a sanction being imposed on the Bourse member firm by the CBV, pursuant to the provisions of Article 8 of Law No. 88–70 of 22 January 1988 pertaining to stock exchanges.

Article 2–2–2

Any person responsible for functions requiring a professional licence under the terms of Article 2–2–1 is expressly notified of this fact.

Article 2–2–3

The professional licence is issued to persons mentioned in Article 2–2–1 upon decision by the CBV taken on the basis of applications submitted by a Bourse member firm and under such Bourse member firm's responsibility.

Prior to issuing a professional licence, the CBV reviews the level of the applicant's professional knowledge.

Any person receiving a professional licence, either for the first time or as a renewal, must acknowledge in writing the receipt thereof. A refusal to provide such acknowledgement prevents the person concerned from being allowed to perform the relevant functions.

Article 2–2–4

By means of an Implementing Regulation, the CBV sets the detailed conditions for issue of professional licences as well as the period of their validity.

Article 2–2–5

The CBV may entrust a committee with the organisation and holding of the examinations provided for in Article 2–2–3, as well as with issuing professional licences.

Article 2–2–6

Each Bourse member firm shall designate among its employees a compliance officer who reports directly to the firm's managing director.

This officer must be authorised by the CBV, and is accordingly issued a special professional licence.

The applicant proposed by the management of the Bourse member firm to carry out the duties of compliance officer, is required to take a professional aptitude examination. The characteristics of such examination are determined by the CBV.

The compliance officer is responsible for ensuring observance by the persons under the Bourse member firm's authority or acting on its behalf of their professional obligations and of applicable ethical standards. To this end, the compliance officer acts as such persons' principal adviser in connection with ethical issues, and as recipient of all the information that such persons must communicate under the regulations to which they are subject.

The management of a Bourse Member firm shall supply the compliance officer with the human and material resources required for carrying out his duties.

The CBV may withdraw its authorisation at any time. Its decision must give the reasons therefor, and both the person concerned and the Bourse member firm's management shall be notified of the decision.

The person authorised as the compliance officer for a Bourse member firm loses such authorisation when leaving such Bourse member firm.

Article 2-2-7

Any suspension or termination of the duties of holders of professional licences shall be notified to the SBF.

Chapter 3
Keeping client accounts – Portfolio management
(1) Opening an account

Article 2-3-1

Prior to opening an account in the name of an individual, a Bourse member firm must verify such individual's identity and address, and ensure that such person has the capacity and status required for carrying out all operations relating to asset management.

Before opening an account in the name of a legal entity, a Bourse member firm must verify the validity of the power of attorney held by the representative of such legal entity, either by virtue of such representative's status as authorised agent, or through a delegation held by him. To this end, the Bourse member firm shall request the filing of any document enabling it to verify the authority of the representative.

The Bourse member firm may ask individuals or legal entities subject to the legislation of a non-Member State of the European Economic Community to submit a legal opinion attesting the legality of the planned activities under such legislation.

(2) Information of the account holder

Article 2-3-2

The Bourse member firm shall inform its clients of the general conditions governing the transactions performed on their behalf, of the conditions governing the use of their account, of the cost of the various services provided, and of the mutual obligations of the Bourse member firm and its clients.

Such conditions and obligations shall be specified in an agreement executed between the Bourse member firm and each client. An Implementing Regulation issued by the CBV specifies those points that must be covered by such agreement.

Article 2-3-3

The Bourse member firm shall inform account holders of each transaction effected.

Furthermore, the Bourse member firm shall regularly send to each client an account statement indicating his securities and cash positions as well as his positions with respect to the futures and options markets. The frequency of such statements, which must be at least quarterly, as well as their contents are provided for by the agreement mentioned in Article 2-3-2.

(3) Discretionary management

Article 2-3-4

Any individual or legal entity may entrust a Bourse member firm, provided such firm so accepts, with a discretionary power to manage, on such person's behalf, portfolios comprised of securities or other financial instruments that such Bourse member firm is authorised to place or to trade , as well as shares or units in collective investment schemes.

The securities which may be traded in connection with a discretionary management agreement are French or foreign securities traded on a regulated market that operates regularly and is open to the public. The other financial instruments which may be traded in connection with a discretionary management agreement are negotiable debt instruments as well as the financial instruments traded on a market mentioned in the list laid down by ministerial order pursuant to the provisions of Articles 23 and 28 of Law No. 88–1201 of 23 December 1988.

Article 2-3-5

The authority for discretionary management of a portfolio entrusted to a Bourse member firm must be in writing, signed for approval by the holder of the managed account and for acceptance by the Bourse member firm. This document shall specify the nature of the transactions left to the discretion of the Bourse member firm, the conditions of account operation, and the terms of remuneration of the manager as agreed between the parties.

When the discretionary authority of management authorises the Bourse member firm to operate on the financial futures market, the traded options market or other derivatives markets, the contract shall mention the risks inherent in such markets and shall contain, in an appendix, the relevant information notices.

In the absence of agreement to the contrary, trades for monthly settlement must be settled at the expiry date, and may not be carried over.

Article 2-3-6

The discretionary management authority is drawn up in the name of the Bourse member firm. It is signed by a person authorised to commit the firm. No delegation of such authorisation is permitted with respect to signature of the discretionary management authority. Any stipulation to the contrary is deemed void.

Article 2-3-7

In addition to the information provided for in Article 2–3–3, the Bourse member firm shall send to its client, in accordance with the frequency provided for in the contract but at least four times a year, a statement showing the management results for the relevant period.

Article 2-3-8

The authority may be terminated at any time by either party by registered letter with acknowledgement of receipt. Termination by the Bourse member firm requires a minimum advance notice of five trading days, starting on the date of receipt of the termination letter.

Upon receiving such letter from the client, or as of the end of the advance notice period where the termination is required at the initiative of the Bourse member firm, and provided the acknowledgement of receipt has been received, the Bourse member firm ceases to be entitled to initiate new transactions.

The Bourse member firm shall close the books of the relevant client as of the date of receipt of the letter or of its acknowledgement of receipt, and on the same date draw up the documents provided for in Article 2–3–7. If the termination is at the Bourse member firm's initiative, the firm provides its client with all necessary explanations about the nature of the outstanding positions.

(4) Vigilance with respect to money-laundering transactions

Article 2-3-9

Every Bourse member firm must put in place such organisation and internal procedures so as to ensure compliance with the requirements for vigilance and information laid down in Law No. 90–614 of 12 July 1990 pertaining to the participation of financial institutions in the repression of drug traffic-related money-laundering, and by application of Decree No. 91–160 of 13 February 1991.

Such internal procedures shall be described in a written document submitted to the SBF.

Modifications made to such document shall also be reported to the SBF.

Article 2–3–10

Each Bourse member firm shall designate the person or persons among its staff responsible for verifying the implementation of the internal procedures mentioned in Article 2–3–9.

These persons, who must hold a professional licence as executive director or as compliance officer, shall in particular act as correspondent with the statutory and self-regulatory authorities in connection with such internal procedures. Their names shall be filed with the department mentioned in Article 5 of the Law of 12 July 1990, and with the SBF acting on behalf of the CBV.

Article 2–3–11

Notwithstanding any provisions creating more restrictive obligations, Bourse member firms must take all necessary measures to maintain for at least five years:

– all documents relating to their clients' identities, from the date of the closing of their accounts or from the date of the termination of their relationship with them;
– written records of the transactions performed on behalf of their clients, from the date of such performance.

When a Bourse member firm acting in accordance with Article 14 of the Law of 12 July 1990 records a transaction, such record is to be kept for five years, with appropriate procedures to ensure confidentiality, and must be promptly reported upon request to the department mentioned in Article 5 of the Law of 12

July 1990 and to the SBF acting on behalf of the CBV.

Article 2–3–12

Bourse member firms must ensure that their employees are properly informed and, where applicable, have been properly trained, so as to be aware of the measures expected from them in identifying money-laundering transactions.

Bourse member firms shall issue all necessary recommendations to their subsidiaries and foreign branches, for the use of appropriate means in order to counter the risk of being used for laundering purposes. The measures adopted as a result of such recommendations shall be reported to the respective Bourse member firms.

Chapter 4
Authorised agents
(1) General provisions

Article 2–4–1

With the exception on the one hand of persons authorised on a non-professional basis by account holders under the terms of an ordinary power of attorney, and on the other of credit institutions governed by Law No. 84–46 of 24 January 1984 pertaining to the activity and supervision of credit institutions, only the following may give orders on behalf of another person to a Bourse member firm:

– a portfolio management firm authorised by the COB, mandated by the account holder and acting in accordance with the provisions of the second section of the present Chapter;
– an order initiator other than a portfolio management firm, acting on behalf of the Bourse member firm in accordance with the provisions of the third section of the present Chapter.

Article 2–4–2

The conditions regarding the opening of accounts, described in Article 2–3–1 of the present Regulations, apply without limitation in circumstances where a third party intervenes. The Bourse member firm shall inform the account holder of the responsibilities incumbent on each of the parties.

The account holder and the portfolio management firm are notified by the Bourse member firm of transactions performed, and each receives all documents provided for in Article 2–3–3 of the present Regulations or in the account agreement between the account holder and the Bourse member firm.

The Bourse member firm sends the account holder and the portfolio management firm any margin call required by the applicable laws and regulations governing the markets on which the transactions have been initiated.

(2) Portfolio management firms

Article 2–4–3

Where an account holder at a Bourse member firm gives an agency to act on his behalf to a portfolio management firm authorised by the COB, the Bourse member firm is informed thereof by means of an attestation signed by both such account holder and such portfolio management firm.

Article 2–4–4

The Bourse member firm is not informed of the terms of the agency agreement between the account holder and the portfolio management firm.

In no event may such Bourse member firm be held liable for the non-compliance with such agency agreement of the orders received and performed.

Article 2–4–5

The termination of the agency by either of the parties shall be immediately notified to the Bourse member firm by the party initiating such termination, by means of a registered letter with acknowledgement of receipt.

Article 2–4–6

The provisions of the present Chapter apply without restriction where the portfolio management firm is a subsidiary of a Bourse member firm.

(3) Order initiators other than portfolio management firms

Article 2–4–7

Prior to the carrying out by a Bourse member firm of any order on behalf of an order initiator other than a portfolio management firm and prior to any remuneration of such order initiator by such Bourse member firm, the Bourse member firm and the order initiator must have executed a contract defining their relationship.

The remuneration provided for in the contract shall be determined on a basis compatible with professional ethical principles.

Article 2–4–8

The Bourse member firm shall be liable to the client for the transmission of the orders accepted by any order initiator which is not a portfolio management firm, and for the observance by such order initiator of the obligations to which it is subject. In this connection, the Bourse member firm is responsible for making sure the orders it executes are identical to the orders entrusted to the order initiator by the client.

Chapter 5
Prudential rules

Article 2–5–1

The CBV shall issue an Implementing Regulation laying down the minimum standards regarding shareholders' equity applicable to Bourse member firms.

Article 2–5–2

The CBV shall issue Implementing Regulations laying down the prudential rules applicable to Bourse member firms, particularly as regards their solvency, their liquidity, and the balance of their financial structure.

Such prudential rules apply to Bourse member firms as specific legal entities.

Such prudential rules apply to each Bourse member firm with respect to all of its activities, including that of principal trader and irrespective of which French exchanges it trades on.

Such rules also apply to any majority-held subsidiary of the Bourse member firm having the status of principal trading firm or falling within Law No. 84–46 of 24 January 1984, pertaining to the activity and supervision of credit institutions, on the basis of such subsidiary's net shareholders' equity.

Article 2–5–3

Each Bourse member firm is responsible for ensuring compliance with the rules issued by the CBV, and shall keep the SBF informed of changes in its situation with respect to such rules, under the conditions set forth in the corresponding Implementing Regulations.

In the event of non-compliance with any of these rules, and having taken into account the relevant information gathered by the SBF, the CBV may urge the Bourse member firm to take appropriate measures to re-establish compliance with such rules.

Should the Bourse member fail to re-establish compliance with such rules, the CBV shall decide on the sanctions to be taken, pursuant to the provisions of Article 8 of Law No. 88–70 of 22 January 1988, and in particular suspension of all or part of its activities.

Article 2–5–4

The SBF, by means of audits made at its discretion, monitors compliance by Bourse member firms with the relevant prudential rules as well as with such firms' information obligations towards the SBF.

Failure by a Bourse member firm to comply with such prudential rules or to properly inform the SBF may result in sanctions being imposed by the CBV, pursuant to the provisions of Article 8 of Law No. 88–70 of 22 January 1988, pertaining to stock exchanges.

Article 2–5–5

Compliance with the prudential rules set forth in the present General Regulations does not release the Bourse member firm or its subsidiaries mentioned in Article 2–5–2 from the duty of complying with any other rule issued by another competent authority, which rule might in any given circumstances be more stringent.

Article 2–5–6

The SBF is empowered to adopt any appropriate measures with respect to market security and to intervene, in this connection, *vis-à-vis* Bourse member firms and traders.

In particular, the SBF may limit a trader's positions in a given security, if the market situation with respect to that security so requires.

The SBF shall indicate the reasons supporting any such decision and report thereon to the CBV.

Chapter 6
Ethical rules

Article 2–6–1

All activities that Bourse member firms are authorised to conduct and which they perform either directly or through their subsidiaries are to be carried out with diligence, fairness, neutrality and impartiality.

In performing such activities, Bourse member firms must give priority to their clients' interests while respecting the market's integrity.

The organisation of Bourse member firms and of their subsidiaries must allow fulfilment of these requirements.

The application of the provisions of the present Chapter extends to companies a majority of whose capital is held by two or more Bourse member firms.

(1) Measures relating to Bourse member firms

Article 2–6–2

Bourse member firms determine and adopt legal, personnel and technical structures allowing for the respect of the principles set forth in Article 2–6–1, in particular where functions are performed that could give rise to conflicts of interest.

To this end, the functions of trader, authorised agent and principal trader are to be carried out in accordance with rules and procedures designed to ensure their independence.

Article 2-6-3

Bourse member firms and their subsidiaries shall make their best efforts to determine their clients' expectations and to supply them with clear, rapid and complete information concerning the transactions performed for their account.

Bourse member firms and their subsidiaries shall ensure that their clients are informed of the risks inherent in the nature of the transactions that they contemplate.

(2) Measures relating to individuals

Article 2-6-4

Any person acting on behalf of a Bourse member firm or of any of its subsidiaries, whether party to an employment contract or not, must observe professional secrecy.

Article 2-6-5

Any person acting on behalf of a Bourse member firm or of any of its subsidiaries, whether or not party to an employment contract, and authorised to execute market transactions on his own account may hold a securities account to carry out such transactions only at an institution approved by such Bourse member firm. Such approval implies that such institution shall issue account statements at the required intervals, and that such Bourse member firm shall have access to any information concerning the relevant transactions.

Article 2-6-6

Market transactions performed by any person on his own account and acting in connection with his duties on behalf of a Bourse member firm or of any of its subsidiaries may not be performed under privileged conditions by comparison with the conditions under which customer transactions are performed. To this end, orders must be transmitted, carried out and recorded in the books in a form and pursuant to rules allowing verification of compliance with the principles set forth in Article 2-6-1.

These provisions apply to transactions performed on any account which can be activated by such person acting privately.

Article 2-6-7

The persons responsible for a trading function may not operate on their own account in connection with securities for which they are responsible.

Article 2-6-8

The executives of Bourse member firms shall ensure compliance with the rules set forth in Articles 2-6-1 to 2-6-7.

They shall inform the SBF of any disciplinary sanctions taken against an employee of the firm for non-observance of his professional obligations. The identity of the sanctioned person and the reasons for the sanction shall be disclosed.

Article 2-6-9

The CBV may decide to adopt further rules binding on all Bourse member firms and on persons acting on their behalf or on behalf of their subsidiaries, whether or not such persons are party to an employment contract, in addition to the provisions decided by each Bourse member firm within the framework of its internal regulations.

Title 3
Admission to listing and delisting

Chapter 1
Admission of securities

Article 3–1–1

Except in the case of French Treasury bonds, which are automatically admitted to the Official List, applications for admission of securities to the Official List or the Second Market shall be submitted to the CBV through an approved intermediary appointed by the issuer thereof to handle the admission procedure.

The SBF examines applications for listing and prepares a report for the CBV.

Article 3–1–2

The entity applying for listing of its securities undertakes:

– to address a copy of the minutes of each annual and extraordinary meeting of shareholders to the CBV, translated into French where applicable;
– to inform the CBV of any changes to its articles of association and of any decisions pertaining to its securities;
– to obtain approval from the CBV for dates of issue and subscription regarding any financial transaction with pre-emptive or priority subscription rights;
– to inform the CBV of any event affecting its assets, financial position or business and which may materially affect significantly the price of its securities;
– to provide the CBV with copies of all announcements, press releases and other publications emanating from the issuer, as well as with copies of all documents that it may publish containing information of a financial or economic nature;
– to make provision for administrative services relating to its securities, in particular payment of dividends or interest, at the place of listing and at no cost to holders of securities, as well as to inform the CBV of any change in the identity of the entities appointed to act as paying agent;

– where the securities are listed abroad, to provide the CBV with the same level of information as is provided to the authorities of the relevant foreign markets.

The applicant also undertakes to abide by all regulations issued by the COB relating to investor protection and information.

Article 3–1–3

The SBF is entitled to require further information from the issuer at its discretion.

Article 3–1–4

Admission of a security to the Official List or Second Market is subject to the conditions of the present Regulations.

Should however the CBV judge this to be in the interest of the market or of investors, it may make admission subject to particular conditions which it notifies to the applicant issuer.

The CBV may reject a listing application if it considers admission to be contrary to the interests of the market and investors.

Article 3–1–5

The CBV may on its own initiative decide to admit a security to the Official List.

It may decide to admit to the Official List or the Second Market securities having the same characteristics as securities already listed and for which no application for listing has been made, unless satisfactory reasons are given for not admitting them.

Article 3–1–6

The CBV sets down conditions for the quotation and trading of newly listed securities.

Article 3–1–7

The CBV informs applicants of its decision regarding admission within six months after receipt of the application or, in the event further information has been requested within this period, within six months of receiving this information.

If no decision is made within six months, the application is deemed to have been refused.

The admission decision of the CBV remains valid for three months. At the issuer's request, this validity can be extended, unless the COB opposes such extension.

Article 3–1–8

Admission to listing is announced in the form of an official notice issued by the CBV, specifying the market on which the security is to be listed, the conditions under which it is to be traded, the date on which it will first be quoted, and the procedure to be followed for initial quotation.

Article 3–1–9

A security not listed on the Official List or on the Second Market may be traded on the *hors-cote* market; the first such trade is made at the initiative of the Bourse member firm having received the corresponding order.

An offer or bid price must be published in the daily statement of *hors-cote* transactions for a minimum length of time set by the SBF before the first quotation may take place.

(1) Admission to the Official List of equity securities issued by French companies

Article 3–1–10

Equity securities are deemed to include ordinary and preferred shares, preferred dividend shares with or without voting rights, non-voting investment certificates (*certificats d'investissement*), depository receipts for shares and warrants for the subscription of equity securities.

Equity warrants may not be admitted to the Official List unless the underlying equity has itself been quoted on the Official List or on the Second Market for at least six months.

Article 3–1–11

Except with the approval of the CBV, the company must have published or filed its annual financial statements for the three fiscal years preceding its application and have had its financial statements for the two preceding fiscal years certified by statutory auditors.

If the last fiscal year closed more than nine months prior to the date of admission, the financial statements for the preceding half-year must also have been so certified.

Article 3–1–12

The CBV shall be informed of any transfer of securities during the year preceding initial listing thereof, and may require that they be temporarily withheld from trading.

Article 3–1–13

The same rights are attached to all equity securities for which listing has been requested and which are of the same class. Their sale may not be subject to any approval clause. Company articles may confer double voting rights on shares held in registered form and in the same name for a given minimum period, at most four years.

Admission shall be requested for all equity securities of the same class that have been issued. Unless the CBV decides otherwise, any issue of securities of the same class as those already listed must be the object of a listing application.

The preceding paragraph does not apply to securities which are non-negotiable pursuant to a legal provision.

Article 3–1–14

Except with the approval of the CBV, admission to the Official List is conditional on shares representing at least 25% of the company's issued capital being held by the public on the first day of listing at the latest.

(2) Admission to the Official List of debt securities issued by French entities

Article 3-1-15

Debt securities are deemed to include bonds, convertible bonds, bonds which may be exchanged for or redeemed in equity, bonds with warrants attached, perpetual participating notes (*titres participatifs*), subordinated bonds or warrants entitling the holder to debt securities.

All debt securities issued in France by French entities are subject to the present Regulations regardless of the currency in which they are denominated.

Article 3-1-16

Except with the approval of the CBV, securities entitling their holders to a portion of a company's equity may be admitted to the Official List only if the related equity securities have been admitted to the Official List or the Second Market.

In any event, the issuer shall undertake to apply for the admission of the relevant equity securities to the Official List or to the Second Market prior to the time when such entitlement becomes effective.

Article 3-1-17

The issuer's financial statements for the two last fiscal years must have been certified by its statutory auditors.

Article 3-1-18

The CBV may require that an application for admission to the Official List be accompanied by a rating for the issue, produced by an agency recognised by the CBV.

It may also require the issue of a guarantee for principal and interest.

Article 3-1-19

The application concerns all debt instruments belonging to the same issue.

Article 3-1-20

The amount of the issue must be at least equal to 100 million French francs.

(3) Admission to the Official List of securities issued by foreign entities – Equity securities – Debt securities issued in France

Article 3-1-21

Securities issued by entities subject to the law of a State which is not a member of the Organisation for Economic Co-operation and Development may only be listed in France with the prior authorisation of the French Economy Minister.

Article 3-1-22

The admission to the Official List of a security issued by an entity subject to the law of a State which is not a member of the European Economic Community may be made conditional on the security's prior admission to another stock exchange.

Article 3-1-23

Except with the approval of the CBV, the company must have published or filed its financial statements for the three fiscal years preceding the application for admission, and have had its financial statements for the two preceding fiscal years certified by statutory auditors.

If the last fiscal year closed more than nine months before the date of application, the financial statements for the prior half-year must also have been so certified.

The French translation of the financial statements and notes shall be verified by a firm of statutory auditors registered as such in France.

Article 3-1-24

A portion of securities admitted to the Official List must be held by the public, either before admission or at the latest on admission. Such holdings by the public must ensure the existence of a regular market and regular quotation of the securities.

(4) Admission to the Official List of securities issued outside France

Article 3-1-25

Application for admission to the Official List of securities issued outside France

231

must include an undertaking by the issuer certifying that the issue shall not be or has not been publicly offered for subscription in France.

This undertaking is given in a letter to the CBV.

Article 3-1-26

Except with the approval of the CBV, securities giving entitlement to a portion of a company's equity may not be admitted to the Official List unless the related equity securities are listed on a stock exchange.

(5) Admission of securities to the Second Market

Article 3-1-27

The following securities may be listed on the Second Market:

- equity securities issued by French companies, including ordinary and preferred shares, preferred dividend shares with or without voting rights, investment certificates (*certificats d'investissement*), depository receipts for shares and warrants for the subscription of equity securities which have been listed on the Second Market for more than six months;
- bonds issued by companies whose equity securities are already listed on the Second Market;
- convertible bonds or bonds with equity warrants attached, issued by a company whose equity securities are not listed on the Second Market provided the issuing company undertakes to apply for listing of the corresponding equity securities before the beginning of the conversion or subscription period;
- perpetual participating notes (*titres participatifs*) issued by co-operatives subject to the Law of 10 September 1947, provided that the issue amounts to at least 15 million French francs;
- equity securities issued by foreign companies, admission being however conditional on ministerial authorisation for companies incorporated in States which are not members of the OECD.

Article 3-1-28

In addition to the undertakings referred to in Article 3-1-2, the entity applying for admission of its securities to the Second Maket also undertakes to bring its accounting and statutory auditing procedures into compliance with the standards set by the COB within three years from the date of initial listing.

The applicant also undertakes, if applicable, to publish consolidated accounts no later than three years after the date of initial listing.

Article 3-1-29

Except with the approval of the CBV, the issuer must have published or filed its financial statements, certified by statutory auditors, for the two fiscal years preceding application for admission to the Second Market.

Article 3-1-30

The CBV shall be informed of any transfer of securities during the year preceding initial listing thereof, and it may require that they be temporarily withheld from trading.

Article 3-1-31

Admission to the Second Market requires a minimum number of securities being held by the public. Except with the approval of the CBV, the company must show proof of the following:

- either that at least 10% of its issued capital is already held by the public or will be so held following a financial transaction undertaken at the time of listing on the Second Market; or
- that one or more shareholders have entrusted the approved intermediaries in charge of the initial listing with the task of making this minimum percentage of its capital available to the market, either acting on behalf of these shareholders themselves or following an underwriting transaction.

The provisions of Article 3-1-13 apply to equity securities admitted to the Second Market.

Article 3–1–32

The intermediaries appointed by the issuer to handle the admission procedure are responsible for the placement and initial quotation procedures.

Article 3–1–33

At the end of a three-year period, the SBF, together with the issuer and its intermediaries, reviews the following items:

– the quality of information provided to investors;
– accounting and statutory auditing procedures;
– the degree to which the security is in public hands and to which a market for it exists, the market criteria being frequence of quotation and trading volume.

In the light of this review, the SBF may recommend to the CBV that the security remain listed on the Second Market, or be removed from this list and transferred to the *hors-cote* market, or be admitted to the Official List if the issuer so requests and the required conditions for such listing are met.

(6) Admission to the Official List of units of debt securitisation funds (*fond commun de créances*)

Article 3–1–34

Application for admission to the Official List shall concern all units of the debt securitisation fund belonging to the same issue and publicly placed.

Article 3–1–35

At the date of application, the remaining life of the issue of units of the debt securitisation fund shall be at least one year.

Article 3–1–36

The amount of the issue for which admission to the Official List is requested shall be at least 100 million French francs.

Chapter 2
Procedures for placement and initial quotation

Article 3–2–1

Initial quotations on the Official List or on the Second Market are announced by means of an official notice published by the SBF describing in particular the procedure to be used for the initial quotation of securities admitted to trading and any related operations.

Article 3–2–2

Securities are traded on the *hors-cote* market under the supervision of the SBF, at the initiative of and under the responsibility of the Bourse member firm entrusted with trading the security.

(1) Placement procedures

Article 3–2–3

The public placement of securities admitted to trading can be realised, in whole or in part, concurrently with their first quotation on the market or during the immediately preceding period.

Article 3–2–4

With the approval of the CBV, the placement of securities during the period immediately preceding their initial quotation may be made through an underwriting transaction by one or more entities legally authorised to do so.

Article 3–2–5

The CBV may allow a placement to be effected partly under the procedure described in the preceding article, the securities being proposed to one or more categories of investors, provided that the main placement procedure be the offer for sale procedure described in Articles 3–2–14 *et seq.* and provided also that the aforementioned securities represent at least 20% of the capital of the relevant company or an amount of 500 million French francs.

In such an event, the placement of the securities shall be made at a price at least

233

equal to the price which has been fixed for the offer for sale.

Article 3–2–6

The lead manager for the placement transactions referred to in Articles 3–2–4 and 3–2–5 shall transmit to the SBF a statement detailing the results of the placement, which are then published by the SBF in a notice.

(2) Initial quotation procedures

Article 3–2–7

The initial quotation of securities on the Official List or the Second Market is effected through one of the the following three procedures: the auction procedure with a minimum price (*procédure de mise en vente*), the offer for sale procedure with a predetermined price (*procédure d'offre publique de vente*) and the ordinary procedure (*procédure ordinaire d'introduction*).

(a) Common provisions

Article 3–2–8

The initial quotation of securities admitted to the Official List or to the Second Market is announced in a notice issued by the SBF which discloses the name of the issuer and of the intermediaries entrusted with the listing and quotation procedures, the number, type and characteristics of the admitted securities, the price stipulated by the issuer or by the sellers, the procedure selected for the initial quotation and, generally, all details necessary for the proper information of the public.

This notice is published at least two trading days before the date set for the initial quotation.

Article 3–2–9

Unless otherwise stated in the notice referred to in Article 3–2–8, those purchase orders which are not filled on the first day of trading and which include no specified time limit, are considered valid until the end of the current calendar month unless cancelled before then.

Article 3–2–10

Whatever the procedure followed, the SBF is entitled to require that persons placing purchase orders lodge a sufficient deposit with the intermediary with whom their orders have been placed. The SBF fixes the percentage of the orders represented by this deposit and the length of time during which such funds are to remain blocked. The SBF may also require to receive directly such deposits from the intermediaries. The SBF fixes the minimum period for the deposit or the unavailability of such funds.

Should the SBF, in the light of the number of purchase orders received, deem that the rules for the selected initial listing procedure would lead to the quotation of a price abnormally exceeding the offer price or to an excessive scaling down of purchase orders, it shall postpone the initial quotation date. In a notice, the SBF shall announce the new date and, where applicable, the selected initial quotation procedure and the new conditions for carrying out such quotation. Notwithstanding Article 3–2–9, all purchase orders must in such case be renewed.

Article 3–2–11

The results of the initial listing procedure are published in a notice issued by the SBF, stating in particular the quoted price or the indicative price recorded, the number of securities traded and the conditions governing trading on the following days.

(b) The auction procedure with a minimum price

Article 3–2–12

The official notice by the SBF of a new listing under the auction procedure (*mise en vente*) states the number of securities to be made available to the market by those seeking the new listing – shareholders and management of the issuer, financial intermediaries – as well as the minimum offer price at which they are prepared to sell. This notice must be published at least five trading days before the date set for initial quotation.

Those seeking the new listing may, with the approval of the SBF, reserve the right to modify the minimum offer price initially stipulated, provided such possibility was mentioned in the listing notice and that the final offer price be published at least two trading days prior to the date set for the initial quotation. These new terms are announced in a notice published by the SBF which describes the conditions governing the confirmation of outstanding purchase orders.

Article 3–2–13

To effect an auction, the SBF centralises purchase orders sent to it by Bourse member firms. It may accept only limit orders, and may exclude those orders at a limit which it considers abnormally higher than the minimum offer price.

The SBF may divide the securities offered on the market into several lots and assign each lot to accepted bids by order of limits set; original orders may be scaled down if market conditions so require.

The initial price quoted is the limit set on the last order met. There is only one price on the first day of quotation.

(c) The offer for sale procedure with a predetermined price

Article 3–2–14

The official notice by the SBF of a new listing by offer for sale (*offre publique de vente*) is generally made at least five trading days before the date set for initial quotation and states the number of securities to be placed on the market by those seeking the new listing and the price at which they are to be offered.

Those seeking the new listing may, with the approval of the SBF, reserve the right to modify the offer price initially stipulated, provided such possibility was mentioned in the listing notice and that the final offer price be published at least two trading days prior to the date set for the initial quotation. These new terms are announced in a notice published by the SBF which describes the conditions

governing the confirmation of outstanding purchase orders.

Article 3–2–15

On the day set for the offer for sale, the SBF centralises the purchase orders sent to it by Bourse member firms. Only orders placed at the offer price are accepted. If the conditions of the offer are met, the price quoted is the offer price.

Article 3–2–16

With the approval of the CBV, those seeking the new listing may divide the purchase orders tendered in connection with the offer for sale into several different categories.

Such categories may be defined according to the number of securities requested and to the type of investor originating the order.

A notice published by the SBF sets out the eligibility criteria for acceptance of purchase orders by financial intermediaries. This notice also describes the conditions governing the transmission of such orders to the SBF as well as the level of detailed information on the identity of order originators which the SBF may require from the financial intermediaries. Furthermore, the notice describes the criteria used by the SBF for, on the one hand closing the order book, and on the other, allocating the securities offered amongst those placing orders, either according to a straight proportional formula or by according preferential treatment to smaller orders.

(d) The ordinary procedure

Article 3–2–17

The initial quotation of securities using the ordinary introduction procedure (*procédure ordinaire d'introduction*) is carried out under the usual conditions for trading and quotation on the market.

With the approval of the SBF, and for the initial quotation of equity securities, the ordinary procedure may allow that a stated number of the securities offered be sold on the market on the date of initial

235

quotation on behalf of the selling shareholders or of the underwriters.

Notice of a new listing is published at least two trading days before the date set for the initial quotation and states the number of securities to be placed on the market by those seeking the new listing and the minimum price at which they are to be sold. The notice also describes the conditions governing the centralisation of orders by the SBF as well as the maximum price variation that it is prepared to authorise in light of market conditions, where necessary through a scaling down of orders.

Chapter 3
Delisting of securities

Article 3-3-1

At the request of the issuer or on its own initiative, and on the basis of a report from the SBF, the CBV may remove a security from the Official List or the Second Market.

The delisting decision is notified to the issuer unless the COB opposes such notification.

Article 3-3-2

The removal of a security from the Official List or the Second Market is announced in a notice issued by the CBV stating the date on which such delisting takes effect.

Article 3-3-3

The CBV may decide to remove equity securities issued by a French entity from the Official List on the basis of the following criteria:

– average daily trading volume expressed in French francs and number of shares, together with the number of trading days per year that the shares have been quoted;
– payment of dividends over the three preceding fiscal years;
– the percentage of capital held by the public;

– fulfilment of disclosure undertakings given either on first listing or at the time of more recent financial transactions;
– compliance with the terms of the present Regulations.

Article 3-3-4

The CBV may decide to remove securities issued by a foreign entity from the Official List on the basis of the following criteria:

– average daily trading volume expressed in French francs and number of securities, together with the number of trading days per year that the securities have been quoted;
– market capitalisation in French francs of the securities held through SICOVAM, as well as the number of such securities;
– fulfilment of disclosure undertakings given either on first listing or at the time of more recent financial transactions;
– compliance with the terms of the present Regulations.

Article 3-3-5

Threshold levels used as criteria for delisting are set by the CBV, different levels applying to securities listed on the Paris Bourse and those listed on regional Bourses.

These levels are revised periodically. Revisions are announced in a notice published by the CBV.

Article 3-3-6

Unless the CBV decides otherwise, delisting of a given equity security automatically entails the delisting of all other securities defined in reference to that security, such as convertible bonds, bonds exchangeable for or redeemable in equity securities, or warrants relating to any of these securities.

Article 3-3-7

Unless the CBV decides otherwise, debt securities issued by French entities shall remain on the Official List until final redemption.

Article 3–3–8

On the first day of each month, securities appearing on the daily statement of the *hors-cote* market for which no price has been quoted and no indication of bid or offer price given during the preceding month, are removed from this statement.

Title 4

The markets

Chapter 1
General rules

Article 4–1–1

The market for securities admitted to the Official List or the Second Market, or traded on the *hors-cote* market, as well as the market for traded options on certain securities and stock market indices, known as the MONEP, are organised under the authority of the CBV.

The conditions for processing orders and trading securities are defined by Implementing Regulations issued by the CBV.

Article 4–1–2

Each security is attributed to a given exchange.

That exchange is designated by the CBV, at the request of the issuing entity.

Article 4–1–3

Trading of securities is generally conducted on a computerised system.

Exceptionally, and where the SBF so decides, trading in a security may be conducted by open outcry or by written procedures.

Any modification made in the trading procedures for a given security is announced in a notice published in the BOC.

Article 4–1–4

Transacted prices result from matching during the trading session of purchase orders and sell orders on the market presented by Bourse member firms, under the supervision of the SBF.

Orders are produced on the market without prior netting of purchase and sell orders.

Article 4–1–5

For each security admitted to the Official List or to the Second Market, the CBV designates a Bourse member firm to act as specialist, on the basis of a proposal made by the issuing entity.

The Bourse member firm acting as specialist for an issue is responsible for monitoring quotations thereon and on the related secondary issues (rights, warrants, new shares, convertible bonds, etc.).

The specialist for a security traded on the cash settlement market of the Official List or on the Second Market is responsible for stabilising the market for the security by means of principal transactions, under the conditions set forth in Title 6, Chapter 4, of the present Regulations.

The CBV may withdraw from a Bourse member firm its status as specialist in one or several securities.

Article 4–1–6

Depending on market conditions for a given security, the SBF may decide to publish only a bid or offer price for the security, without any transactions taking place.

If the applicable trading procedure so allows, the SBF may agree to the fixing of a single price, with a proportional reduction on the purchasing or selling side of orders eligible for execution.

Article 4–1–7

By means of an Implementing Regulation, the CBV determines the maximum price variations allowed by the SBF, depending on the type of securities and the applicable trading procedures, as well as the measures which the SBF is empowered to adopt in the event such variations occur.

Article 4–1–8

By means of a delegation from the CBV, the SBF may suspend trading in one or several securities, as well as trading in one or several series of traded options on the MONEP.

In particular, the SBF may suspend trading in one or several series of traded options on a stock market index when information relative to said index is unavailable, or when quotations on futures contracts on the same index are suspended. A co-ordinated suspension measure may also be applied to quotations on the component securities of said index.

Any suspension of quotations is reported in a notice published in the BOC.

Article 4–1–9

Before the end of every year, the CBV decides on the days on which French Stock Exchanges are to be open during the next year.

The opening and closing times of the trading sessions are set by the SBF.

These decisions are reported in notices published in the BOC.

Article 4–1–10

The SBF determines the format and headings of the BOC.

The BOC reports the first and last prices, as well as the highest and lowest prices transacted for each security during the day's trading session.

No corrections may be made after publication of the BOC, except for omitted or cancelled prices and in respect of errors.

The BOC includes a daily report on the *hors-cote* market, containing information relative to the securities traded thereon, about which the SBF has been informed either by the issuing entities, the paying agents, or the Bourse member firms centralising the market.

Chapter 2
The securities markets

Article 4–2–1

The Official List consists of a cash settlement market and a monthly settlement market. A given security is traded either on the cash settlement market or on the monthly settlement market. The CBV decides on the market on which each security is to be traded.

The Second Market and the *hors-cote* market are also cash settlement markets.

1) The cash settlement markets

Article 4–2–2

On a cash market, the buyer is accountable for the funds and the seller for the securities as soon as the order is executed.

Article 4–2–3

On a cash market, the unit of trading is one security, unless otherwise decided by the SBF.

Article 4–2–4

On the *hors-cote* market, for securities in which the latest transaction occured more than three months previously, a bid or offer price is published at least one day before a trade can take place.

2) Monthly settlement market

Article 4–2–5

On the monthly settlement market, the buyer is irrevocably committed at the time of execution of the order to pay the price of the securities to which he will receive title only when such securities are registered in his account, *i.e.* at the end of the month, provided however that the corresponding position has been closed out and not carried over; the seller is irrevocably committed at the time of execution of the order to deliver the securities to which he retains title until the end of the month, provided however that such securities be in his account.

Article 4–2–6

Except as otherwise provided by Articles 4–2–10 and 4–2–11, the payments and deliveries described in Article 4–2–5 take place within the framework of the monthly settlement schedule in accordance with the provisions of Article 4–2–7.

Article 4–2–7

Transactions on the monthly settlement market are settled on the last trading day of the month.

On the first day of the settlement schedule, which is also the last trading day of the current account, known as expiration day, a general netting is made of all trades entailing monthly settlement.

On the second day of the settlement schedule, which is also the first trading day of the new account, the monthly settlement positions in the current account may be carried over into the new account.

Article 4–2–8

The monthly settlement schedule is determined by the SBF and is published in the BOC before the beginning of every year.

During the year, the SBF may modify the settlement schedule. Any such modification is published in the BOC.

Article 4–2–9

Unless otherwise provided for by the SBF, the securities on the monthly settlement market are traded by round lots and in multiples of such lots.

The SBF determines the round lot for each of the securities traded on the monthly settlement market.

Article 4–2–10

Orders for a number of securities that is less than the round lot are executed for immediate settlement by a Bourse member firm acting as principal and remunerated therefor by a specific fee.

Article 4–2–11

A client whose order is for one or more round lots of securities may stipulate that execution of the order shall be for immediate settlement, a specific charge being made for such service.

Bourse member firms may decline execution for immediate settlement of purchase orders.

Article 4–2–12

By means of a decision published in the BOC, the SBF may suspend with respect to one or several securities the option of electing immediate settlement.

Furthermore, the SBF may suspend, until a given date and at the latest until the date scheduled for deliveries of the closest monthly settlement, any deliveries following purchases stipulated as being for immediate settlement in respect of one or several securities.

Article 4–2–13

The buyer or the seller of securities traded on the monthly settlement market who has not closed out, in whole or in part, his position before the expiration day by means of an offsetting transaction, must either pay the funds in the case of a purchase or deliver the securities in the case of a sale, or carry over his outstanding cash or securities position.

Article 4–2–14

Carryover is the option granted to a holder of a monthly settlement position to postpone execution of his commitment from one account to the following account. A buyer who carries over his position sells at the end of the current account and at the settlement price the securities he has acquired and undertakes to repurchase them at the same price at the end of the following account. A seller who carries over his position buys at the end of the current account at the settlement price the securities he has sold and undertakes to resell them at the same price at the end of the following account.

The settlement price is determined by the SBF and is published in the BOC. Except in special circumstances, this price is equal to the first price, rounded off, quoted on the first day of the settlement schedule.

Article 4–2–15

For each security, the positions carried over on the purchase and sell sides are compared on the carryover (contango) market, between Bourse member firms, under the supervision of the SBF.

From this comparison arise the rates of intervention by providers of funds and securities. These rates are published in the BOC.

Chapter 3
The traded options market (the MONEP)
(1) Definitions

Article 4–3–1

All traded options of the same type (American or European) with the same range of maturity (short or long term) and relating to the same instrument constitute a class of traded options. The underlying instrument may be a given security, or an index on securities.

An option is said to be of the American type when the buyer may exercise it at any time until expiration.

An option is said to be of the European type when the buyer may exercise it only at the expiration date.

The CBV decides on the creation and cancellation of a class of traded options. Its decision is published in the BOC.

Article 4–3–2

All traded options of one and the same class with identical standard specifications constitute a series of interchangeable traded options. The standard specifications of the series of traded options are: the amount of the underlying instrument covered by the option, the nature of the option (call or put), the strike price, and the date of expiration.

Each series of traded options gives rise to a traded price, known as the premium.

Creation and cancellation of series of traded options as well as all modifica-

tions of the standard specifications of the existing options series are published in the BOC.

Article 4–3–3

The expiration dates, the standard intervals separating the strike prices of two series of traded options (depending on the unit value of the underlying instrument) and the conditions for creating series characterised by a new strike price (depending on changes in price of the underlying instrument) are determined by an Implementing Regulation issued by the CBV.

(2) The SCMC and market participants

Article 4–3–4

The SCMC (*Société de Compensation des Marchés Conditionnels*), constituted by the SBF, is entrusted by the latter, by means of a general delegation and under its supervision, with the following tasks:

– ensuring the operation and supervision of the traded options market, on which it may order the halt of trading in one or several series;
– recording all transactions in traded options on a given security or on an index of securities;
– ensuring clearing of transactions between clearing members, as well as the processing of exercises and assignments.

Article 4–3–5

By agreement with the SCMC, Bourse member firms are trading members and/or clearing members.

The SBF may allow intermediaries who collect orders but are not MONEP trading members to become clearing members. By agreement with the SCMC, such intermediaries then directly hold clearing accounts and undertake to comply with all provisions of the present Regulations.

Article 4–3–6

The SBF and the SCMC are empowered to carry out all monitoring operations at

MONEP trading and/or clearing members, and to obtain all required documents from them, including those relating to the identities of the clients.

(3) Closing out a position – Exercising an option

Article 4–3–7

A client holding an open long or short position in a series of traded options may close out that position at any time up to the last trading day for the series by re-selling or repurchasing the relevant contracts on the market.

When he buys or sells a traded option, the client must inform the Bourse member firm responsible for effecting the trade as to whether the trade has the effect of opening or of increasing a position, or of closing it, in whole or in part.

An open position in traded options may be closed out only through the intermediary through which the transaction opening such position was recorded.

Article 4–3–8

A holder of a buy position in traded options may exercise his option at the expiration date, in the case of European options, and may do so at any time until the expiration date in the case of American options, even if trading is halted on the series in question. To that end, he gives exercise instructions to the intermediary with whom the transaction opening such position is recorded.

This exercise has the effect of closing the client's long position.

The assigned account is determined at random from among the accounts of the clearing members holding an open short position in the same series of traded options.

An assigned order-collecting intermediary, in turn, designates at random those among his clients to be assigned.

Article 4–3–9

Any option on a security that is exercised or assigned is automatically converted into a trade in the underlying instrument, either on the monthly settlement market or on the cash settlement market, depending on the market on which said security is traded, in the corresponding amount of securities and at the option strike price. Such a trade cannot be stipulated for immediate settlement when the security is traded on the monthly settlement market.

The option buyer becomes either a buyer, in the case of a call, or a seller in the case of a put, of the underlying security. The option seller become either a seller, in the case of a call, or a buyer in the case of a put, of the underlying security.

The conditions regarding delivery of the underlying securities and payment of the funds are set forth in Title 8 of the present Regulations, following trades on the cash settlement market or on the monthly settlement market, depending on the market on which the underlying instrument is traded. Only exercise instructions transmitted to the clearing house by the day immediately preceding the last trading day of the current account period, give rise to settlement and delivery within the framework of the current account.

Article 4–3–10

As an exception to the rule set forth in the previous Article and if circumstances so require, the SBF may decide that the exercise and assignment of traded options on a given security shall give rise to a cash settlement of the difference between the option strike price and the price of the underlying instrument.

This decision is reported in a notice published in the BOC, which shall state the conditions thereof.

Article 4–3–11

The exercise and assignment of a stock index option have the effect of attributing, to the exercising buyer and to the assigned seller, an amount in cash corresponding to the difference between the value of the settlement index or the value of the liquidation index and the option strike price.

The value of the settlement index is determined daily, while the value of the liquidation index is determined on the day the options expire.

(4) Trading in options

Article 4–3–12

Trading in options is carried out either by open outcry, or on a computerised system, or using a combined trading procedure.

The SCMC decides on the trading procedure or procedures to be applied to each options class, and publishes a relevant notice in the BOC.

Article 4–3–13

All orders are produced on the market without prior netting, under the supervision of the SCMC representative, who is also empowered to execute orders on behalf of an intermediary.

Article 4–3–14

Trading in a series of options that are expiring ceases in accordance with the schedule and under the conditions published in the BOC.

Expiration may be deferred, if circumstances so require.

Article 4–3–15

Price variations are recorded according to market supply and demand, no price limits being applicable either with reference to the previous day's closing price or with reference to the preceding transaction price.

Article 4–3–16

Only Bourse member firms and principal-trading fims in which Bourse member firms hold a majority of the voting rights are entitled to engage in market-making activities, which consist in carrying out principal transactions in connection with one or several classes of options during trading sessions with a view to ensuring smooth market operation.

Market-makers are authorised by the CBV. The authorised firms undertake to meet the commitments laid down by the CBV, and in particular to respect the integrity of the various markets on which they operate.

Any failure to meet these undertakings may lead the CBV to withdraw its authorisation.

Article 4–3–17

Persons responsible for carrying out principal transactions on behalf of a Bourse member firm or a principal-trading firm, under the conditions set forth in Article 4–3–16, are authorised by the CBV.

The authorised persons must undertake to comply with the professional and ethical rules set by the CBV. Any failure to observe such rules may lead the CBV to withdraw its authorisation.

Article 4–3–18

The unit of trading for options is one contract.

Article 4–3–19

A buyer of an option is immediately debited for the amount of the premium corresponding to his purchase. The seller is immediately credited with the amount of the premium corresponding to his sale.

(5) The clearing of traded options

Article 4–3–20

As soon as a transaction takes place, the purchase or sale of an option gives rise to the assessment of a clearing fee.

In the case of an index option, exercise may give rise to assessment of a fee.

Article 4–3–21

The SBF may set a maximum limit for the net open position that a given clearing member or order originator may be allowed to hold in any one class of options. It may also set a maximum limit for the overall open interest, and decide that as from a given date only orders tending to close outstanding positions will be accepted.

Article 4–3–22

The SBF effects payments between clearing members which result from all trades in options on the one hand, and from exercises and assignments of index options on the other hand, under the conditions and in accordance with the schedule it sets.

Article 4–3–23

The SCMC determines for each clearing member its net daily position and the amount of the corresponding margin requirements, taking into account all trades, exercise instructions, and assignments recorded in the members' accounts.

Among the operations recorded in their accounts, clearing members separate operations carried out by their authorised agents acting as market-makers, operations carried out on their own account, operations carried out on behalf of their direct clients, and operations carried out on behalf of order-collecting intermediaries that are not clearing members.

Article 4–3–24

The SBF receives in deposit and is responsible for margin payments made to it by clearing members. It determines the conditions regarding the composition, calling up, and payment of margins by such members.

Article 4–3–24 bis

In the event of failure by a clearing member to meet its margin or payment obligations in full within the timetable set by the SBF, the SBF may decide the total or partial liquidation of such member's positions. To this end, all guarantees of any nature granted by such member to guarantee its positions may be foreclosed, in whole or in part.

Positions recorded in the clearing accounts related to the clients of a defaulting member, whether such clients are direct clients or order-collecting firms, may be transferred to another clearing member. The defaulting member may be suspended or excluded from clearing operations.

Chapter 4
Corporate actions
(1) Subscription or allotment rights

Article 4–4–1

Unless otherwise provided for by the SBF, a subscription or an allotment right is detached for the relevant security on the day on which the subscription or allotment operations start.

Article 4–4–2

Unless otherwise provided for by the CBV, a subscription or allotment right detached from a security that is negotiable on the monthly settlement market is traded solely on the cash settlement market.

Article 4–4–3

When a subscription or allotment right is detached from a security underlying a traded option, the option strike price and the number of securities covered by the option are adjusted under the conditions set forth in an Implementing Regulation issued by the CBV.

As regards those operations which do not give rise to a detachment of rights but which have an effect on the price of the security, such operations give rise, in appropriate cases, to those adjustments required so that the situation of buyers and sellers is not modified, subject however to roundings.

Article 4–4–4

As an exception to the provisions of Article 4–1–4, the CBV may authorise intermediaries holding purchase and sell orders for the same right at the same price, to off-set them and produce on the market only the net balance.

(2) Coupons

Article 4–4–5

Detachment of an interest or dividend coupon takes place on the day it becomes payable.

243

However, with respect to a security issued by a foreign entity, the SBF may set a date for coupon detachment which is different from the payable date.

Article 4–4–6

All deliveries of securities traded on the monthly settlement market are made ex-coupon, whether the trade is effected before or after the coupon is detached. A person who purchases a security before the coupon ex-date is credited with an indemnity whose amount is equal to the net amount of the coupon paid and the seller is debited accordingly.

Article 4–4–7

For detachment of a coupon payable in foreign currency, the SBF calculates the equivalent of this coupon in French francs, using as the basis the exchange rate on the day of detachment in France.

The equivalent value in French francs of the coupon as determined in this way on the day of detachment is published in the BOC. This does not in any way guarantee the value the coupon will have on the day the beneficiary actually cashes it in.

Article 4–4–8

Detaching a dividend coupon from the security underlying a traded option does not modify any of the standard specifications of such option.

(3) Common provisions

Article 4–4–9

With respect to a security traded on the monthly settlement market, no effect may be given to any corporate action on carryover (contango) day.

Furthermore, with respect to a security traded on the monthly settlement market, no detachment of a subscription or of an allotment right or of an interest or dividend coupon may be carried out on the last day of the current account or on the previous trading day.

Chapter 5
Orders
(1) Order terms

Article 4–5–1

Any order must include an indication of whether it is a purchase or sell order, the designation or the characteristics of the security to be traded, the number of securities to be traded, and in a general way all details required for proper execution.

In the case of traded options, the order must include whether it is a buy or sell, opening or closing order, the complete identification of the series, *i.e.* the class, whether it is a put or a call, the strike price, the date of expiration, as well as the number of contracts of the series to be traded.

Article 4–5–2

On markets on which trading is continuous, orders are termed "at market price" or with a limit price.

On markets on which trading is provided by open outcry, or by a written procedure, the orders may be termed "at best", with a limit price, or with a limit price together with the indication "stop".

Article 4–5–3

An "at best" order does not contain any price indication. It is carried out at the first transacted price after it is received.

Article 4–5–4

An order at the market price does not contain any price indication.

At market opening, such an order may be executed in full or in part, or not at all, depending on the orders presented on the market. In case of non-execution or partial execution, the order or fraction of an order that has not been executed becomes a limit order at the opening price.

After the opening, such an order may be executed, in full or in part, at the price of the best limit on the opposite side of the market at the time it is presented or not at all when there are no orders on the opposite side of the market. In case of partial execution, the unexecuted part of the order becomes a limit order at the last transacted price.

Article 4–5–5

An order at a limit price is one by which the buyer sets the maximum price he is prepared to pay, and the seller the minimum price at which he agrees to sell his securities. The order is executed if market conditions allow.

Article 4–5–6

On markets on which trading is provided by open outcry, or by written procedures, an order at a limit price together with the indication "stop" is one in which the client indicates his willingness to buy or sell from a given price – at that price and above in the case of a purchase, or at that price and below in case of a sale.

A stop order becomes an "at best" order, carried out as such, once the set price limit has been reached. However, in the event of non-execution of the order or only partial execution, such an order is not executed in full or for the balance at a later price if that price is less than the set limit in the case of a buy order, or greater in the case of a sell order.

Article 4–5–7

The amount due in respect of a dividend or interest coupon is deducted from the limit price set by the client on the day of detachment of such coupon, in the absence of instructions to the contrary from such client.

(2) Order transmission

Article 4–5–8

An order may be transmitted by any means convenient to the client and to the Bourse member firm, under the conditions set forth in the client account agreement concluded between them and mentioned in Article 2–3–2 of the present Regulations. The SBF or the Bourse member firm may require orders transmitted verbally to be confirmed in writing.

The client may modify or cancel his order at any time before execution.

Article 4–5–9

Every order is time and date stamped when received by the Bourse member firm. The conditions under which this is done are set forth in Implementing Regulations issued by the CBV.

(3) Order validity

Article 4–5–10

An order with an expiration date lapses at the end of the stipulated period, if it has not been executed during that period.

Article 4–5–11

An order good till cancelled is valid until the last trading day of the calendar month where it relates to a security traded on the cash settlement market or a traded option the underlying security of which is traded on the cash settlement market, and until the last day of the current account period where it relates to a security traded on the monthly settlement market or a traded option the underlying security of which is traded on the monthly settlement market.

Article 4–5–12

In the absence of any indication of duration, an order is deemed to be:

– good till cancelled, in the case of a security,
– valid for the day only, in the case of a traded option.

If the client specifies a validity duration in his order, that duration may not, in any case, exceed the validity of a good till cancelled order transmitted the same day.

Article 4–5–13

The validity of an order automatically expires upon detachment of a subscription or allotment right, and, generally speaking, of any special advantage in connection with the security in question.

By special decision, the SBF may set a deadline after which orders which are not executed in connection with a given security must be renewed by the clients.

Such a decision is reported in a notice published in BOC, which states the new conditions, if any, regarding transmission and renewal of orders.

(4) Cancellation of trades

Article 4–5–14

The SBF may cancel a traded price and hence all transactions made at that price. It may also cancel a given transaction, in the case of a security traded on a computerised system. In the first case, the cancellation is published in the next day's BOC. In the second case, the cancellation is made public at once.

Chapter 6
Guarantees and margins
(1) Constitution of initial margins

Article 4–6–1

A Bourse member firm may demand, at its own initiative or at the request of the SBF, that funds or securities be deposited before any trade on the settlement cash market or giving rise to immediate settlement.

Article 4–6–2

At the latest by the day following execution of his order on the monthly settlement market, a client must deposit margin with his Bourse member firm. The margin basis, minimum rate and composition must comply with the rules set forth in an Implementing Regulation issued by the CBV.

The Bourse member firm may require the deposit of such margin before the order is executed.

Under the supervision of the SBF, this margin is calculated by referring to the overall amount of risk incurred by the client.

Article 4–6–3

As an exception to the previous Article, the CBV may establish special rules applying to orders transmitted by a credit institution.

It may also, in connection with any security and any type of operation, increase the minimum guarantees that may be demanded from clients to cover their commitments.

Article 4–6–4

The SBF may require the guarantee provided for in Articles 4–6–1 and 4–6–2 to be deposited in its accounts.

(2) Reconstitution of guarantees and liquidation of positions

Article 4–6–5

Throughout the account period, a client's positions must be margined at all times, in accordance with the rules mentioned in Article 4–6–2.

Failure by a client to have completed or reconstituted his margin deposit within one trading day after a request to do so by the Bourse member firm of which he is a client results in such firm liquidating his positions.

Article 4–6–6

When the client, either on the day following the trade with respect to trades on the cash settlement market or giving rise to immediate settlement, or on the first day of the new account period with respect to trades for monthly settlement, has not delivered the securities or funds, as applicable, to the relevant Bourse member firm, the latter shall proceed, without further notice, to buy-in the undelivered securities sold or to sell-out the unpaid securities bought, at the expense and risk of the defaulting client.

As of the first day of the new account period, the Bourse member firm shall exercise the same rights with respect to a client whose positions have been carried over, in full or in part, and who, before that date, has not settled his debit balance and constituted or completed the margin relating to the carryover operation.

Article 4–6–7

In the absence of any agreement to the contrary between the Bourse member firm and the client, all of the securities and assets held in the client's account(s) are automatically assigned as margin for guaranteeing all of his commitments. The Bourse member firm may sell them without notice in order to close out his positions.

(3) Traded options

Article 4–6–8

With the exception of clearing members, clients on the traded options market must deposit a minimum margin amount with the trading Bourse member firm assigned for the sole purpose of guaranteeing their positions on that market, pursuant to the request to that effect made to them by said Bourse member firm.

This margin amount, updated daily, is calculated for each class with a view to allowing the possible close-out of the positions as of the following trading session based on the most unfavourable price change possible in the underlying instrument.

The SBF determines the list of eligible collateral to meet the margin requirements and publishes the list in the BOC.

Article 4–6–9

The SBF determines and publishes the rules for calculating margin requirements on open positions in traded options.

For every class or series of options, it may increase the minimum margin amount to be required from clients to guarantee their positions.

Article 4–6–10

Positions in traded options must be covered in full, at all times, by the client.

The Bourse member firm shall liquidate positions that are insufficiently covered at the close of a session, no later than the end of the following trading day.

Article 4–6–11

All securities held in the client's account(s) are automatically assigned as margin in order to guarantee his open positions in traded options, and may be

sold without notice in order to close out such positions.

Chapter 7
Put-throughs (cross-trades)

Article 4–7–1

A put-through (*application*) is a trade involving a purchase and a sale executed simultaneously in connection with the same amount of a given security, on the same date and at the same price, on behalf of clients who have asked one or several Bourse member firms to record in their books the trade to be concluded between them.

Article 4–7–2

With respect to securities that are not continuously traded, any put-through must be carried out at the last transacted price for the relevant security.

Article 4–7–3

With respect to securities that are traded continuously, a put-through may be carried out during the trading session only at the limit set by the best bid or offer price existing at the time the put-through is carried out, or at a price lying within such spread.

Outside the trading session, a put-through involving a security that is traded continuously may be carried out only at the limit set by the best bid or offer price existing at the close of the last trading session, or at a price lying within such spread.

Article 4–7–4

By exception to the provisions of Article 4–7–3, a put-through in respect of a block of shares as defined at Article 6–3–1 of the present Regulations and effected during the trading session, may be carried out either at a price within the spread, limits included, of the weighted average buy and sell prices available on the market for the normal block size of the relevant security.

Where a put-through in respect of a block of shares is effected outside market operating hours, it must be carried out at

247

a price within the spread, limits included, of the weighted average buy and sell prices at the close of the most recent trading session for the normal block size of the relevant security, or under the conditions set forth in Article 6–2–4 of the present Regulations.

The weighted average spread and the normal block size referred to above are defined in Articles 6–3–1 *et seq* of the present Regulations.

Article 4–7–5

Put-throughs referred to in Articles 4–7–2, 4–7–3 and 4–7–4 of the present Regulations are reported to the SBF and published in accordance with the terms of an Implementing Regulation issued by the CBV.

Article 4–7–6

Put-throughs are forbidden in connection with a security traded with a proportional reduction of orders.

Article 4–7–7

With respect to traded options, no put-through may be recorded outside the market and outside trading hours.

A put-through may be carried out on the traded options market only at the limit set by the best bid or offer price existing at the time the put-through is made, or at a price lying within such spread.

Title 5
Public tender offers

Chapter 1
General rules

Article 5–1–1

The provisions of the present Title relate to public tender offers for equity securities or debt securities issued by a company incorporated under French law and admitted to the Official List or the Second Market, or traded on the *hors-cote* market, such tender offers being made by a person acting alone or in concert within the meaning of Article 356–1–3 of Law No. 66–537 of 24 July 1966.

Article 5–1–2

Companies having their registered office on French territory whose equity securities are admitted to the Official List or the Second Market must notify to the CBV the total number of existing voting rights, under the conditions set forth in Article 356–1–1 of Law No. 66–537 of 24 July 1966.

Such information, once received, is published by the SBF in the form of a notice.

Article 5–1–3

The shares and voting rights mentioned in Article 356–1–2 of Law No. 66–537 of 24 July 1966 are considered as shares and voting rights owned by a person acting alone or in concert.

Chapter 2
Purchase tender offers and exchange tender offers for equity securities – Normal procedure

Article 5–2–1

The proposed tender offer is submitted to the CBV by one or several credit institutions governed by Law No. 84–46 of 24 January 1984 which guarantee the irrevocable nature of the commitments made on behalf of the person or persons who initiate the operation.

As soon as the proposed tender offer is filed with the CBV, the SBF suspends trading in the equity securities of the company or companies concerned. It informs the Economy Minister (*Direction du Trésor and Direction Générale de la Con-*

248

currence et de la Consommation) and the COB that the proposal has been filed.

The public tender offer period begins with publication of the notice of filing of a proposed offer, indicating its main provisions, and particularly the identity of the initiator, of the institution or institutions submitting the offer and of the target company, the number of equities already held by the bid initiator, and the proposed price or terms of exchange.

Article 5-2-2

The public tender offer must be for the totality of the equity securities and of any securities giving access to equity securities or to voting rights in the target company.

Article 5-2-3

The public tender offer may be either a purchase offer[1], or an exchange offer[2], or an alternative offer[3], or an offer which is primarily a purchase offer or an exchange offer but secondarily an exchange offer or purchase offer respectively.

Article 5-2-4

When the initial tender offer is a mixed offer – an alternative offer, a purchase offer with partial payment in securities, or an exchange offer with partial payment in cash – the specific rules that are applicable are those relating to purchase offers or exchange offers, depending on the primary characterisation of the offer by the initiator, subject to the approval of the CBV.

(1) General provisions applicable to purchase offers and exchange offers

Article 5-2-5

In support of the proposed tender offer, the institution or institutions presenting

---

[1] An offer the consideration for which is cash (*offre publique d'achat* or OPA).
[2] An offer the consideration for which is other securities (*offre publique d'échange* or OPE).
[3] An offer the consideration for which is cash or securities at the discretion of the tendering securities holders.

the offer must submit a dossier specifying the following:

– The initiator's objective and intentions on the day of the filing, and the number and nature of the initiator's current holding of securities of the target company, if any.
– The minimum number of securities to be tendered in response to the offer below which the initiator reserves the right to withdraw the offer, where any such reserve is made.
– The price or the terms of exchange at which the initiator is offering to acquire the securities, the factors used to determine such price or terms, and the proposed conditions regarding payment or exchange.

Where required, the dossier must also contain a copy of the preliminary declaration provided for by regulations concerning foreign investments or by regulations calling for intervention by a French or European authority empowered to authorise or to approve the contemplated offer.

The dossier, prepared in accordance with the rules laid down by an Implementing Regulation of the CBV, is submitted by means of a letter to the CBV, guaranteeing under the signature of the submitting institution(s) the irrevocable nature and the terms of the commitments made by the initiator.

If the offer is an exchange offer in connection with which the initiator, a stock company, proposes to offer securities to be issued in exchange for securities of the target company, the irrevocability of the initiator's commitments entails an obligation on the part of its management to propose a resolution to the general shareholders' meeting calling for issue of the securities to be delivered as consideration under the conditions set forth in the tender offer.

Article 5-2-6

The CBV has a period of five trading days following the day on which the dossier is filed to announce its decision on the acceptability of the tender offer. At the end of this period, the CBV announces its decision in a notice published by the SBF.

Article 5-2-7

During the period provided for in Article 5-2-6, the CBV is empowered to demand that the submitting institution supply any further explanations and guarantees, and to demand a guarantee deposit, in cash or in securities.

The CBV may also ask the initiator to reconsider the proposed offer if it considers unacceptable any of the following:

- The proposed price or exchange ratio, on the basis of generally accepted objective evaluation criteria and the target company's characteristics.
- The threshold, expressed as a minimum number of securities tendered, below which the initiator reserves the right to withdraw the offer.
- The nature, the characteristics or the market for the securities proposed in exchange.

Article 5-2-8

As a general rule, trading resumes in the securities of the company or companies concerned two trading days after publication of the notice of acceptability (*avis de recevabilité*).

Article 5-2-9

If the CBV has declared the tender offer acceptable, the SBF publishes a tender offer opening notice, after having been informed of approval of the prospectus by the COB, as well as, where applicable any authorisations or decisions required by law.

Article 5-2-10

The tender offer opening notice specifies the identity of the initiator, the name of the submitting institution(s), the number of shares already held by the initiator, the minimum number of securities to be tendered below which the initiator reserves the right to withdraw its offer, the proposed price or terms of exchange, the offer closing date, the proposed conditions for delivery of the securities and payment of the funds, and generally,

the schedule for the transaction as a whole.

The time between the opening of the offer and the closing of the offer may be no less than 20 trading days.

Orders of persons tendering their securities are received by intermediaries up to and including the closing date.

At any time during the offer period, the CBV may extend the closing date. A notice issued by the SBF announces the new schedule for the tender offer and any consequences thereof.

Publication of the tender offer opening notice does not mean approval of the offer from the viewpoint of merger control law. Pursuant to Ordinance No. 86-1243 of 1 December 1986, the initiator has the option of notifying the proposed offer to the Economy Minister (*Direction Générale de la Concurrence et de la Consommation*), who, even failing such advance notification, retains his supervisory power.

Article 5-2-11

Persons wishing to tender their securities in response to the offer forward their orders to the intermediaries of their choice. Such orders may be cancelled at any time until and including the day on which the offer closes.

Article 5-2-12

Intermediaries deliver to the SBF the securities tendered by their clients in response to the offer, at the latest by the date set in the timetable published in the tender offer opening notice. This delivery is accompanied by a letter certifying that the deposit is being made under the conditions of the offer, and by a form restating, for each client account, the number of securities tendered.

Article 5-2-13

The result of the tender offer is announced in a notice issued by the SBF. The notice indicates either that the offer has failed (*sans suite*) or that it has succeeded (*suite positive*).

If the offer has failed, the same notice, or

a later notice, states the date on which the securities tendered in response to the offer will be returned to the custodian intermediaries.

If the offer has succeeded, the notice indicates the number of securities acquired by the initiator.

During the period between the closing date and either the date of publication of the notice announcing that the offer has succeeded or the date on which the securities are to be returned to the custodian intermediary, the initiator and the persons who have acted in concert with it may neither sell on the market securities of the target company held on the closing date nor purchase securities of the same company at a price higher than the offer price.

Article 5–2–14

A tender offer competing with an offer already in progress may be submitted to the CBV and declared acceptable, provided it complies with the rules set forth in Articles 5–2–1 to 5–2–5 above and it is filed at least five trading days before the closing date of the earlier offer.

Article 5–2–15

Publication of a notice of suspension of trading due to the filing of a competing tender offer results in a cancellation of all tenders of securities made in response to the earlier offer, addressed to intermediaries following publication of such offer.

The initiator of an earlier offer must inform the CBV, no more than five trading days following publication of the competing offer opening notice, as to whether the initial proposal is maintained or withdrawn or modified.

Article 5–2–16

Where two or more tender offers are successively made, the CBV ensures that the date or dates for the closing of the earlier offer or offers coincide with the closing date of the most recent offer.

Article 5–2–17

During the period of a public tender offer

for securities that are traded on the monthly settlement market:

(a) monthly settlement orders must be 100% margined in cash in the case of purchase orders, and must include advance deposit of the securities in the case of sell orders. However, these provisions are not applicable to orders aimed at unwinding positions that have been taken, on the buy or sell side of the market either before or after publication of the notice mentioned in Article 5–2–1;

(b) if the securities of the target company underlie traded options, orders for selling call options can be received by the intermediaries only if advance deposit of the securities capable of giving rise to delivery is made. This provision is inapplicable to orders aimed at unwinding open positions, whether they were taken before or after the publication of the notice mentioned in Article 5–2–1;

(c) the provisions of paragraphs (a) and (b) above are inapplicable to trades made by market-makers within the framework of their regulatory obligations on the MONEP.

Article 5–2–18

For the duration of the tender offer, all orders must be transmitted to the market. Principal trading in blocks of shares is forbidden throughout the offer period.

Put-throughs and other principal transactions[4] are authorised only during trading sessions. They are reported to the market as soon as they are completed.

Recording of any option agreement[5] is prohibited for the duration of the offer. Any option agreements recorded before publication of the notice mentioned in Article 5–2–1 may be exercised.

The validity of orders that are not executed during the offer automatically expires at the close of the offer.

---

[4] See Title 6 for the definition of the various types of principal trading.
[5] See Title 7, Chapter 2 for the definition of option agreements.

Article 5–2–19

Trades that must be reported, pursuant to rules laid down by the COB, by companies involved in a tender offer, their directors, any persons holding 5% or more of the capital or voting rights at ordinary shareholders' meetings and any other persons acting in concert with such persons, directly or indirectly, are published in a notice issued by the SBF, in principle the day after the trade day. The notice also specifies the total number of securities of the companies concerned that were traded during the previous session.

The same rule applies to persons who have acquired, since the filing of the offer, directly or indirectly, an amount of securities in one of the companies concerned representing 0.5% or more of the capital or voting rights at the company's general shareholders' meetings.

Article 5–2–20

In the case of an exchange tender offer whereby the initiator proposes shares or other equity securities to the holders of securities of the target company, the declarations and publications by means of a notice issued by the SBF are to be understood as applying to trades involving the securities proposed in exchange and to those involving the equity securities of the companies concerned.

Article 5–2–21

When more than ten weeks have elapsed following publication of the offer opening notice, the CBV, with a view to hastening the filing of successive tender offers and with due observance of the order of their filing, may set a deadline for filing each successive higher offer. Such deadline may be no less than three trading days starting on the date of publication of each acceptability notice. The decision of the CBV is published in a notice issued by the SBF.

(2) Specific provisions for purchase offers

Article 5–2–22

The initiator of a purchase offer may improve the terms of such offer until the closing date. The new conditions and, where applicable, the new closing date set for the offer are published in a notice issued by the SBF.

Article 5–2–23

For the duration of the offer, the initiator as well as any persons acting in concert with it are authorised to trade on the market in the securities of the target company, except where the initiator has reserved the right of withdrawal referred to in the second indent of the first paragraph of Article 5–2–5.

Where the initiator trades on the market at a price higher than the offer price, the offer price is automatically increased to the higher of 102% of the current offer price or the price actually paid on the market, regardless of the number of securities bought, and the initiator is not allowed to modify any other terms of the offer.

The same rule applies to the market in subscription rights to any issue of equity securities by the target company: where the initiator trades on the market at a price higher than the amount by which the offer price exceeds the issue price, the offer price is automatically raised to the higher of 102% of the current offer price or the offer price implied by the price actually paid for the subscription rights, under the same conditions as in the previous paragraph.

Article 5–2–24

Competing purchase offers as well as higher bids made by the same initiator are made at a price that is at least 2% higher than the price stipulated for each of the securities of the target company by the previous purchase offer or higher bid.

However, a competing purchase offer or an amended offer by the same initiator may be declared acceptable if the condition requiring that a minimum number of securities be tendered in response to the offer is withdrawn, even though the offer price is not modified.

(3) Specific provisions for exchange offers

Article 5–2–25

The initiator of an exchange offer may modify the terms of such offer until the closing day.

If the CBV declares the modified offer acceptable, this decision as well as the new conditions and timetable are published in a notice issued by the SBF.

Article 5–2–26

Where an exchange offer is in competition with one or several other tender offers, the CBV appreciates whether any modifications made therein significantly improve the stipulated terms of exchange and make it necessary to extend the offer period.

Article 5–2–27

For the duration of the offer, the initiator, as well as any persons acting in concert with it, may not trade on the market directly or indirectly, as principal or as agent, in the securities of the target company, in the securities proposed in exchange should these be listed, and in a general way in the securities of the companies concerned by the offer.

Chapter 3
Purchase tender offers and exchange tender offers for equity securities – Simplified procedure

Article 5–3–1

For acquisition of equity securities and of voting rights and of securities giving access to equity securities of a company whose equity securities are admitted to the Official List or to the Second Market, or traded on the *hors-cote* market, the CBV may authorise use of a simplified procedure for a purchase or exchange tender offer.

Subject to the specific provisions set forth in the present Chapter, the provisions of Chapter 2 of the present Title are applicable to tender offers carried out in accordance with the simplified procedure.

Article 5–3–2

The use of the simplified offer procedure may be authorised only in the following cases:

(a) an offer made by a person holding directly or indirectly, alone or in concert, at least half of the target company's capital and voting rights;

(b) an offer made by a person, acting alone or in concert, who acquires or has agreed with one or several shareholders of the target company, the sellers, to acquire a block of shares in such company giving such person or persons a majority of the capital or voting rights of the company, taking into consideration any securities or voting rights already held by such person or persons;

(c) an offer for at most 10% of the voting equity securities or voting rights of the target company, taking into consideration any voting equity securities or voting rights the initiator already holds, directly or indirectly;

(d) an offer made by a person, acting alone or in concert, for preferred shares, investment certificates or voting right certificates;

(e) an offer made by a company to purchase its own shares, pursuant to Article 217 of Law No. 66–537 of 24 July 1966.

Article 5–3–3

A simplified purchase offer is carried out by means of purchases on the market, according to the terms laid down in the offer opening notice, except in those cases of a limited offer provided for in Articles 5–3–2, paragraphs (c) and (e), and Article 5–3–9.

A simplified exchange offer is centralised by the SBF or, under its supervision, by a financial institution.

With the approval of the CBV, the duration of a simplified tender offer may be limited to ten trading days in the case of a purchase offer, and to fifteen trading days in the case of an exchange offer, a mixed offer or an alternative offer, except for a purchase offer made by company with a view to reducing its own capital.

Article 5–3–4

If the tender offer is a purchase offer made pursuant to paragraph (a) of Article 5–3–2, and subject to the provisions of Article 5–2–7, the price stipulated by the initiator may not be less, except with CBV approval, than the volume-weighted average of transaction prices on the exchange over the 60 trading days preceding publication of the notice of filing of the proposed offer.

Article 5–3–5

To carry out a purchase offer pursuant to paragraph (b) of Article 5–3–2, the person who has acquired or has agreed to acquire the block of securities in question may apply to the CBV to be authorised to carry out a price guarantee procedure (*garantie de cours*), whereby such person undertakes to acquire on the market, for a period of ten to fifteen trading days, all the securities offered for sale at the price at which the sale of the securities has been or is to be made, and only at that price, unless the CBV authorises a lower guaranteed price where the sale includes a guarantee clause covering an identified risk or a deferred payment clause affecting any or all of the relevant payments. In case of deferred payment, the discount rate used may not be greater than the market rate at the time of the sale.

At the end of the price guarantee period, the initiator reports the number of shares acquired during such period to the SBF which ensures publication thereof.

Article 5–3–6

The acquisition, from one or several given persons, of a block of shares capable of ensuring majority control of the capital or of the voting rights of a company whose equity securities are traded on the *hors-cote* market gives rise to implementation of the price guarantee procedure referred to in Article 5–3–5.

Article 5–3–7

Individual or legal entities acting alone or in concert are required to comply with the procedures set forth in the present Chapter when, in taking control of a company, they come to hold, directly or indirectly, a majority of the capital or of the voting rights in a French company whose equity securities are admitted to the Official List or the Second Market, or are traded on the *hors-cote* market, where the equity securities held by the company the control of which is acquired make up an essential part of its assets.

Article 5–3–8

In the case of a simplified tender offer made pursuant to paragraphs (c) and (e) of Article 5–3–2, the initiator undertakes *vis-à-vis* the CBV to refrain from any intervention on the market for the duration of the offer.

Article 5–3–9

In the case of a tender offer made for investment certificates or voting right certificates, the initiator is authorised to use the simplified procedure and to limit the transaction to the acquisition of an amount of voting right certificates or of investment certificates equal to the number of investment certificates or of voting right certificates already held by it.

Orders submitted in response to the offer are centralised by the SBF or, under its supervision, by a financial intermediary.

Article 5–3–10

In cases in which the initiator of a simplified tender offer has been authorised to reserve the right to reduce sale or exchange orders that are presented in response to its offer, the reduction is made on a proportional basis, subject to the necessary adjustments.

Chapter 4
Purchase tender offers and exchange tender offers for equity securities – Mandatory offers

Article 5–4–1

When an individual or legal entity, acting alone or in concert, comes to hold more than one-third of the equity securities or more than one-third of the voting rights in a French company whose equity securities are admitted to the Official List or the Second Market, such person is required, at its own initiative, to inform the CBV of this fact immediately, and to file a proposed tender offer for all equity securities and any securities giving access to equity securities or voting rights of such company, the offer being drawn up in such terms as can be approved by the CBV.

The proposed tender offer may not contain any clause providing for the tender of a minimum number of securities for the offer to go through.

Article 5–4–2

The determination of the threshold of one-third of the number of equity securities, referred to in the present Chapter, is made on the basis of voting equity securities where the capital of the company concerned consists partly of non-voting equity securities.

Article 5–4–3

Individuals or legal entities acting alone or in concert are required to comply with the requirement set forth in Article 5–4–1 when, in taking control of a company, they come to hold, directly or indirectly, more than one-third of the equity securities or more than one-third of the voting rights in a French company whose equity securities are admitted to the Official List or to the Second Market, where the equity securities held by the company the control of which is acquired make up an essential part of its assets.

Article 5–4–4

The requirement set forth in Article 5–4–1 applies to individuals or legal entities, acting alone or in concert, who either hold, directly or indirectly, between one-third and one-half of the total number of equity securities or voting rights of a company and increase, within a period of less than one year, the number of equity securities or voting rights they hold by 2% or more of the total number of equity securities or voting rights of the company, or who come to

hold an absolute majority of this total number.

The persons referred to in the present Article are to inform the SBF of any variations in the number of equity securities or voting rights that they hold.

Article 5–4–5

Subject to the provisions of Article 5–4–1, the provisions of the Articles in the present Title that relate to purchase or exchange tender offers are applicable to mandatory offers.

Article 5–4–6

The CBV may grant an exemption to the mandatory filing of a proposed tender offer, if the person(s) mentioned in Articles 5–4–1 and 5–4–4 prove to the CBV that one of the following conditions has been met:

(a) The acquisition results either from a transfer for nil consideration, or from a capital increase in cash reserved to designated persons, or from a merger or a capital contribution of assets approved by the shareholders of the company whose securities have been acquired.

(b) The acquisition of equity securities or voting rights above the one-third threshold does not exceed 3% of the total number of equity securities or voting rights of the company, and the acquiror(s) undertake(s) to dispose of the excess securities or voting rights within 18 months.

(c) The increase in the percentage held of the total number of equity securities or voting rights results from a reduction in the total number of the company's equity securities or voting rights.

(d) The person(s) previously held control of the company within the meaning of the third indent of the first paragraph of Article 355–1 of Law No. 66–537 of 24 July 1966 pertaining to commercial companies.

(e) The company is already majority-controlled by one or by several shareholders acting in concert, other than the person(s) referred to in the present Chapter.

255

(f) The person(s) acquire the equity securities or voting rights on their own account from one or several sellers outside the group to which such persons belong, and this group already controls the issuing company the accounts of which are consolidated with those of the other companies of the group.

(g) The persons controlling the issuing company dispose of equity securities to other members of their group, without such disposal having the effect of significantly modifying the balance among the members of the group.

(h) The exceeding of the threshold results from a concert party agreement that has been reported to the CBV and published by the SBF, and the signatories of such agreement have not made, directly or indirectly, in the year preceding such reporting, any significant acquisition of voting securities and undertake not to make any significant modification, for two years, in the respective balance of their holdings within the concert.

Article 5–4–7

The aforementioned exemption, if granted by the CBV, is published by the SBF in a notice indicating in particular the reasons for granting it and the terms of any undertakings made by the purchaser.

Chapter 5
Public buy-out offers

Article 5–5–1

Subject to the provisions set forth in the Articles constituting the present Chapter, and subject to any contrary provisions, public buy-out offers (*offres publiques de retrait*) are to be carried out pursuant to the provisions of Chapter 3 relating to the simplified tender offer procedure.

Article 5–5–2

When an individual or a legal entity, or a group of individuals or legal entities acting in concert are shareholders of a company whose equity securities are admitted to the Official List or the Second Market or were previously admitted to the Official List or the Second Market and subsequently traded on the *hors-cote* market, and of which they hold 95% or more of the voting rights, the holder of one or more voting equity securities or one or more voting rights certificates not belonging to the majority shareholder or group, may request the CBV to require said majority shareholder or group to file a proposed buy-out offer.

After having made the necessary investigations, the CBV acts on the request filed with it. If it considers the request admissible, it notifies the majority shareholder or group.

It examines with this shareholder or group, as well as with the institutions appointed to guarantee the transaction, the terms and the conditions for implementation of a buy-out offer. Such offer must be for the totality of the equity securities or securities giving access to equity securities as well as any voting rights certificates not held by the majority shareholder or group.

If the CBV decides that the proposed offer is acceptable, the SBF publishes the opening notice for the buy-out offer.

Article 5–5–3

An individual or legal entity, or a group of individuals or legal entities acting in concert, who hold 95% or more of the voting rights in a company whose securities are admitted to the Official List or the Second Market, or were previously admitted to the Official List or the Second Market and subsequently traded on the *hors-cote* market, may file with the CBV a proposed buy-out offer for the totality of the equity securities or securities giving access to equity securities as well as any voting rights certificates not held by said persons.

After having made the necessary investigations, and receiving approval from the CBV with respect to the acceptability of the proposed buy-out offer, the SBF publishes the buy-out offer opening notice.

Such notice indicates that, after the close of the offer, and whatever its outcome, a delisting from the Official List or the Second Market of all equity securities or securities giving access to equity securities as well as any voting rights certificates of the company shall be ordered.

Article 5–5–4

One or several individuals or legal entities holding a two-thirds majority of the voting rights of a stock company (*société anonyme*) whose equity securities are admitted to the Official List or the Second Market, and which is transformed into a partnership limited by shares (*société en commandite par actions*), are required to file a proposed buy-out offer as soon as the shareholders' general meeting adopts the resolution to transform the company.

The CBV decides on the acceptability of the proposed buy-out offer.

The buy-out offer opening notice published by the SBF may indicate that the majority shareholder or group has reserved the right, at the end of the offer and depending on its outcome, to request that all of the company's equity securities or securities giving access to equity securities as well as any voting rights certificates be delisted from the Official List or the Second Market.

Article 5–5–5

The person or persons controlling a company whose equity securities are admitted to the Official List or the Second Market inform the CBV and consider with it the possibility of a buy-out offer in the following cases:

– when they propose to ask an extraordinary shareholders' meeting to approve one or several significant modifications of the company articles, particularly the provisions relating to the company's legal form as well as conditions regarding the transfer of its equity securities, and any other rights pertaining to such securities;
– when they decide on the principle of a sale or capital contribution to another company of all or most of the assets of the company, of a change in its business activities, or of the suppression for several financial years of any remuneration of the equity securities.

The CBV appreciates the consequences of the proposed changes in the light of the rights and interests of the holders of the company's equity securities and voting rights. With the approval of the person(s) controlling the company, the CBV determines the conditions for implementation of a buy-out offer. The SBF ensures publication of such conditions.

Article 5–5–6

If, at the time of filing a proposed tender offer, the initiator has indicated its intention to request maintenance of the listing of the company's securities once the offer has been completed, the CBV may grant the initiator a period of time to ensure sufficient dissemination of the securities among the public to create a market. During that period, no request for a buy-out offer pursuant to Articles 5–5–2 and 5–5–3 may be declared acceptable by the CBV.

Chapter 6
Compulsory buy-out procedures

Article 5–6–1

At the close of a buy-out offer carried out in accordance with Articles 5–5–2 or 5–5–3 above, securities not tendered by the minority shareholders may be transferred to the majority shareholder or group, subject to an indemnity being paid to such minority shareholders.

When a proposed buy-out offer is filed, the initiator informs the CBV whether the decision to apply for a compulsory buy-out will depend on the outcome of the offer, or if immediate application is made to implement a compulsory buy-out at the close of the offer.

In support of its proposed buy-out offer, the initiator supplies the CBV with a valuation of the securities of the target company, based on the objective methods usually applied to asset sales and taking into account the following factors which shall be weighted in a manner appropriate to the individual case: the value of the company's assets, its earnings and market capitalisation, as well as its subsidiaries and business prospects. This valuation must be accompanied by the assessment of an independent expert.

The CBV examines the proposed buy-out offer in accordance with the conditions set forth in Article 5–2–7. If it declares the offer acceptable, the conclusions upon which this decision is based are published in the notice issued by the SBF.

Article 5–6–2

If, upon filing a proposed buy-out offer, the initiator reserves the right to apply for a compulsory buy-out at the close of the offer, notice shall be given to the CBV within ten days following the close of the offer whether it waives this right or not. The decision taken in this regard is indicated in the notice describing the outcome of the offer that is published by the SBF.

If the initiator decides to effect a compulsory buy-out, the CBV is informed of the proposed price to be paid in compensation. This price must be at least equal to that of the buy-out offer, and is higher in cases where events of a nature to affect the value of the securities have occurred after the offer was declared acceptable.

The decision of the CBV concerning the compulsory buy-out is made public in a notice published by the SBF setting out conditions for implementation, in particular the date on which the buy-out becomes effective; the time which elapses between the date of the decision and the date on which it becomes effective may not be less than that prescribed in paragraph 2, article 3 of the Decree of 7 May 1988. The decision to effect a compulsory buy-out results in the delisting of the relevant securities from the Official List or Second Market, and the striking off the daily *hors-cote* statement of any securities which may have been included therein.

Custodians effect the transfer of securities not tendered in response to the buy-

out offer to the majority shareholder or group, which pays the amount corresponding to the indemnity into a reserved account opened for this purpose in accordance with conditions set forth in an Implementing Regulation of the CBV.

Article 5–6–3

If, upon filing a proposed buy-out offer, the initiator applies to the CBV for compulsory buy-out procedures to be implemented as soon as the offer closes, whatever its outcome may be, the buy-out offer opening notice indicates the conditions applying to the compulsory buy-out, in particular the date on which it becomes effective.

As soon as the buy-out offer closes, the relevant securities are withdrawn from the Official List or the Second Market, or struck off the daily *hors-cote* statement. On the same date, custodians effect the transfer of securities not tendered in response to the buy-out offer to the majority shareholder or group, which pays the amount corresponding to the indemnity into a reserved account opened for this purpose in accordance with conditions set forth in an Implementing Regulation of the CBV.

Chapter 7
Purchase or exchange tender offers for debt securities or non-equity warrants

Article 5–7–1

With the approval of the CBV, purchase or exchange offers for debt securities or non-equity warrants admitted to the Official List or the Second Market or traded on the *hors-cote* market, are carried out in accordance with the simplified tender offer procedure.

Such tender offers may be either purchase or exchange offers, with or without partial payment in cash.

Article 5–7–2

The initiator sends the CBV a letter containing an irrevocable undertaking to acquire or accept in exchange, for a minimum period of ten trading days, all or part of the securities that might be tendered. Where the offer is only for a part of the existing securities, the orders in response to the offer are centralised by the SBF or, with its approval and under its supervision, by a financial intermediary.

In the aforementioned letter, the initiator states the reasons for the offer and the conditions under which the securities holders who do not tender their securities will remain company creditors and able to trade their securities, once the offer is completed.

The initiator also states either the proposed price for the securities, or the proposed terms of exchange, stating in particular the characteristics of the securities offered in exchange, the proposed exchange ratio, and the amount of any partial payment in cash.

The initiator's commitments must be guaranteed by one or several credit institutions governed by Law No. 84–46 of 24 January 1984. The CBV may require advance deposit with the SBF of the funds or securities to be offered in exchange by the initiator.

Article 5–7–3

The tender offer opening notice published by the SBF indicates, in particular, the identity of the initiator, the number of securities for which the offer is made, the name(s) of the submitting credit institution(s) having guaranteed the transaction,

the price or exchange terms proposed and the duration of the offer.

Article 5–7–4

For the implementation of a simplified purchase or exchange offer for debt securities or non-equity warrants with partial payment in cash, the CBV may authorise the use of an auction procedure.

In the case of a purchase offer, the initiator undertakes to acquire, at a given price, all of the securities tendered at that price, and reserves the right to acquire, at the limit price set by each person tendering securities, all or part of the securities tendered at a price higher than the offer price.

In the case of an exchange offer, the initiator undertakes to exchange all of the securities tendered at the specified conditions with respect to parity and partial payment in cash, and reserves the right to exchange securities tendered at the same parity but with a partial payment in cash higher than the partial cash payment initially offered.

An Implementing Regulation issued by the CBV lays down the conditions for application of this auction procedure.

Article 5–7–5

Subject to the special provisions set forth in the present Chapter, the provisions of Chapter 3 of Title 5 are applicable to purchase or exchange tender offers for debt securities or non-equity warrants.

Title 6
Principal trading in equity securities

Chapter 1
General provisions

Article 6–1–1

A principal transaction is defined as the purchase or sale of securities by an institution acting for its own account within the context of its activity as intermediary.

The intermediary is not allowed to buy or sell equity securities from or to a client as a principal when it manages the client's account on a discretionary basis and hence can take the initiative for investments and disinvestments carried out in such account.

Article 6–1–2

All the equity securities or other securities giving access to equity securities which are admitted to the Official List or the Second Market, or appear in the daily statement of the *hors-cote* market, may be traded under the principal trading rules described in the present Title.

Article 6–1–3

Unless specifically authorised by the SBF in which case notice thereof is published in the BOC, the following principal transactions in respect of a security are forbidden:

– when the SBF has ordered a trading halt in the security;
– when an imbalance between purchase orders and sell orders has prevented transactions in the security occuring during the last or current trading session, and has resulted in only a bid or offer price being displayed.

Article 6–1–4

The intermediary who fills a client order by means of a principal transaction is allowed to issue a confirmation notice with the net price, without brokerage or other fee.

The intermediary may pay stamp duty, if any, on behalf of its client with respect to the part of the transaction concerning such client.

Article 6–1–5

The intermediary acting as principal must time- and date-stamp all transactions.

Unless it relates to principal trading in blocks of securities as defined in Chapter 3 of the present Title, a principal transaction carried out during a trading session is executed on the market, where appropriate as a put-through. For a security which is traded continuously on a computerised system, the put-through is entered immediately in the trading system, pursuant to the provisions of Article 4–7–3 of the present Regulations.

Where a principal transaction relates to a block of securities, such a trade requires a specific recording under the conditions set forth in an Implementing Regulation issued by the CBV.

A principal transaction carried out outside a trading session must be recorded as a put-through before the opening of the next trading session.

Article 6–1–6

Where the intermediary acting as principal is not a Bourse member firm, the market trade or the recording which are mentioned in Article 6–1–5 are carried out by a Bourse member firm acting as bookkeeper (*domiciliatrice*) for the principal transaction.

Article 6–1–7

The Bourse member firm acting as bookkeeper issues a trade confirmation notice to the intermediary acting as principal.

Such notice states whether the transaction took place outside the trading session. It also mentions the transaction price and details on related stamp duty and other charges.

Article 6–1–8

When a Bourse member firm carries out a client order, it must inform its client where applicable that it has acted as principal in executing all or part of such order, under the conditions set forth in an Implementing Regulation issued by the CBV.

Article 6–1–9

Principal transactions are recorded by Bourse member firms in a specific account for each intermediary acting as principal, including those transactions where the Bourse member firm itself acts as principal.

Article 6–1–10

Principal transactions are subject to all applicable regulatory provisions relating to the guaranty of trades on the cash market or for immediate settlement, to the margin requirement for trades made on the monthly settlement market, as well as to the delivery of securities and payment of funds.

Article 6–1–11

The Bourse member firm requested by an intermediary acting as principal to execute a principal transaction must ensure that such transaction satisfies the provisions of the present Title.

Article 6–1–12

The Bourse member firm effecting a principal transaction for its own account or on behalf of other intermediaries must report such principal transaction to the SBF, under the conditions set forth in an Implementing Regulation issued by the CBV.

Article 6–1–13

The SBF monitors the regularity of principal transactions. It includes such transactions in the daily market statistics.

Article 6–1–14

The CBV must be informed of any contract between a Bourse member firm or an intermediary authorised to act as principal and an issuer, whereby such Bourse member firm or intermediary would intervene on the market for the equity securities of such issuer under particular conditions.

The existence of any such contract is published by means of a notice in the BOC.

Chapter 2
Ordinary principal trading

Article 6–2–1

The only intermediaries authorised to carry out principal transactions, as defined in the present Chapter, are Bourse member firms, credit institutions licensed as banks, mutual or co-operative banks, specialised financial institutions, securities firms (*maisons de titres*), and the Caisse des Dépôts et Consignations, such institutions being members of SICOVAM and entitled to maintain securities accounts on behalf of their clients, as well as principal firms (*sociétés de contrepartie*) in which said intermediaries hold a majority of the voting rights.

Article 6–2–2

An intermediary which is not a Bourse member firm must be authorised by the CBV to act as principal. In order to obtain such authorisation, such intermediary must confirm the existence of an agreement concluded with one or more Bourse member firms whereby all principal transactions will be recorded in the books of this or these firms, which furthermore are recognised by such intermediary as authorised agents for executing principal transactions on the market.

A specific authorisation for the opening of any new principal trading account with a Bourse member firm by an authorised principal must be granted by the CBV.

The operation of such account or accounts is governed by the rules laid down by the CBV and takes place under its supervision.

Any failure to comply with these provisions may result in a decision by the CBV to suspend or withdraw the relevant authorisation.

Article 6–2–3

For securities traded continuously on a computerised system, principal transactions made during the trading session may be carried out only at the limit stipulated by the best bid or offer price existing at the time the principal transaction is carried out, or at a price lying within such spread.

With respect to other securities, principal transactions may be executed at any price transacted during the trading session.

Article 6–2–4

Outside trading sessions, a principal transaction in a security that is traded continuously on a computerised system may be carried out only at the limit set by the best bid or offer price existing at the close of the last trading session, or at a price lying within such spread. This limit may be reduced or increased by a margin for which the CBV sets the maximum rate.

With respect to other securities, a principal transaction may be carried out at any price transacted during the last trading session. Such price spread may be reduced or increased by a margin for which the CBV determines the maximum rate.

Chapter 3
Principal transactions in blocks of equity securities

Article 6–3–1

During a trading session, a Bourse member firm may execute a principal transaction at a price within the spread, limits included, of the weighted averages of current market bid and offer prices for a block of standard block size (*taille normale du bloc*) provided the following conditions are met:

– the transaction relates to a security which is included in a list drawn up by the CBV and published in a notice issued by the SBF;
– the transaction concerns a number of securities at least equal to that defined as the standard block size for the security concerned.

The weighted average spread of bid and offer prices is to be understood as the average of bid and offer prices, weighted in accordance with the number of securities for each limit order displayed on the central market, and corresponding to a total number of securities equivalent to the standard block size for the security concerned.

The weighted average bid/offer spread is calculated and disseminated by the SBF on a continuous basis.

For each security which may be the object of principal block transactions, the standard block size is determined on the basis of criteria defined in an Implementing Regulation issued by the CBV and published by the SBF.

Article 6–3–2

In the event that the weighted average bid/offer spread cannot be calculated due to a temporary lack of orders on the central market, a transaction falling

within the scope of Article 6–3–1 of the present Regulations may be effected at a price which does not vary from the best bid or offer price by a percentage greater than that set down for this purpose in an Implementing Regulation of the CBV.

Article 6–3–3

Provided the conditions enumerated in Article 6–3–1 above are met, a Bourse member firm may carry out a principal transaction outside the trading session at a price within the spread, limits included, of the weighted averages of bid and offer prices for a standard block size for the security at the close of the last preceding trading session, or in accordance with the provisions of Article 6–2–4.

Chapter 4
Principal transactions with a view to ensuring smooth market operation

Article 6–4–1

Only the Bourse member firm appointed by the CBV as the specialist in an equity security pursuant to the provisions of Article 4–1–5 of the present Regulations is authorised to execute principal transactions in such security with a view to ensuring smooth market operation (*contrepartie en régularisation de marché*).

Such principal transactions, the purpose of which is to ensure continuity of trading and market liquidity, are carried out during the trading session, for the account of the Bourse member firm acting as a specialist itself, or on behalf of a firm acting as principal in which it holds a majority of the voting rights, pursuant to the rules laid down by the CBV and under its supervision.

Article 6–4–2

An Implementing Regulation issued by the CBV sets out the undertakings that a Bourse member firm must comply with when carrying out such principal transactions.

The Bourse member firm may act within

the framework of a liquidity contract to which the issuer, one or more of its shareholders, as well as its financial intermediaries may be parties.

Article 6—4—3

Such principal transactions must be recorded by the specialist Bourse member firm in a specific account for each security.

Title 7
Special operations

Chapter 1
Offers for sale

Article 7—1—1

A proposed offer for sale involving securities admitted to the Official List or the Second Market, or traded on the *hors-cote* market, must be described in an application submitted to the CBV by the person holding the securities to be sold.

As soon as the CBV is informed of the proposed offer, the SBF informs the Economy Minister (*Direction du Trésor*) and the COB.

Article 7—1—2

Except with the approval of the CBV, particularly in view of the number of securities offered or of their value, an offer for sale must relate to an amount of securities representing either at least 10% of the total number of equity securities of the same category in the relevant company, or at least 20 times the average daily trading volume recorded on the market during the six months preceding the filing of the offer.

Article 7—1—3

The application submitted to the CBV must specify the following:

– The initiator's objective.
– The number and specification of the securities offered for sale.
– If applicable, the minimum number of securities that must actually be sold by the initiator for the tender to be declared successful.
– The price at which the initiator offers to sell the securities.
– The conditions regarding payment of the price.

The application is submitted through a covering letter addressed to the CBV, specifying the irrevocable nature of the initiator's undertakings. Such irrevocability is effective on the date of publication of the notice referred to in Article 7-1-4. The CBV may request that a surety issued by a credit institution governed by Law No. 84–46 of 24 January 1984 be granted, or that the securities offered for sale be deposited in advance with the SBF.

Article 7—1—4

The CBV may suspend trading in the security concerned by an offer for sale as soon as the proposed offer is filed. The CBV decides on the acceptability of the offer.

If the CBV declares the offer acceptable, the SBF publishes a notice stating the identity of the initiator, the number of securities offered for sale, the price at which they are offered, and all other terms and conditions of the offer necessary for the information of the public.

Such notice is published at least four trading days before the date set for carrying out the offer. Furthermore, the duration of the offer to investors cannot be less than three trading days.

With prior approval of the SBF and provided that such possibility be stated in the notice published by the SBF, the initiator may reserve its right either to set a minimum number of securities to be sold as a condition for declaring the offer successful and completing it, or to increase the number of securities offered by up to 25% of the number of securities initially offered in view of the demand.

Article 7–1–5

On the day set for carrying out the offer for sale, the SBF centralises the purchase orders transmitted to it by Bourse member firms. The SBF accepts only orders at the offer price, stipulated as in response solely to the offer of sale, and valid for one day only.

Article 7–1–6

The result of the offer for sale is reported in a notice published by the SBF. If the offer is declared successful, the notice indicates any reduction applied to the purchase orders.

If trading has been suspended, it is resumed as of the first trading day following the day on which the offer was carried out.

Article 7–1–7

The provisions of Articles 5–4–1 and 5–4–7 regarding the mandatory filing of a proposed public tender offer are applicable to any individual or legal entity which, following an offer for sale, may hold, directly or indirectly, more than one-third of the equity securities or voting rights in the company having issued the securities sold.

Article 7–1–8

With the approval of the CBV, the initiator may provide that the orders issued in connection with the offer for sale will be divided into different categories under the conditions set forth in Article 3–2–16.

Article 7–1–9

In parallel with the offer for sale, where such offer involves at least 20% of the equity securities of the relevant issuer or an amount of 500 million French francs, the CBV may authorise that the offering of the securities be carried out partly through an underwritten placement (*placement garanti*) as defined in Article 3–2–4, such securities being offered to one or more categories of investors.

In such case, the placement price of the securities must be at least equal to the price fixed for the offer for sale.

Article 7–1–10

Further to completion of the placement, the lead underwriter must report to the SBF a detailed statement describing the results thereof. Such results are published in a notice issued by the SBF.

Chapter 2
Option contracts – Transactions in structural blocks

Article 7–2–1

The SBF registers option contracts on securities admitted to the Official List or the Second Market, or traded on the *hors–cote* market. Such contracts give one of the parties an option, either to sell or to purchase a given number of securities at a price quoted on the market on the day of the contract or at a price quoted on the market on the day of expiration or at a price equal to the average of the prices quoted between those two dates, or to forego such transaction without penalty.

The application for registration of an option contract indicates the identity of the parties, the period during which the option can be exercised, the exercise price, and the number of securities involved. The expiration of an option contract may not exceed two years after the date of its registration.

If the option contract refers to a price quoted on the day on which it is filed with the SBF, that filing must be made before the opening of the following trading session.

If the contract has a duration of more than three months, the parties may agree on an average price based on prices for the three months preceding the date at which the option is exercised.

The application for recording an option contract is supported either by the contract itself, signed by the parties, or by an exchange of letters between the parties, filed by a credit institution governed by Law No. 84–46 of 24 January 1984 or by a Bourse member firm, acting as guarantor of the transaction.

264

Article 7–2–2

The SBF is also empowered to register option contracts on securities admitted to the Official List or the Second Market with a view to their resale (*reclassement*) to one or several investors who have not yet been identified.

The registered contract or contracts indicate, under the responsibility of the intermediary or intermediaries handling the resale, the maximum number of securities to be resold, the price and expiration date of option contract, and the identity of the seller or sellers of the securities.

The option contract must be filed for registration, at the latest, before the opening of the trading session following the session during which the price set for the resale was quoted. The expiration of the option contract may not exceed three months after the date of its registration.

On the day on which the option contract is exercised, the intermediary or intermediaries involved inform the SBF of the conditions under which the resale operation was carried out and the identity of the acquirors of the securities.

Article 7–2–3

The SBF is empowered to register transactions effected off the central market and concerning structural blocks (*blocs structurants*) of shares. A block of shares is deemed structural where it exceeds an amount determined by an Implementing Regulation of the CBV. Applications for registration of such a transaction must meet the following conditions:

– It must be presented to the SBF through a Bourse member firm.
– It must concern a security admitted to the Official List or the Second Market.
– The seller as well as the buyer or buyers must be identified.
– The transaction must be at price which varies from the best bid/offer spread by a percentage not exceeding that determined by an Implementing Regulation of the CBV. As an exception to this rule, transactions may be effected at a price which does not meet this condition with the prior approval of the CBV.

An Implementing Regulation of the CBV determines the conditions applying to publication by the SBF of information concerning such transactions in structural blocks of shares.

Chapter 3
Deferred settlement transactions – Repurchase agreements

Article 7–3–1

Transactions providing for deferred settlement for all or part of the securities in question are submitted to the SBF before the opening of the trading session following that during which the price of the relevant securities was quoted.

The SBF registers such transactions in its books, and verifies the outcome thereof.

Article 7–3–2

The SBF registers in its books repurchase agreements (*opérations liées*) by which one of the contracting parties buys or sells a given number of bonds and undertakes *vis-à-vis* the other party to sell or buy the same amount of securities at an agreed date.

The undertaking may be irrevocable or may include an option clause.

The initial trade is registered at a price quoted on the day on which the agreement is concluded, the price of the second trade being increased or decreased in a proportion not exceeding a maximum set by the CBV and published in a notice issued by the SBF.

A repurchase agreement cannot be registered by the SBF if, on a date lying between the day on which the transaction is filed and its due date, a special advantage or a given charge, such as detachment of a coupon or the opening of a drawing right is attributed to the security to which such agreement relates.

Chapter 4
Mandatory sales

Article 7–4–1

Mandatory sales of securities are carried out, at the request and under the responsibility of the seller, in accordance with one of the following three procedures:

– public offer for sale under the conditions set forth in Chapter 1 of the present Title;
– Direct sale on the market;
– Sale at public auction.

Article 7–4–2

Direct sale on the market applies, in principle, to securities admitted to the Official List or the Second Market where the quantity of securities to be sold does not exceed normal market capacities.

The Bourse member firm designated by the CBV proceeds with the sale of the securities under the conditions normally observed on the market, under the supervision of the SBF.

Article 7–4–3

A sale at public auction is made on the date and under the conditions determined by the CBV.

Such sale is announced in a notice issued by the SBF, which also indicates the quantity of securities to be sold, whether they are divided into lots, the category and specificity of the securities, the minimum price sought, and the option if any for combining lots.

Bids are submitted through Bourse member firms.

The award is made by the SBF as soon as the bids come to an end. The award price is published in a notice.

An Implementing Regulation issued by the CBV sets forth the conditions for carrying out sales through public auctions.

Title 8
Payment of funds and delivery of securities

Chapter 1
General principles

Article 8–1–1

The provisions of this title apply to payments of funds and deliveries of securities resulting from trades.

Article 8–1–2

Any purchase or sale of securities results in a payment of funds and a delivery of securities. Said payment and delivery are correlative and simultaneous.[6]

However, if the market situation with respect to a given security precludes making the corresponding delivery of securities, the CBV may decide that the obligation to deliver securities shall be settled in the form of pecuniary compensation, the amount of which is determined by the SBF.

Article 8–1–3

With respect to purchases and sales on

the cash settlement market or for immediate settlement[7], the payment of funds and the delivery of securities between intermediaries take place within a fixed maximum period following the trade date. This period may depend on the nature of the security. It is specified by an Implementing Regulation issued by the CBV.

Article 8–1–4

With respect to purchases and sales on the monthly settlement market, the payment of funds and the delivery of securities are made on the same day between intermediaries and between intermediaries and clients, pursuant to the schedule set forth by the SBF.

Article 8–1–5

The CBV issues an Implementing Regulation laying down the general rules with respect to setting the conditions under which corporate actions affect pur-

---

[6] Delivery versus payment (DVP).

[7] As regards trades made on the monthly settlement market.

chases and sales which have not yet given rise to payment of funds and delivery of securities.

Pursuant to the said Implementing Regulation, the SBF determines and publishes the trade date as of which the buyer is entitled to and the seller is no longer entitled to corporate actions. This date applies to all securities, whether in registered or bearer form.

Article 8–1–6

All deliveries of securities traded on the monthly settlement market are made ex-dividend or ex-right. The purchaser of an equity security before the ex-dividend date is credited with an indemnity[8] whose amount is equal to the amount of the dividend paid, and the seller is debited accordingly.

Article 8–1–7

Institutions authorised to keep securities accounts in their name and in the names of their clients must hold and manage, in distinct accounts, the securities belonging to their clients and to themselves.

Chapter 2
Settlements and deliveries between clearing house members

Article 8–2–1

Trades between Bourse member firms are affirmed under the conditions set forth by the SBF.

With respect to certain trading procedures, the SBF may provide for automatic affirmation.

Article 8–2–2

Payment of funds and delivery of securities resulting from an affirmed trade between Bourse member firms in connection with a security admitted to listing by the CBV are to be made, unless the CBV decides otherwise, through the SBF, acting as a clearing house.

---

[8] This indemnity is not considered as a dividend for tax purposes.

Article 8–2–3

Bourse member firms are *ex officio* members of the clearing house.

An Implementing Regulation issued by the CBV lays down the conditions governing membership of the clearing house for institutions other than Bourse member firms, and particularly membership of financial institutions affiliated with SICOVAM, as well as foreign institutions whether national or international, involved in the clearing and guarantee of securities markets.

The membership of a financial institution gives rise to a contract between such institution and the SBF.

The SBF shall determine the conditions regarding the assumption of trades by Bourse member firms on behalf of clearing members other than Bourse member firms.

Article 8–2–4

The SBF, acting as a clearing house, computes the net position in terms of securities and cash for each clearing member at the end of each trading day.

Payment of funds and delivery of securities carried out at the clearing house's initiative are made on a net basis.

With respect to securities admitted to SICOVAM, the SBF sends SICOVAM instructions regarding payment of funds and delivery of securities on a net basis.

Such instructions may give rise to partial settlements and deliveries.

Article 8–2–5

The SBF, acting as a clearing house, guarantees to clearing members payment of funds and delivery of securities due to them according to their net positions.

To this end, the clearing members make deposits with the clearing house, pursuant to its calls.

Such deposits are calculated on the basis of net positions and are adjusted daily, notification being sent to clearing members every trading day before the market opens.

If the adjustment has not been made by the opening time of the same day's trading session, the SBF may proceed with the partial or total liquidation of the defaulting member's positions, in the name and at the risk of such member, until reconstitution of the required deposit is made.

The cash deposits are remunerated by the SBF. They are invested in liquid assets that present no capital risk.

Article 8–2–6

Any net position that has not given rise to payment of the funds and delivery of the securities within the required period is known as a net fail (*suspens*).

Article 8–2–7

Any net fail is subject to a penalty for late delivery, levied on the defaulting member by the SBF.

Article 8–2–8

The SBF, acting as a clearing house, makes a daily updating of the equivalent value of the net fails, on the basis of a reference price that it sets daily.

It credits or debits the difference between the day's value and the value of the previous day in the clearing members' accounts in buy position by debiting or crediting the accounts of the members in sell position and issues new instructions regarding payment of funds and delivery of securities to the SICOVAM.

Article 8–2–9

The net fails may, at the initiative of the SBF acting as clearing house, give rise to the borrowing of securities at the expense and risk of the defaulting clearing members.

Article 8–2–10

The net fails may be the object, at any time, of a buy-in or a resale at the initiative of the SBF, acting as a clearing house. In any case, such buy-in or resale occurs at the end of a period set by the CBV.

Expenses and costs connected with the buy-in or resale of the securities are borne by the defaulting clearing members.

Article 8–2–11

A Bourse member firm that does not receive delivery within the prescribed period of the securities due to it from another Bourse member firm and resulting from a trade not assumed by the clearing house puts the defaulting Bourse member firm on notice to make such delivery in accordance with the procedure laid down by the CBV.

If the Bourse member firm has not been satisfied at the end of the period provided for under this procedure, it buys the securities on the market, at the expense and risk of the defaulting Bourse member firm.

Chapter 3
Settlements and deliveries between Bourse member firms and order collectors

Article 8–3–1

In the present Title, the term "order collector" refers to institutions which are authorised to hold securities accounts in their own name and in the names of their clients, and send their orders to Bourse member firms for execution. Bourse member firms may be order collectors with respect to orders they do not execute themselves.

The provisions of the present Chapter apply to all Bourse member firms acting as broker-dealers and to all order collectors, notwithstanding any agreement to the contrary.

Article 8–3–2

Execution by Bourse member firms of buy or sell orders transmitted by order collectors results in an affirmation in accordance with the procedures and within the timetable determined and published by SICOVAM.

Article 8–3–3

Payment of funds and delivery of securities between order collectors and Bourse member firms acting as broker-dealers are made within the period laid down by the CBV:

– In the case of securities admitted to SICOVAM, pursuant to the procedures laid down by SICOVAM.
– In the case of securities not admitted to SICOVAM, pursuant to the procedures defined by the SBF.

Article 8–3–4

The instructions for payment of funds or delivery of securities that are not carried out on due date because of a lack of a provision in the form of cash or securities, are known as fails.

All fails are subject to a penalty for late delivery, levied on the defaulting party by SICOVAM, pursuant to its regulations.

Article 8–3–5

An order collector that does not receive delivery of the securities due to it on the due date, puts the defaulting Bourse member firm acting as a broker-dealer on notice to make such delivery pursuant to the procedures laid down by the CBV.

If, at the end of the period provided for by this procedure, it has not been satisfied, it has the securities purchased on the market, at the expense and risk of the defaulting Bourse member firm involved.

Article 8–3–6

A Bourse member firm acting as a broker-dealer that does not receive delivery of the securities due to it on due date puts the defaulting order collector on notice to make such delivery in accordance with the procedure laid down by the CBV.

If, at the end of the period provided for by this procedure, it has not obtained satisfaction, it purchases the securities on the market, at the expense and risk of the defaulting order collector.

Article 8–3–7

Orders executed by a Bourse member firm on behalf of an order collector may give rise to partial payments and deliveries between such Bourse member firm and such order collector, under the conditions laid down by the SBF.

Article 8–3–8

A client who has securities and cash on deposit in an institution other than a Bourse member firm may directly give a buy or sell order to a Bourse member firm, which accepts it, subject to said Bourse member firm being informed of the identity of the custodian institution for the securities and cash, and said custodian being informed of the characteristics of the order and the due date for settlement and delivery agreed with the Bourse member firm. With respect to payment of the funds and delivery of the securities resulting from execution of such an order, the institution holding the securities and cash must comply with the provisions of the present Chapter applicable to order collectors.

As soon as it becomes aware of the order, the custodian may require the client to set aside provision in the form of cash or securities required for payment of the funds or delivery of the securities.

Chapter 4
Settlements and deliveries between institutions authorised to hold securities accounts in the name of third parties and their direct clients

Article 8–4–1

Any financial institution that holds securities accounts in the names of third parties shall credit into or debit from such accounts the securities that are purchased or sold on behalf of its clients, and register all movements of funds.

Article 8–4–2

In the case of securities that are bought or sold on the cash market, or for immediate settlement[9], the credit or the debit of the securities in or from the

---

[9] As regards trades made on the monthly settlement market.

account and the accounting for the corresponding fund movements takes place on the day the order is executed, or, at the latest, the next day.

As of the day following the day the order is executed, securities purchased on the cash market benefit from any advantage and bear any charge entailed in owning them.

Subject to the provisions of Article 8–1–6, securities that are purchased or sold for immediate settlement, ownership of which entails either a special advantage or a given charge, benefit from the same advantages or bear the same charges as the securities traded on a monthly settlement basis on the same date.

Any securities purchased may not be transferred to another institution before the expiration of the standard delivery periods between institutions.

Article 8–4–3

For those securities bought or sold on the monthly settlement market, the credit or debit in the securities account and the accounting for the corresponding fund movements occur on the day specified in Article 8–1–4 .

Chapter 5
Special cases

Article 8–5–1

When a drawing, involving the designation of redeemable securities is to occur for an issue, the securities traded on the market take part in the drawing for the seller's account, and no longer the buyer's, as of a date known as the ex-drawing date.

The ex-drawing date is prior to the drawing date by a number of days at least equal to the period specified in Article 8–1–3, increased, where necessary, by a period allowing for the suspension of movements in SICOVAM accounts.

The ex-drawing date is set by the SICO-

VAM, and is published in a notice in the BOC.

Article 8–5–2

Transactions relating to certificated securities are paid and delivered as provided by the SBF.

Article 8–5–3

Any claim between Bourse member firms relating to the material condition of delivered securities must be submitted, at the latest, on the second trading day following their delivery.

Article 8–5–4

Certificated securities delivered with attached coupons may be refused by the purchaser if one or several of these coupons bear different numbers from those of the security to which they are attached.

Article 8–5–5

Certificated securities, whether French or foreign, denominated in foreign currencies, are delivered with coupon attached, except where the coupon amount is covered by an entry in the monthly settlement accounts.

Such coupon may, however, be replaced by another coupon with the same maturity, bearing a different number from that of the security, where its payment does not require proof of ownership.

If the seller is unable to deliver the securities with attached coupons under the conditions set forth in the previous paragraphs, the SBF may levy a penalty for late delivery.

Chapter 6
Interim provisions

Article 8–6–1

The provisions of the present Title shall come into force on dates to be indicated, for each security or category of securities, in one or more decisions issued by the the SBF.

Title 9
The bond market

Chapter 1
General provisions

Article 9–1–1

The scope of the provisions of the present Title is the secondary market for securities not giving access to equity securities and admitted to the Official List or the Second Market, or traded on the *hors-cote* market, as well as *fonds communs de créance* (asset-backed securities) admitted to the Official List.

Article 9–1–2

The secondary market mentioned in Article 9–1–1 consists of:

– Trades made by Bourse member firms on the market organised by the SBF within the framework of centralised matching of orders and in accordance with the provisions of Title 4 of the present Regulations.
– Principal transactions carried out under the conditions set forth in Chapter 2 of the present Title at prices linked to central market prices.
– Market-making transactions carried out under the conditions set forth in Chapter 3 of the present Title at prices freely set as between the market-makers and their clients.

A principal transaction is defined as the purchase or sale by an institution acting for its own account within the framework of its activity as intermediary.

Market-making consists in an undertaking by an institution to supply any person so requesting with bid and offer prices for a given amount of securities, greater than or equal to the minimum block size defined by the CBV, and to fill any orders transmitted by such person in accordance with market practices, within the limits of the spread announced for said amount.

Market-making may relate solely to securities corresponding to pure interest rate instruments.

Article 9–1–3

Every principal transaction is time- and date-stamped by the intermediary carrying it out. Either it is immediately recorded with a Bourse member firm, or it is declared to the SBF under the conditions laid down by the latter.

Every market-making transaction must be time- and date-stamped by the intermediary carrying it out and be reported to the SBF under the conditions laid down by the latter.

Article 9–1–4

The SBF compiles and disseminates, at least once a day, statistical information concerning the market as a whole for each security.

Chapter 2
Principal trading in bonds

Article 9–2–1

The only intermediaries authorised to act as principals, as defined in the present Chapter, are Bourse member firms, credit institutions licensed as banks, mutual or co-operative banks, specialised financial institutions, securities firms (*maisons de titres*), and the Caisse des Dépôts et Consignations, such intermediaries being members of SICOVAM and entitled to maintain securities accounts on behalf of their clients, as well as principal firms (*sociétés de contrepartie*) in which said intermediaries hold a majority of the voting rights.

Article 9–2–2

An intermediary which is not a Bourse member firm must be authorised by the CBV to act as principal.

An Implementing Regulation issued by the CBV indicates the conditions for authorisation of principals, and particularly the required minimum shareholders' funds.

271

A principal is required to observe the provisions of the present Regulations and any further texts adopted for their implementation, under the supervision of the SBF. Such principal complies with the prudential rules laid down by the CBV or, where applicable, any equivalent rules on which agreement has been reached between such principal's supervisory authority and the CBV.

Article 9–2–3

The SBF verifies observance by principals of the provisions of the present Regulations and of any further texts adopted for their implementation. In particular, the SBF ensures that all principal transactions carried out are actually reported to it with due observance of the rules set forth in Article 9–1–3, and that they respect the price rules set forth in Article 9–2–7.

A principal acknowledges that the SBF is entitled to require any regular or exceptional information enabling it to make such verifications.

The SBF may carry out on-the-spot inspections, in conjunction, in appropriate cases, with the supervisory authority of the intermediary concerned.

Article 9–2–4

Should a principal fail to observe the provisions of the present Regulations or of any further texts adopted for their implementation, the CBV may publicly disclose such inobservance, or may decide on temporary suspension or on withdrawal of its authorisation.

Article 9–2–5

Except with the express authorisation of the SBF published in a notice appearing in the BOC, principal transactions in connection with a security are forbidden when the SBF has ordered a trading halt in the relevant security.

Article 9–2–6

The intermediary is not allowed to buy or sell securities from or to a client as a principal where it manages the client's account and hence can take the initiative for investments and disinvestments carried out in such account.

Article 9–2–7

A principal transaction is carried out at a price within the spread, limits included, equal to the last transacted price at the time of its execution, plus or minus the maximum percentage on that day for the security in question, set by the SBF pursuant to the provisions of an Implementing Regulation issued by the CBV.

If the transaction occurs outside trading hours, or if the security is not traded during the current session, the reference to be used corresponds to the last price recorded by the SBF for the security.

Article 9–2–8

When the intermediary fills a client's order by means of a principal transaction, the client is informed thereof. The transaction confirmation notice may be issued with a net price, without brokerage or other fee.

Article 9–2–9

The regulatory provisions in force with respect to trade guarantees, delivery of securities and payment of funds are applicable to principal transactions when registered by a Bourse member firm.

Chapter 3
Market-making

Article 9–3–1

The only intermediaries authorised to carry out market-making transactions, as defined in the present Chapter, are Bourse member firms, credit institutions licensed as banks, mutual or co-operative banks, specialised financial institutions, securities firms (*maisons de titres*), and the Caisse des Dépôts et Consignations, such intermediaries being members of SICO-VAM and entitled to maintain securities accounts on behalf of their clients, as well as market-making firms (*sociétés de contrepartie*) in which said intermediaries hold a majority of the voting rights.

Article 9–3–2

Any intermediary mentioned in Article 9–3–1 must be authorised by the CBV to act as market-maker.

An Implementing Regulation issued by the CBV indicates the conditions for authorisation of market-makers, particularly the required minimum shareholders' funds.

The authorisation is given by the CBV for a given number of securities, pursuant to the rules relating to the shareholders' funds that it issues.

An authorised intermediary must comply with the provisions of the present Regulations and any further texts adopted for their implementation, under the supervision of the SBF. It must observe the prudential rules laid down by the CBV or, where applicable, the equivalent rules on which agreement has been reached between its supervisory authority and the CBV.

Article 9–3–3

The CBV must be informed of any contract between a market-maker and an issuer whereby such market-maker would apply special conditions to market-making in the securities of such issuer. The existence of any such contract is published in a notice in the BOC.

Any contract concluded between a market-maker and an issuer must include a condition precedent, which is authorisation of the market-maker by the CBV.

Article 9–3–4

The SBF verifies observance by market-makers of the provisions of the present Regulations and of any further texts adopted for their implementation. In particular, the SBF verifies that all transactions are reported to it, with due observance of the rules set forth in Article 9–1–3, and that the market-maker respects the undertakings made to the CBV at the time of its authorisation.

An authorised intermediary acknowledges that the SBF is entitled to require any regular or exceptional information enabling it to make such verifications.

The SBF may carry out on-the-spot inspections in conjunction, in appropriate cases, with the supervisory authority of the intermediary concerned.

Article 9–3–5

Should a market-maker fail to observe the provisions of the present Regulations or any further texts adopted for their implementation, the CBV may publicly disclose such inobservance, or may decide on temporary suspension or on withdrawal of its authorisation.

Article 9–3–6

By issuing an Implementing Regulation, the CBV lays down the conditions regarding the eligibility of a security for market-making. Such conditions bear on the characteristics of the issuer and the size of the issue, as well as on the minimum number of market-makers required for the market-making to be effective in a given security.

Article 9–3–7

A market-maker may commit itself to the securities of its choice from among those eligible for market-making, subject to providing the SBF with information in advance, and provided that the latter, acting by delegation from the CBV, does not express opposition. Any opposition that might be expressed by the SBF must state reasons therefor, and be notified to the CBV at the time of its next meeting.

Absence of response by the SBF within five trading days following the date of the filing made with it is tantamount to approval on its part.

A market-maker must publicly disclose the securities in connection with which it has committed itself.

Article 9–3–8

A market-maker announces its conditions for each of the relevant securities pursuant to procedures laid down by the SBF.

A market-maker that wants to halt market-making in a given security must announce this fact publicly, and observe a notice period defined in an Implementing Regulation issued by the CBV. It may not commit itself again to the security in question before the end of a period set forth in the same Implementing Regulation.

Article 9–3–9

In the absence of express authorisation from the SBF published in a notice in the BOC, market-making transactions in connection with a security are forbidden when the SBF has ordered a trading halt in the relevant security.

Article 9–3–10

The intermediary is not allowed to buy or sell equitiy securities from or to a client as a market-maker where it manages the client's account and hence can take the initiative for investments and disinvestments carried out in such account.

Article 9–3–11

When the intermediary fills a client's order by means of a market-making transaction, the client is informed thereof. The transaction confirmation notice may be issued with the net price, without brokerage or other fee.

BIBLIOGRAPHY

Books relating to French Securities Law

Dictionnaire Joly, *Bourse et produits financiers*;
Dictionnaire Permanent Epargne et Produits Financiers;
Lamy, *Droit du financement*;
Juris-classeur, *Banque et crédit* (3 volumes);
Francis Lefebvre, *Mémento Sociétés Commerciales*;
Lamy, *Sociétés Commerciales*;
Michel Vasseur, *Droit des Affaires* (Vol II), *Les Cours de Droit*, 1987–88;
Michel de Juglart et Benjamin Ippolito, *Banques et bourses* (3rd ed) Lucien M. Martin, (Montchrestien, 1991);
Alice Pézard, *Droit des marchés monétaire et boursier*, (Editions J.N.A., 1994);
Vauplane (de) et Bornet, *Droit de la Bourse* (Litec, 1994).
Renault, *Les Banques et les opérations sur les valeurs mobilières* (Banque, 1971);
Alain Choinel, *Le Marché Financier–Structures et Acteurs* (Banque, 1986);
Rémi Grenier, *Le Second Marché* (Economica, 1988);
Loyrette etc., *Valeurs Mobilières; Réglementation Boursière, OPA-OPE* (Joly, 1979);
Raymond Perquel, *Manuel des Opérations de Bourse* (Dalloz, 1963);
Dossier Comptable Lefèbvre, *Le Second Marché*, (Francis Lefèbvre, 1989);
Rider J. Drake R., European Financing Laws (London, Chancery Publishing, 1994);
Société des Bourses Françaises, Paris Bourse–Member Firm User Guide, (Société des Bourses Françaises, 1994);
Euromoney, *Issuing Securities. A guide to securities regulation around the world* (London, Euromoney, March 1993);
Euromoney, *World Equity Market* (London, Euromoney, June 1994);
Euromoney, *Private Placements: National and International Markets* (London, Euromoney, 1984);
Euromoney, *International Securities Law* (London, Euromoney, 1992);
Bulletin Joly, *Market Control and Investor Protection Financial Information in Europe* (International Seminar of the European Society of Banking and Financial Law (ESBFL) 23 and 24 September 1993) (Bulletin Joly, Bourses et produits financiers).

Periodicals

Rapports annuels de la COB;
Bulletin mensuel de la COB;
Revue de droit bancaire et de la Bourse;
Bulletin Joly Bourses et produits financiers;
L'Année boursière (SBF, 1994).

Books relating to Tender Offers

Guy Barsi, *Les OPA en France: droit et pratique*, (Nathan, 1988);

Pierre Bezard, *Les offres publiques d'achat* (Masson, 1982);

Alain Viandier, *OPA, OPE, garantie de cours, retrait, OPV (droit des offres publiques)* (2nd ed) (Litec, 1993);

D. Martin and J. P. Valuet *Les offres publiques d'acquisition (OPA, OPE, OPR)*, Brochure ANSA No. 189 in co-operation with GLN-Joly (1993);

Répertoire Dalloz des Sociétés, fascicule Offres publiques (1991, updated 1994);

Jurisclasseur commercial, Traité des sociétés, Vol V, OPA-OPE, Fascicule 112-4-C, mise à jour;

Stefano Mogini and Alessandro Munari, *L'"affaire Perrier"*, Milano, Dott. A. Giuffrè Editore (1993);

Clifford Chance, *Takeovers in Europe*, London (1992);

Michel Fleuret, *Les OPA en France*, Dalloz Gestion Pratique (Paris, Dalloz, 1991).

Index

References in **bold** are to articles of the General Regulation, translated at pages 217–274.